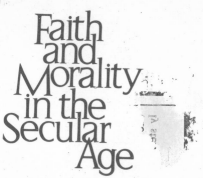

Faith and Morality in the Secular Age

Bernard Häring, C.Ss.R.

In this thoughtful look at the changing roles of faith and religion in the modern world, one of the leading theologians in the Catholic church analyzes the meaning and effect of secularization on the life of the contemporary Christian.

Father Häring believes that it is not possible to proclaim the message of salvation without a thoroughgoing attention to the "joys, hope, griefs and anxieties" of man, and toward that end he traces the relationship of religion to culture from biblical times down to the present. Casting aside the casuistry which has characterized moral theology in the past, he then presents an in-depth consideration of faith in our ecumenical age and shows how, with a proper understanding, secularization can be transformed into a true time of favor for the people of God.

(continued on back flap)

FAITH AND MORALITY
IN THE SECULAR AGE

FAITH AND MORALITY

IN THE SECULAR AGE

By BERNARD HÄRING, C.Ss.R.

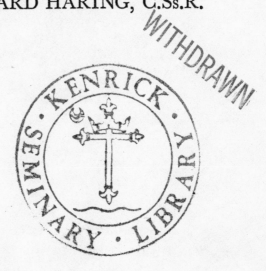
DOUBLEDAY & COMPANY, INC., GARDEN CITY, NEW YORK, 1973

ISBN: 0-385-03837-2

Library of Congress Catalog Card Number 73-79876

ACKNOWLEDGMENTS

I am greatly indebted to my students at Union Theological Seminary in New York for the contents of this book, which evolved from a course on the subject in 1967. The theme was chosen by the Academic Senate of the school from a number of proposed courses. Dialogue with professors and students from different churches has greatly helped me come to a better understanding of the breadth and depth of the vast problem of secularization.

Over the past few years, I have taught the same course twice for graduate students of Christian Ethics at the Academia Alfonsiana in Rome, which serves students from all continents. Again, formal discussion and informal dialogue enriched my understanding of the complexity of the phenomenon by revealing to me the many different expressions of it in various cultures. The last time I taught the course was in 1971 for the summer school of the University of San Francisco, where I enjoyed a very receptive and responsive audience.

A number of the chapters presented here were first written in Italian and translated into English by Sister Gabrielle L. Jean (Ph.D.); the whole was then repeatedly re-edited. I wish to express to Sister Jean my heartfelt gratitude for the patient and intelligent work in the preparation of this book.

B.H.

CONTENTS

KEY to Conciliar Documents

AA: *Apostolicam Actuositatem,* Decree on the Apostolate of
   the Laity

AG: *Ad Gentes,* Decree on the Church's Missionary Activity

CD: *Christus Dominus,* Decree on the Bishops' Pastoral
   Office in the Church

DH: *Dignitatis Humanae,* Declaration on Human Freedom

DV: *Dei Verbum,* Dogmatic Constitution on Divine
   Revelation

GE: *Gravissimum Educationis,* Declaration on Christian
   Education

GS: *Gaudium et Spes,* Pastoral Constitution on the Church
   in the Modern World

IM: *Inter Mirifica,* Decree on the Instruments of Social
   Communication

LG: *Lumen Gentium,* Dogmatic Constitution of the Church

NA: *Nostra Aetate,* Declaration on the Relationship of the
   Church to Non-Christian Religions

OE: *Orientalium Ecclesiarum,* Decree on Eastern Catholic
   Churches

OT: *Optatam Totius,* Decree on Priestly Formation

PC: *Perfectae Caritatis,* Decree on the Appropriate Renewal
   of the Religious Life

PO: *Presbyterorum Ordinis,* Decree on the Ministry and Life
   of Priests

SC: *Sacrosanctum Concilium,* Constitution on the Sacred
   Liturgy

UR: *Unitatis Redintegratio,* Decree on Ecumenism

INTRODUCTION

All parts of Christianity evince a growing awareness that it is not possible to proclaim the message of salvation without a thoroughgoing attention to the "joys, hopes, griefs and anxieties" of man in this age. This is particularly true for the transmission of the New Testament's moral message. Admittedly, time cannot alter the spirit, truth and intrinsic value of Christian morality; at all times, we are to live according to the Gospel message and to strive for that maturity measured by nothing less than the full stature of Christ. But as disciples of the Word Incarnate, Christians face the challenge of incarnating morality in the concreteness of present life conditions with a conscious and critical acceptance of contemporary reality.

Herein we have to follow Christ. He almost always spoke in "parables"; that is, his message was presented as one that not only illumines the daily personal and social experiences of his listeners but makes life itself a part of the challenging message. Moral theology must do likewise; to be faithful to its mission of messenger of salvation and wholeness, it must courageously, critically and loyally open itself to the spirit of the times, to all new experiences including language, culture, new interpersonal, social and international relations. Only thus will it be able to communicate the abiding orientation which faith, hope and redeemed love can give. A closed mind and a predominantly polemic or defensive attitude would irreparably jeopardize its *diakonia* (ministry).

One of the knottiest of contemporary problems is that of modern atheism in its variety and complexity of tones, forms and motives. Distinct from it, yet variably linked to it, is the other multifaceted phenomenon of secularization. Both have far-reaching and serious repercussions in the field of morality. It behooves moral theology to study them with courage and serenity.

In these pages, our reflection will not be concerned with new cases nor will it be limited to the contemporary problems confronting us, just as it will not be applying to them methods and perspectives of the moral casuistry of the last three centuries. It is vitally important that, first of all, we be informed of the historic-cultural and socio-religious presuppositions which grounded the earlier types of moral theology. These aspects will then stand comparison with the contemporaneous. Christian ethics must be fully cognizant of the evolution of historical conditions and thinking if it wishes to proclaim convincingly Christ's message in our times.

A conscious and critical acceptance of today's newness will alone enable Christians to distinguish "eternal realities from their changing expressions" (GS, Art. 52). Yet they need to approach with sympathy and discernment whatever man discovers, achieves and creates on his own, accepting gratefully all human accomplishments in the sincerity of a heart filled with faith and hope. The Church can then successfully offer a credible testimony of Christ to the world of today.

In this spirit, the following pages will pursue the new perspectives for a timely Christian ethics; we shall then attempt to face some concrete problems posed by the socio-cultural changes. We will assume the *fact and process of modern secularization* as the specific object of our study. Once aware of its complex ramifications, we will be in a strategic position to commit ourselves so as not to degenerate into "secularism" while grasping wholeheartedly the just exigencies of "secularity." Within a perspective of faith and vigilance for the "signs of the times," secularization will be transformed into a propitious opportunity, a true *kairos* (time of favor) for the people of God (Chapter 1).

After having synthesized all the components of the phenomenon of secularization, we will then endeavor to specify the meaning of the biblical term "world" (*saeculum, mundus, cosmos*) in historical context and according to the broad lines of the history of salvation (Chapter 2). Our study will then relate the "sacred" to be the "profane" throughout history. Ecclesiastical teaching and legislation are reflected in a certain hierarchy of ethical values and both are influenced by the time-bound concepts of "sacred" and "profane" in each specific historical era. Because of this, they invariably contain many elements contingent on those periods. Even a superficial comparison of the nineteenth and twentieth centuries reveals clearly that today's understanding of the "sacred" and the "profane" in their mutual interdependence denotes sufficiently profound changes to warrant attentive consideration in the moral field (Chapter 3).

The multiple *interactions of culture, socio-economic structures and religion* will enter our analysis. In fact, a serene review of these factors is indispensable for an understanding of the change in emphasis and perspective in the historical course of our Judeo-Christian morality. The energy expended for a grasp in depth of these interacting cultural parameters is justified only if a correlative effort is exerted to span the gap separating religion from life. Under "religion," we understand religious expressions such as official teachings, theology, catechism, devotions, ecclesial structures. Under "life," we include not only daily activities but the whole stream of culture, the economy, the "spirit of the times" that exerts such a strong influence on the personal and social life. A true theology strives to actualize faith in today's world as the "salt of the earth" (Chapter 4).

On the theological as well as on the pedagogical level, it is not easy to find that bridge which will allow the man of today to unite faith, prayer (liturgy) and daily life, to synthesize love of God with effective love of neighbor. Because secularized man is subjected to the influence of both secularity and secularism, he encounters great difficulty relative to the many

inherited forms of prayer, devotion, liturgy, preaching and religious teaching, especially when there is no evidence of the
living and vivifying link between faith and the concrete reality
of life including tangible opportunities for promoting a more
genuine brotherhood based on the dignity of all men. In this
perspective, we re-examine the doctrine on "salvation by faith
alone" and do so in an ecumenical spirit (Chapter 5).

The discourse on *sanctity in daily life* under varying conditions and in different situations will be cast in the same perspective, specifying that which is the authentic relationship of
Christian morality to the totality and concreteness of every-
man's life today. An attempt will be made to describe a "holy
worldliness" in the light of the declarations of Vatican II, all
the while treasuring the insights of men like Dietrich Bonhoeffer and Teilhard de Chardin. Our study will consider the problem of the priestly ministry and the charisms of "religious life"
without neglecting the arduous vocations in the secular world.
The presentation will seek to bring boldly into relief the universal vocation to holiness of all the people of God; it wants to
make clearly perceptible the "common holiness" in marriage,
in private and professional life, in the many social relationships: civic, political, economic and other (Chapter 6).

The whole problematic issue of faith and life in a secularized
culture comes to a climax in the understanding of *prayer*.
Secularization compels us to search for an adoration of God in
Spirit and in truth, yielding neither to horizontalism nor to
alienation in any form. Reflection on prayer in a secular age
should make visible the link between prayer, meditation and
the wholeness of life while capitalizing on the new directions
suggested by the present era (Chapter 7).

Finally, we intend to indicate a direction for the true *ethical-
religious dialogue with secular man* in a language adequate
to the demands of religious truth on the one hand and those of
the mentality of modern man on the other. Points of privileged
encounter in this dialogue could well be: the dignity of man,

the centrality of conscience, human freedom and the brotherly solidarity of all men (Chapter 8).

Along these lines, moral theology will be able to renew itself in fidelity to the Gospel so as to offer to the modern world a live and convincing testimony of Christ, Lord of history and of the world.

B.H.

Rome
September 1972

CHAPTER 1

SECULARIZATION TODAY[1]

In the wake of the French Revolution, secularization was frequently mentioned but with a very limited meaning ascribed to the term; inspired by the principles of its proclamation, Napoleon confiscated vast territories from the Church's possessions (mortmain) inclusive of all the rights and obligations, and transferred them to the civil authority. The name of *secularization* was given to this huge operation; since the Church's privileges and possessions were all considered to be "sacred," a transfer to the "profane" civic society was deemed sacrilegious. With the affirmation of the secular state, the process of secularization gained breadth. The annexation of territories of the Papal State by the young Italian government (1870) represented the most clamorous exploit; it culminated in the proclamation of Rome as capital of the Italian kingdom.

Every phase of this process of secularization was accompanied by recriminations, threats and grave sanctions for those responsible for it.[2] Today, we can be more dispassionate in our

[1] Berger, P. L., *The Sacred Canopy* (New York: Doubleday, 1969).
Meland, B. E., *The Secularization of Modern Cultures* (New York: Oxford, 1966).
Richard, R. L., *Secularization Theology* (New York: Herder & Herder, 1967).
Richardson, H. W., *Toward an American Theology* (New York: Harper & Row, 1967).
——, *Theology for a New World* (London: SCM Press, 1968).
Schillebeeckx, E., *God: The Future of Man* (New York: Sheed and Ward, 1968).
[2] The strong sanctions protecting Church property and clerical privileges are still enforced by the Code of Canon Law; see Canons 2345, 2346.

assessment of it, realizing that on the whole, it was providential. It has contributed much to the renewal of the Church by purifying her witness and promoting her credibility. Over and above all else, it has rendered more evangelical the religious and prophetic ministry of the successor of Peter and that of the bishops, priests and religious.

With the secularization process, the hierarchy and the religious have found freedom and the prophetic *parrhesia* in the field of social justice, i.e., the fundamental rights of every human person, covering political life and international relations. However, the secularization of ecclesiastical wealth and power is only one aspect of the immense human course which we designate today by that term; secularization actually embraces the whole of man: his way of perceiving, of thinking and of acting. Therefore, it is a complex human phenomenon pregnant with Christian and human values but also bearing contrary elements.

Methodologically, I feel it would be fairer to start by analyzing the positive aspects of secularization. Once aware of the positive realities of the phenomenon, we will be in a better position to face the unacceptable aspects and review the causes.

I. LINES OF BIBLICAL SECULARIZATION[3]

Secularization can signify triumph over a false sacralization and attainment of a more genuinely religious orientation. It is in this sense that one can also speak of a biblical secularization. In fact, the monotheism which we find in the Sacred Scriptures, in both the Old and the New Testament, overcomes the superficiality of common sacralization in the various forms of animism and pantheism. Authentic religiousness gains nothing, but rather loses much, with the "sacred cows," "sacred plants," the various and multiple taboos.

[3] Cf. Loretz, O., *Schöpfung und Mythos, Mensch und Welt nach den Anfangskapiteln der Genesis* (Stuttgart, 1968).
Rad, G. von, *Theologie des Alten Testaments,* Vol. I (Munich, 1962), pp. 70–82; 105–15; 153–67. Vol. II (Munich, 1965), pp. 357–79.

Animism perceives souls and divinities everywhere in the world surrounding man. It therefore proscribes the use of many things necessary for man and indispensable to his progress. In this manner, animism and similar forms of superstition hamper man's mastery over the world and he consequently remains incapable of rendering it more humane.

The "Karma" accounts for the fact that the craftsman of India dared not change the methods of work or the various instruments and tools at his disposal. Every tradition became so "sacred" that he could not dissociate himself from it. This in turn made it impossible to abolish the caste system: the pariahs had to remain outcasts forever.

Some forms of pantheism and, to a certain extent, Stoicism view the universe in its whole and in parts as a direct presence of the divine Spirit in the world. The laws governing nature therefore become "sacred" for the Stoics; they are laws to which man must be submitted and which he cannot subdue or administer responsibly.

Biblical theism contrarily views all things, even the most beautiful and most imposing, as mere creatures. Therefore, everything becomes desacralized; in fact, acknowledgment of their creaturely state is an assertion that they have no divine character. Man stands serenely free before them: "God blessed them and said to them, 'Be fruitful and increase, fill the earth and subdue it, rule over the fish in the sea, the birds of heaven, and every living thing that moves upon the earth" (Gen. 1:28).

The fact that God created all things for man implies that they are neither "profane" nor "indifferent." In no way do they, by themselves, disavow or dismiss God the Creator. No one person or group can dispose of them egotistically without acting against their intrinsic purpose. They are a gift of God, and a selfish abuse by any creature offends by doing violence to their inherent significance. This is particularly true with respect to the dignity of the human person made to the image and likeness of God.

Like every created thing, man himself constitutes a gift and a message of love. Man and the universe serve as an appeal to

praise and witness to that love from whence they have originated. This intrinsic dignity does not allow man to transform
a worldly reality into an idol or a taboo; it would destroy his
own dignity and freedom. Every creature, according to its own
true nature, is intended for the praise of God's glory in the
service of man, of brotherhood, solidarity and human progress.

Christ states it even more emphatically: there do not exist
"pure" and "impure" things; before God, only love and sincerity of heart count insofar as they determine attitudes toward
fellowmen and all created things. Jesus upbraids the Pharisees
in rather harsh terms: "But you say, 'If a man says to his
father or mother, "anything of mine which might have been
used for your benefit is set apart for God," then he must not
honor his father or his mother.' You have made God's law null
and void out of respect for your tradition. What hypocrisy!"
(Mt. 15:5-7). Since God is the creator of all men and all
things, we cannot deny our neighbor that which he absolutely
needs. We praise God with our possessions when we place
them generously in the service of the most needy of our brethren. We fail to praise God through his creation if we restrain
man's progress. True praise of God lies in mastering the created
universe in a brotherly spirit, in sharing one's accomplishments
and in setting the harnessed physical forces in the service of
all men.

For those who look over various foods for the purpose of
sorting them out as pure and impure, Christ is no less forceful: "Do you not see that whatever goes in by the mouth passes
into the stomach and so is discharged into the drain? But what
comes out of the mouth has its origins in the heart, and that
is what defiles a man. Wicked thoughts, murder, adultery, fornication, theft, perjury, slander—these all proceed from the
heart, and these are the things that defile a man; but to eat
without first washing his hands, that cannot defile him" (Mt.
15:17-20).

St. Paul continues the secular discourse relative to the desacralization of various human traditions and the differentia-

tion of things as clean and unclean (I Cor. 8). That which counts for the Apostle is the purity of intention, fruit of charity: "If we are in union with Christ Jesus, circumcision makes no difference at all, nor does the want of it; the only thing that counts is faith active in love" (Gal. 5:6).

If, on the one hand, the biblical desacralization affirms man's freedom before all things and all human traditions, it demands of man, on the other, greater responsibility and a stronger determination to overcome a selfish profanation of creation. The Bible expects that in the use of created things, man will be guided by genuine love, seeking the glory and praise of God.

In a certain sense, Christ has desacralized the priesthood itself. He abolished the hereditary priesthood and, as a consequence, every priestly caste or class; he transformed it into a service of the brethren, a *diakonia*. He stressed the kind of witness befitting all messengers of the Good News. Priestly holiness, earlier understood as separation, yielded to a holiness of service in fraternity, a *koinonia*.

We shall return to these points in greater detail as we progress in our study of ethics in a secularized era. Our brief panoramic glimpse will serve to orient us in the interpretation of today's secularization.

II. THE COMPLEXITY OF TODAY'S SECULARIZATION

Modern secularization, be it in contents or in methods, does not always correspond to the biblical form. Notwithstanding, an authentic Christian renewal of the world, of society and of the Church will come to valuate it positively. The whole People of God will be committing itself loyally to witness to the secular applications contained in Christ's message in such a way as to penetrate, like yeast, the whole human phenomenon of today.

Before initiating an analytic study of its contents and of its applications, we must remember that the process of secularization is not affirmed with the same depth or emphasis in all contemporary human groupings. In certain areas, the process is barely beginning, as in Africa and parts of Asia, while in others it is firmly implanted, as in North America, northern and western Europe. There are also regions officially characterized as secularist, manifesting a positively anti-religious secularism. In them, however, we must distinguish carefully between an official position and the concrete reality.

In the secularization process of today, the pressures for demythologizing are strong. Modern man pledges himself to demolish the various myths of the past such as "sacred empire," "sacred power," "holy war," and "sacred dynasty." The epoch of "sacred alliances" between civil and religious powers is over or is gradually being overcome. Today, there exists a common conviction that political life, such as forms of authority, structures and ordinances, ought to be guided solely by criteria of service to the common good of the whole of humanity. "Religious" ideologies, which in the past had sacralized and seemingly justified privileges or actions regardless of the well-being of the community, are now being set aside. However, one can no longer ignore how these superficially sacrosanct ideologies are replaced by many others, even if more pragmatic, such as communism. They continue to canonize, in a quasi-religious way, actions destructive of the dignity and authentic vocation of man, even fostering the systematic exploitation of man by man.

Another wellspring of secular views and attitudes comes from the physical sciences and modern technology. A technocratic mentality analyzes, shapes natural phenomena coldly and without emotion, including the most stupendous, which, in the past, would have spontaneously evoked in pre-scientific man a "sense of the sacred," a sense of awe. Where yesterday one spoke of sacred illness (*morbus sacer*), today the psychologist and psychiatrist carry on their dispassionate analyses. The field of illness is no longer that of exorcism or magic but one of analyses, drugs and surgery.

Modern man is smitten by secondary causes; their action and laws rule him but he can come to control them, whereas in the past, his thought went directly to an active and immediate presence of God or his angels. That which was so often before accepted simply as "the will of God" is today perceived primarily as a challenge to man's power and ingenuity in transforming nature and mastering the world.

In the past, the field of piety and liturgy emphasized relics, religious objects, sacred stones, holy places, sacred vestments and the like. There was scrupulous concern for the observance of the eucharistic fast. In liturgical functions, attention focused on the exact pronunciation of the various standard formulas and on a perfect performance of all the rubrics, even when a concrete situation divested them of all significance. There was strong insistence on keeping Latin as a sacred language.

Today, on the contrary, we proceed with a vivid realistic sense in the liturgical domain; both signs and liturgical language are placed in the service of the proclamation of the Gospel. And this is their *raison d'être;* when they no longer adequately serve such a purpose, they lose their value. For the mature Christian of today, there is nothing magical in liturgical celebrations; there is the "kerygma," the proclamation of the Good News and the response of faith which it evokes. It centers on the mystery of human solidarity of all the brethren before the one God and Lord.[4]

A similar critical tendency and demythologizing effort are aimed at the formulas of revealed truth inherited from the past. In fact, it is true that for a time, there existed for many a kind of formulas-idolatry. There was undue insistence on fidelity to the formulas without ever evincing concern of equal urgency as to whether in the concrete socio-religious situation, they expressed the living message of salvation. The security found in formulas seemed greater than the security found through trustful faith in Christ, Lord of history. Secularization's critical sense and consequent demythologizing of every theoretical formulation not in keeping with the rhythm of life can be of

[4] Bernard Häring, *Vita Cristiana nella luce dei sacramenti* (Vicenza: Favero Editore, 1970).

great help in the search for a living religious language, one capable of proclaiming Christ's message of life.

Another central component of the process of secularization is found in a greater awareness of the specific competency and autonomy of the laity in the earthly city and in the Church. In the Constantinian era and later in that of Charles the Great, Otto the Great and their successors, the clergy was "secularized." However, it was a process diametrically opposed to that of today; it was a slow and not always justified extension of the competency of the Church hierarchy over temporal matters. The clergy invaded *en masse* the civil, political and cultural life, often monopolizing it in an overall perspective of "sacred power."

It came to the point where popes and bishops arrogated for themselves the "direct power over the temporal sphere," (*potestas directa Ecclesiae in temporalia*). At the same time, the Church was identified with the hierarchy; the divine mission of the Church was confused with the all too worldly claims of a socially privileged or "sacred" class. Thus did the clergy fall unconsciously into that false messianism about which Christ had so frequently reproached the apostles and Peter himself (Mt. 16:23), a messianism much too earthbound for men supposed to be "in the world" but not "of the world" (cf. Jn. 17:14–17).

The *Constitution on the Church in the Modern World* definitively accepts the process of emancipation and of autonomy of the secular city; it recognizes as just the independence of the sciences and of the whole terrestrial reality in relation to the hierarchy and the Church herself. However, the conciliar document deplores the occasional lapse into atheism or secularism, that is, an affirmation, either on the theoretical or the practical level, of the total autonomy and independence of man before God (GS, Art. 36).

In addition to a totalitarian conception of theology, the clericalism of the past greatly limited and even negated the autonomy of the layman in his own scientific pursuits. Such a monopolistic tendency obscured the depth and the integrity of the message of salvation and made "worldly" the religious mission of the Church. The curricular offerings of the medieval universities not only allocated first place to theology, but all the other sciences were subordinated to it to the point of subjecting them to the methods proper to theological research and to strict clerical control. The case of Galileo is but one of the many recorded to prove to us the difficulties which had to be overcome to free the positive sciences from theological tentacles and methodology.

If at times theology proved a major hindrance to the development of the mathematical-physical and behavioral sciences, clericalism dominated the political domain. Time has witnessed the Church's becoming a "force for order," bound in a "sacred alliance" with the privileged classes and with forms of power favoring a questionable status quo. At the hierarchical level, the Church was thus party to the countless social injustices then in existence. Not only was the alliance between "throne and altar" a deterrent from its becoming a prophetic voice; it was even unwilling to listen to prophetic men and women who were not, for the most part, members of the hierarchy. Very significant in this respect was the protest which the people of the French Revolution directed against the diverse monopolies and privileges of the higher clergy. A portion of the lower-echelon clergy had sided with those protesting against the status quo.

The *Declaration on Human Freedom* (Dignitatis Humanae) of Vatican II brought an end to the long period in which first the Roman emperor and his various successors posed, if not as Pontifex Maximus, at least as powerful protector of religion and of the Church's earthly privileges. The document solemnly renounces every practice or claim which arises from such a pattern. It consciously disclaims any "sacred alliance" between the priesthood and political power; it rejects every assertion of a "sacred power" which would subordinate to itself multiple sectors of life. In daily practice, however, the enticements and temptations are not wanting, but they are now officially unmasked and condemned as anti-evangelical.

Among the most positive results of the process of secularization can be listed: the emergence of a purer religious sense, greater trust in the work of the Spirit and in the power of the Gospel, a more humble witness of a servant Church to the Servant-Messiah, and a better, simpler, and more wholehearted following of Christ, servant of God and of man. One must admit, however, that in many parts of the modern world, the process of secularization has cost a loss of synthesis and loss of the sense of mystery resulting in loss of the sense of sin. The various forms of anti-clericalism have not all disappeared even if they have gradually diminished wherever the Church has truly overcome the past forms of clericalism and does not yield too readily to the temptation of new forms.

Modern totalitarian ideologies which replaced the earlier superficially sacralized visions of life are still strong. Distrust often remains and repeatedly the accusation is made that religion is a source of alienation from real life since it seems to encourage disengagement from the great unresolved problems of humanity. The same charge is leveled even when a good number of believers grow in enthusiastic commitment to the brotherhood of all men and thus truly honor the one Creator and Lord of all men.

It may be that for a time yet the Church, particularly in her hierarchy, will remain surrounded by suspicion, by jealousy of man's autonomy and progress. She will be confronted by the pervasive fear of new forms of clericalism or some other undue extension of her competence. Besides a convincing proclamation of the kingdom of God, much more will be asked of her; secular man will readily ask: is she truly thinking of the kingdom of God or is this a pretense for contriving new forms of power in the earthly city? Does the practice of the hierarchy confirm the doctrine of the autonomy of the whole temporal sphere?

Even if it seems aprioristic, we assert that believers have the vocation to prove the impossibility of a true and authentic secularity when man withholds gratitude and adoration to the true God. When man forgets everything about God, when he obliterates even within himself the sense of God, then the terrestrial city becomes a gigantic golden calf, the new and terrible divinity which demands of man the sacrifice of his own personal dignity. The man who does not pray and who displays no sensitivity whatsoever to the religious problem inevitably becomes enslaved to his self-made idol. Such is also the fundamental thesis of the theology of secularity of Friedrich Gogarten and Dietrich Bonhoeffer.

Therefore, the Church cannot assume a defensive attitude or globally refuse today's secularization. As a matter of fact, the Church can be greatly helped by it in her quest for self-understanding, in her continuous pledge to conversion and renewal in view of an ever increasing fidelity to the Gospel for the world's salvation. She must not even keep aloof through indifference and disinterest; she is called to contribute to the process of secularization in a constructive way. The Church can and ought to introduce all men to those secular applications contained in the Gospel message which otherwise would be left out; they are indispensable to guard from secularization's degenerating into the creation of new idols.

Such a presence and testimony on the part of the Church demand that she evince courage and take two indispensable steps. First and foremost, she ought to commit herself to seek a live integrative vision which embraces all spheres of life, all human tasks as well as the unadulterated newness of the contemporary world. In this quest, theology pledges itself unreservedly on the basis of its particular role and responsibility (GS, Art. 43, 62). Besides, the Church must readily renounce all forms, structures and claims which would obscure or fail to serve the purity of her testimony: "She does not lodge her hope in privileges conferred by civil authority. Indeed, she stands ready to renounce the exercise of certain legitimately acquired rights if it becomes clear that their use raises doubts about the sincerity of her witness or that new conditions of life demand some other arrangement" (GS, Art. 76).

III. SECULARIZATION AND ATHEISM[5]

An epoch of secularization like ours is not necessarily an atheistic epoch; it can even become an era favorable to a more personal, deeper and more committed faith. Prior to today's secularization, religion was often a primarily sociological-cultural fact. The structures, customs, traditions and collective convictions were so permeated by religion that for an individual person, being a member of a certain population or family signified also being "religious," a member of the Church. One's religious affiliation was not so much the fruit of a personal choice as something received from society; it was a religion of birth, not of choice. One became a member of the Church by the mere fact of insertion into a social milieu and by a ritualistic reception of the sacraments.

These remarks are not intended to negate the personal values of religiousness found in the earlier "Church of the people." It would not even be fair to be extremist about them or to generalize them unduly. I wish only to underline how, in the past, the socio-religious components of Christianity were strong and often predominant. The prevalence of socio-religious factors is not a phenomenon specific to Christianity; on the contrary, there were times when such influences were decidedly stronger outside of Christianity.

In the same context, the very choice of the priesthood or religious life was not so much a personal choice as a social-familial one. In no way am I insinuating that, in the past, dedication and personal commitment were wanting in the clergy or in religious orders; however, attention is called to the extent to which the situation was fraught with grave dangers.

With the process of secularization, the religious sphere has

[5] Marty, M. E., *The Modern Schism: Three Paths to the Secular* (New York: Harper & Row, 1969).
Mascall, E. L., *The Secularization of Christianity* (New York: Holt, Rinehart & Winston, 1966).

become characterized ever more as one of responsibility, of choice and personal commitment. In religious decisions, the social-familial factors are toned down. Today, to be a believer is ever more visibly the result of a definite personal choice. The declaration on religious freedom issued by Vatican II is to be read in this perspective and new context. Even today, faith and conscience remain what they were before secularization insofar as essentials. However, new aspects are uncovered and realized which pose new questions. If the believer is presented new opportunities, he also faces new perils for his faith.

It is inevitable that in a sociologically compact epoch where religion is characterized by a "Church of the people" or a "religion of the state," faith would encounter grave hazards of clericalism, simony, careerism and hypocrisy. We must recognize, however, that today such dangers can be overcome more easily by a personal choice on the part of believers. Notwithstanding, we cannot forget or underestimate the new perils to which faith is exposed in a secular age, such as secularism, atheism, loss of the sense of God, loss of the sense of sin, immanentism and horizontalism.

The secularization and secularity of culture, politics, economics and social life are not necessarily *secularism*. Autonomy, freedom and responsibility are defended not against God but against undue interference of the Church as a socio-religious institution and these vindications are particularly addressed to the hierarchy. Such claims coincide, at least fundamentally, with specific evangelical exigencies.

The *raison d'être* of the Church is the proclamation of and testimony to the kingdom of God, which differs radically from all forms of political, economic or cultural power of this world. "The pharisees asked him, 'When will the kingdom of God come?' He said, 'You cannot tell by observation when the kingdom of God comes. There will be no saying, "Look, here it is!" or "There it is!," for in fact the kingdom of God is among you!'" (Lk. 17:20–21).

The humble proclamation of God's kingdom cannot rest on an earthly reality as a form of power, but is a constant strength of enlightenment for the conscience of all men. It is like the leaven that loses itself in the mass, like the salt that dissolves and gives flavor, like the lamp that illumines while consuming itself. With much greater loyalty and sincerity, the Church today recognizes and respects the secularity of the social and political life, with a consequent greater credibility for her *diakonia* of the kingdom.

President John F. Kennedy, while being a sincere Catholic, jealously defended the independence of the political sphere from intrusion by any Church or ecclesiastical hierarchy. Yet no one can accuse him of having lapsed into secularism. So there is a very marked difference, then, between secularity and secularism. There is secularism only when there is present, either on the theoretical or practical level, an explicit negation or neglect of man's ultimate dependence on God. Likewise is there a marked difference between secularism and atheism. Even if in reality they sometimes truly form a unity, such a coincidence is neither total nor always fully realized, at least at the level of conscience and theoretical reflection.

The deism of the seventeenth and eighteenth centuries, for example, did not negate the existence of a personal and transcendent God or the fact that history, in its totality, evolves along the lines of the laws established by the Creator. However, it denied that religion, i.e., the acceptance of this God, can and ought to have somewhat of an influence on the concrete economic, cultural, political and social life. The logical consequence was a pattern of secularism. The *Constitution on the Church in the Modern World* describes a particular form of "atheism" in these terms: "Some laud man so extravagantly that their faith in God lapses into a kind of anemia, though they seem more inclined to affirm man than to deny God" (GS, Art. 19). Such an attitude ought to be called secularism more than atheism. In fact, many theists, theoretically and in the concreteness of life, are governed by what is here described in *Gaudium et Spes;* they are secularists.

Care must be taken not to accuse of either atheism or secularism those political parties and socio-cultural associations which delimit their own programs and task to concrete political and socio-cultural problems, without taking a stance or associating themselves with any religion or ideology. We should give serious and appreciative consideration to the historical evolution of many contemporary socialist parties. Characterized originally by an atheistic ideology or at least by a secularism clearly anti-church and anti-religious, they eventually evolved in a pragmatic, political direction, slowly detaching themselves from every ideology quasi-religious or anti-religious. The process could have been hastened if churchmen had been more alert to the "signs of the times," renouncing all kinds of undue interference in secular matters.

Therefore, we must not be amazed or dismayed if today there occasionally remains in such political movements a practical attitude bearing the stamp of a certain secularism. We must not cry out "scandal" or even passively expect further progress. We must necessarily convince ourselves that secularism's definitive overthrow depends much on the attitude of believers relative to the secularity of political and economic life. The ideological liberation of such parties can proceed only if Christians know clearly how to overcome all the variegated forms of clericalism and all those theoretical-practical attitudes that give the impression or generate suspicion of underlying clerical designs. This problem can be especially illustrated by the political situation in Italy, where the Church, and particularly the hierarchy, have great difficulty in freeing themselves from outdated modes of clerical control over the whole of life.

The commitment to definitive disengagement from clericalism demands constant vigilance, a keen critical sense, generosity and prayer. To be liberated from the religious power ventures of yesterday does not mean that automatically one ceases to be clericalist. In fact, its modes of expression are forever changing, adapting themselves to new social and cultural situations. The Church will be able to steer clear of the new expressions of triumphalism and anti-evangelical clericalism only if she listens attentively and loyally to the petitions—the lovingly or violently critical—which the world puts to her, and if she promotes sincerity for a committed dialogue among all her members. Besides, it is necessary that she continually make it the object of her prayer. The whole Church owes it to herself to pray constantly for fidelity to the humility of her *diakonia* in the world of today, i.e., the proclamation of and testimony to the kingdom according to Christ, who realized it in his death-resurrection.

Many forms of atheism and of secularism are due, at least partially, to the believers' lack of love for neighbor and the triumphalistic and anti-historical structures of religions, including the Christian churches. Another contributing factor came from the excessive and unjust reaction of the Church in taking imprudent official positions when she found herself confronted with secularization, a process necessary for human progress. Until the end of Vatican II, she was more concerned with seeking out secularization's negative aspects and pronouncing global condemnations of it than in capitalizing on the religious and Christian possibilities contained within it.

"Yet believers themselves frequently bear some responsibility for this situation. For, taken as a whole, atheism is not a spontaneous development but stems from a variety of causes, including a critical reaction against religious beliefs, and in some places against the Christian religion in particular. Hence believers can have more than a little to do with the birth of atheism. To the extent that they neglect their own training in the faith, or teach erroneous doctrine, or are deficient in their religious, moral, or social life, they must be said to conceal rather than reveal the authentic face of God and religion" (GS, Art. 19).

We have earlier called attention to the fact that in this article, *Gaudium et Spes* includes under the name of atheism that which would be more properly termed secularism. Even in the secularist deviations of the secularization movement, believers and Church institutions have grave responsibilities. It would therefore be pharisaical to condemn secularism without first recognizing our own errors and sins and converting ourselves in sincerity.

Modern man operates on the basis of facts; words without facts fail to impress him. He likes to see, touch and ascertain more than to listen to an abstract discourse. If religions and communities of believers do not succeed in realizing a living synthesis between faith in God and authentic commitment to the dignity of all men, the man of today will find little credibility in their assertion that religion and faith do not alienate from actual life. Such declarations, even if beautifully expressed in choice language, will have no effect on secular man except perhaps for generating an even more critical attitude toward those institutions which fail to renew themselves.

It is not enough theoretically to prove to contemporary man that faith in God can be a source of human authenticity and true brotherhood. We have to testify, personally and in community, by a style of life and language adapted to his intelligence and achievements. When there is no active synchronization of the Church with the initiatives and brotherhood of today, the secularist temptation becomes seductive, and growing numbers of Church affiliates become ever more marginal to faith as well as to the life and commitment of brotherly love and justice.

An example will help clarify the point. Should dogmatic theology, liturgical celebrations and catechesis be only abstractions removed from daily life, and if moral teaching should deign to stoop slightly to life's demands but with a harsh moralism, are we to be surprised if those who are committed to the evolutionary process of man and the world "use such a method to scrutinize the question of God as to make it seem devoid of meaning" (GS, Art. 19)? It should not astound us, for in final analysis, their methodology resulted from religious forms and structures "devoid of meaning."

In the past both the private and public sectors of life were guided by church and religion. The constant presence of the religious element was such that individuals did not even question themselves on God; they could not avoid giving attention to the religious problem. Informally, they were made aware of the importance and urgency of adhering to the community of faith. In every field of endeavor, at every step, the person came upon something which immediately or indirectly spoke to him of God. It was inconceivable to be personally un-attentive to the problem of God and religion, even if the con-cept of faith and its life-response were influenced in part by socio-cultural pressures and interests.

There is no longer this type of abiding reminder of God in our world wavering between a secular and a secularist outlook. Its structures, plans and commitment speak of the power of the self-conscious man, of his self-determination and responsibil-ity. So very little in culture will lead individuals to question themselves on God unless we believers learn a new language or present a life style revealing of him. In a fragmented mode of living, man is distracted to the point that only with much diffi-culty does he come to question himself on his ultimate destiny and choices. He easily becomes a computerized number in an inflexible, blind and suffocating production system. *Gaudium et Spes* thus expresses itself in this regard: "Some never get to the point of raising questions about God, since they seem to experience no religious stirrings, nor do they see why they should trouble themselves about religion. . . . Modern civiliza-tion itself often complicates the approach to God, not for any essential reason, but because it is excessively engrossed in earthly affairs" (GS, Art. 19).

In a world whose structures and ordinances do not pose the problem of God and fail to suggest its urgency, the principal task of believers is that of becoming points of recollection and of encounter with God for all who live and suffer with them. More than ever today, a fraternal presence and commitment inspired by faith are invaluable. It is urgent for the future of faith that believers individually and as a community become a living testimony of God and of Christ, a courageous witness, fully respectful of and grateful for all the contemporary achievements. Today's world needs a testimony of faith which invites all persons to question themselves on God and Christ in view of life's total experience. The whole Church is called to be such a witness. Her visibility is authentic if it leads contemporary man to meet with the living God, to understand the urgency and the necessity of a decision of faith.

The tragedy of evil and of injustice is particularly felt by to-day's responsible man. He dedicates himself generously and loyally to the search and realization of concrete steps which can overcome social evils. This fraternal commitment is a genuine value that ought to pave the way for a personal encounter with God. Instead, it often becomes a source of alienation, of rebellion and struggle against the Church, religion or God himself. When, in fact, these generous and sincere men encounter in churchmen structures or forms of life which commit them more to a philosophical quest of the meaning of evil than to its eradication, the scandal is then too great and rebellion breaks out. The revolt of people who want to commit themselves for the building of a better world and consequently reject an image of religion that remains sterile is not truly a rebellion against God!

Equally strong are the scandal and protest aroused by an erroneous presentation of eternal life as evasion of the reality of this world and refuge in a tomorrow totally outside history. Man knows not what to make of a hope that distracts from the building up of the earthly city and from commitment to true brotherhood; it is certainly not a Christian hope (GS, Art. 20).

Often in the past, a certain religiosity coupled with faith of an individualistic brand spoke of Christian salvation, limiting it, however, to the spiritual soul, depriving it of the personal-cosmic richness and totality found in Revelation. Salvation and the "states of perfection" seemed to lie in withdrawal from life to the point of neglecting responsibilities for one's immediate surroundings and social life. It is no wonder then that the world with its economy and politics often became the dominion of humanists with no interest in "religion" or that of an inhumane secularism. Even those Christians committed to social and political domains were to find faith and salvation marginally, outside their daily tasks; in the quest of salvation and "piety" they were expected to model themselves on the monks, including their devotions and ascetical practices. Their primary concern for "saving their soul" led them to consider the economic and social life chiefly as a temptation to sin, or, at best, as a realm to be exploited for "virtuous acts" and for gaining "merits" in view of the other world. Such religious individualism certainly did not set the discourse on the world's salvation and the Christian's vocation in the same perspective as the *Constitution on the Church in the Modern World.*

The promotion of a fundamental attitude of individualism, the unjust interferences of a powerful clericalism and the innumerable old superstitions hindering progress ended by veiling the countenance of God and rendering incredible the Gospel of faith and of love preached by the Church. Churchmen then viewed any humanistic commitment as horizontalism if not an atheistic reaction. Thus was contemporary systematic atheism born, founded on the conviction that "it gives man freedom to be an end unto himself, the sole artisan and creator of his own history" (GS, Art. 6).

The most powerful form of modern atheism is the Marxism of the Stalin and Mao type. Their followers are convinced that the construction of the earthly city absolutely demands the elimination of faith in God. They view humanity's commitment as centering on liberation from all forms of alienation, among which religion occupies first place, followed by imperialism and capitalism. This Stalin-Mao Marxism is altogether different from the secularity whose aspects we have enumerated. We note, however, how the hope of an absolute brotherhood contained in Marxism transcends, at least partially, its fundamental dialectical vision of the world and humanity, which posits a situation of perpetual conflict as the basis of historical progress. There are some bridges for dialogue even with communists if we can discern the signs of the time.

CHAPTER 2

THE WORLD AND THE KINGDOM OF GOD

The world of today is more than ever the *kingdom of man*—the field, the material and instrument with which and in which he asserts his power, freedom and responsibility. *Secularism* has rendered this vision so radical as to leave no room for God; the kingdom of God is often looked upon as nonsense or is opposed as an assault to the dignity and capability of mankind. Contrariwise, *secularization* on the whole does not exclude acceptance of God's kingdom, but it does demand that the Church present and incarnate it in such a way as not to curtail the just autonomy of terrestrial realities, personal dignity and freedom. It therefore imposes a specific task to today's theologians, namely, a critical rethinking, in the light of the Word of God and the signs of the times, of the way in which theology has, until now, systematized the world-salvation relationship.

How the world and the kingdom of God are interrelated has always been the object of theological reflection. At every phase of history, theology has offered an answer likely to satisfy at once the exigencies of fidelity to revealed truth as well as the socio-cultural truths of the times. Theology thus addressed itself to the relationship between nature and grace, between the natural and the supernatural, between faith and reason. Every epoch came to discover, however, that whatever systematization had been attained could not be satisfactory forever. It was an accepted fact that man's world and the understanding of the kingdom of God were continually evolving. Reflection on their interrelatedness was therefore to be continuously enriched by newly discovered perspectives and elements.

Today's secularization poses the additional problem of relating the profoundly new terms and contents to those of the past. The fact that man has elaborated a new vision of the world compels the believer to ask himself anew what should be the relationship between the kingdom of God and the world thus conceived. The problem is particularly delicate because of the strongly anthropocentric dimension of today's world view. Man does not stand alone at the center of reality; he molds the created universe with the help of the sciences and technology.

For secular man, the world encompasses human-terrestrial values to be actualized by exploiting the cosmic reality with technical-scientific adroitness. Besides, he senses keenly a liaison between the world's becoming and that of humanity. He is aware that only by shaping the world can he shape man's development.

A conception of the "world" in such a strongly anthropocentric and dynamic way renders man conscious of the need to rethink the relationship of "this world" to the "kingdom of God." He expects a new answer but not by reason of a futile love of novelty for its own sake but because, on the one hand, he has experienced the inadequacy of past solutions and, on the other, he is aware of how much his perception and Weltanschauung differ from past conceptions.

Our quest for a right answer ought necessarily to start from a biblical view of the world and man's activities in the world.[1]

[1] For the problem touched upon in this chapter, see particularly:

Gogarten, F., *Demythologizing and History* (New York, 1955).

Häring, Bernard, *The Church on the Move* (Staten Island: Alba House, 1970).

———, *New Horizons of the Church in the World* (Notre Dame, Ind.: Ave Maria Press, 1968).

Metz, J. B., "A Believer Looks at the World," in *The Christian and the World* (New York: Kennedy, 1965).

Moltmann, J., *The Theology of Hope. On the Grounds and the Implications of a Christian Eschatology* (New York: Harper & Row, 1967).

Williams, C., *Faith in a Secular Age* (New York: Harper & Row, 1966).

I. AMBIVALENCE OF THE WORLD

Salvation bears an intricate relationship to the world. In the Holy Scriptures, its complexity suddenly leaps before one's eyes especially when attention turns to the multiplicity of meanings ascribed to the term "world" (*cosmos, mundus*) and the other related concepts.

A. The World: Work of God

Fundamentally, *the world,* understood as the sum total of all that exists in time and in space, *is good because created by God.* It is the work of God's love, a sign and reminder of his infinite benevolence. God gives being to things, plants and animals because through them he wants to reveal himself to man as LOVE. In response, once man has experienced God as Love, he turns to him, loves him wholeheartedly and opens himself to his supreme gift, namely, participation in the blessedness of the trinitarian communion. God creates the world so as to have sharers of his own love (*"ut habeat condiligentes se"*—Duns Scotus). We ought not, therefore, to be startled by the expression full of admiration with which the sacred author closes the first account of creation: "And God saw all that he had made, and it was very good" (Gen. 1:31).

The world is created in the Word: "and through him all things came to be; no single thing was created without him" (Jn. 1:3). Creation in the Word cannot be understood solely in the light of the categories of causality, which are non-religious categories. To say that reality is created "in the Word" is to say that it reveals God's own dialogue, God's trinitarian life as revelation and loving presence; it expresses creation as a manifestation, a word of goodness and of glory, a gift of God, an inborn invitation to love in return. "The God who created the world and everything in it, and who is Lord of heaven and earth, does not live in shrines made by men . . . for he is himself the universal giver of life and breath and all else . . . for in him we live and move, in him we exist" (Acts 17:24–28). "His invisible attributes, that is to say, his everlasting power and deity, have been visible, ever since the world began, to the eye of reason, in the things he has made" (Rom. 1:20).

If man places himself before creation in this spirit, he will not fail to consider it ever more explicitly in the light of Christ, Lord and Redeemer, and with Teilhard de Chardin, he will justly exclaim, *"Tout est sacré!* [Everything is sacred!]." Likewise, everything invites the psalmist to adoration and gratitude toward Yahweh: "The heavens tell out the glory of God, the vault of heaven reveals his handiwork. Day pours out the word to day and night to night. One day speaks to another, night imparts knowledge; not a word or a discourse whose voice is not heard through all the earth; their voice resounds, and to the ends of the world, their message" (Ps. 19:1–5). "Acclaim our God, all men on earth; let psalms declare the glory of his name, make glorious his praise. Say unto God, 'How fearful are thy words! Thy foes cower before the greatness of thy strength" (Ps. 66:1–3; cf. Psalms 33, 135, 136, 145).

The creation of everything in the Word is the foundation of the whole universe's intrinsic sacredness. The man who knows how to listen to and praise God sees the whole world as sacrosanct and holy. In God's plan, one does not find "things which speak of and lead to him" and others which "do not speak of him and draw away from him." The whole of creation is, in some way, *profane* and *sacred:* profane in the positive sense of secularity because it has its own independence, uniqueness and is entrusted to man's free stewardship; sacred because, according to its own autonomy and individuality, it speaks of God, who has constituted it in the Word.

The heart of the loving and prayerful man truly acknowledges the sacredness and secularity of creation when he uses, transforms and perfects created realities in a spirit of brotherhood and service for all mankind. Conversely, should man's heart be dominated by egotism and proud self-sufficiency, his utilization of worldly things would render them "profane" in a negative sense; he would be alienating them from their goal; no longer would they speak to him of the love of God but instead, they would lead him away from adoration of God and from universal brotherhood.

B. *The Frustrated World*

When man, totally oblivious of God, sets himself up as master in the world, he shapes it in such a way that created reality loses its intrinsic value for the manifestation of God's love. Temptation then grows stronger for man to be ever more forgetful of God; it may even lead him to oppose God's plan of salvific love.

The created universe arouses wonder and delight in man, and the liberating power with which man submits it to himself suggests gratitude toward the Lord and service to one's neighbor. Religious admiration and thanksgiving toward the Creator do not detract from service to the neighbor. When one disregards this synthesis, both aspects of sacredness become falsified. Religion becomes alienation, an empty sacralization of things and rites, while genuine love and service yield to pride and to a lust which is blind, selfish and oppressive to the brethren. Thus does man get entangled in a deadly interdependence; turning away from God, he also drags creation into his rebellion. On the other side, "frustrated creation," i.e., all the investments of sin in our milieu, tempts man to move ever farther away from God. Through man's sin, the original salvific plan uniting the cosmos and humanity is transformed into a desperate solidarity of sin and death.

The first chapters of Genesis explain well the frustration of the world by linking it strictly to man's decision self-sufficiently and determinedly to seek his own wisdom independently of God: "The serpent said, 'Of course you will not die. God knows that as soon as you eat it, your eyes will be opened and you will be like gods knowing both good and evil'" (Gen.

3:4–5). Consequently, the first homicide is found rooted in insatiability for material possessions. Cain selfishly disposes of his goods and chooses to give God second-rate offerings. An inordinate, selfish lust for earthly goods can thus become a source of rebellion against God and lead to oppression of fellowmen (cf. Gen. 4:3 ff.).

Egotistic, self-centered men are no longer capable of living in the world as among brothers in a spirit of gratitude and adoration. By their life "they are stifling the truth" (Rom. 1:18); they pervert fraternal rapports and deprive created things of their true splendor and genuine value. They are without "possible defense for their conduct; knowing God, they have refused to honor him as God, or to render him thanks. Hence all their thinking has ended in futility, and their misguided minds are plunged in darkness. . . . For this reason, God has given them up to the vileness of their own desires, and the consequent degradation of their bodies, because they have battered away the true God for a false one" (Rom. 1:20–25).

The *Pastoral Constitution on the Church in the Modern World* justly states that the Council "gazes upon that world which is the theater of man's history, and carries the marks of his energies, his tragedies, his triumphs" (GS, Art. 2). The sin-death solidarity of men profoundly affects the whole cosmos. Our contemporary world is plunged in sin and death despite the many efforts and vexatious longing of true believers to open it up to Christ and love. It is not that creation has fully lost the fundamental value and basic goodness which were originally in God's plan. Created realities do not become bad in themselves; they remain intrinsically good, but because of man's sinfulness and constant abuse of them their goodness is concealed and submerged in sinful solidarity. Therefore, evil and sin inhere not so much in things *per se* as in the human agent utilizing them. It is a case of men's hearts dominated by sin and the noxious solidarity of iniquity; they have resolved to avail themselves of created things in an unjust and selfish way.

When sin reigns in the heart of individuals and spreads to

the whole of mankind, it molds, orders and structures the world in such a way that it becomes sin's domain, an investment of sinfulness. The depth of wickedness in humanity at large and in individuals engenders a greater assertion and overall facilitation of evil in the world. Therefore, man has been unjust toward the Creator by doing violence to created things; he has failed to comply with God's plan as regards creation: "It was made the victim of frustration, not by its own choice, but because of him, who made it so" (Rom. 8:20). That is why the world needs redemption.

Neoplatonism placed the salvation of man in a prodigious effort of evasion, liberation from the physical body and worldly reality. Even among Christians, models of salvation strongly influenced by the excessive spiritualism of a Neoplatonic or Manichaean stamp were not lacking in theological reflection and spirituality. The reality of salvation which Christ wrought for man pertains not only to the "spiritual soul"; it is salvation of the whole man in his psychosomatic integrity. St. Paul writes: "Now if this is what we proclaim, that Christ was raised from the dead, how can some of you say there is no resurrection of the dead? If there be no resurrection, then Christ was not raised . . . But the truth is, Christ was raised to life—the first fruits of the harvest of the dead" (I Cor. 15: 12–13, 20).

Man's solidarity with the world is redeemed just as truly as his solidarity with fellowmen. Holy Scripture never refers to man's solidarity binding the world to his deadly fate without projecting it in the hope of a redemption to come. The salvation of the world has already begun with Christ's triumph over sin and death, since he died for all. However, it is not yet fully realized. The world awaits with man the fullness of salvation; it is in hope that "the universe itself is to be freed from the shackles of mortality and enter upon the liberty and splendor of the children of God. Up to the present, we know, the whole created universe groans in all its parts as if in the pangs of childbirth. Not only so, but even we, to whom the Spirit is given as firstfruits of the harvest to come, are groaning inwardly while we wait for God to make us his sons and set our whole body free" (Rom. 8:21–23).

This expectation of fullness is not without promise and strife. Christian hope connotes a determination to fight courageously "against the authorities and potentates of this dark world, against the super-human forces of evil in the heavens" which exploit evil scattered even in the air which man breathes, to block his development and his opening up to God (cf. Eph. 6:11–20). The man redeemed in Christ extends his dominion over the cosmos in an attitude of adoration and brotherly service, freeing it ever more from all types of sinful investment which erring men have wrought. Salvation for the Christian does not lie in "liberation from the world" but in living in the world with a heart renewed by Christ in brotherhood and responsibility for one's environment so as to destroy the power of deadly sin and extend the kingdom of Christ.

C. Selfish Existence in the Bodily Reality

Evil does not reside one-sidedly in the body or in the cosmic reality, nor is either one evil in itself. The cosmos and the human body were created as "very good" by God. Evil comes from within man, from his heart, his pride and egotism: "But what comes out of the mouth has its origin in the heart; and that is what defiles a man. Wicked thoughts, murder, adultery, fornication, theft, perjury, slander—these all proceed from the heart" (Mt. 15:18–19).

Springing from the heart of man, sin diffuses itself throughout the body and whole being of the person. Because it is rooted in the whole man, sin enslaves him and expresses its sovereignty in a set of consequences which Paul calls "the law of the flesh [sarx]." Sarx can also be translated as "incarnate sinfulness." "For I know that nothing good lodges in me—in my unspiritual nature [sarx], I mean—for though the will to do good is there, the deed is not. The good which I want to do, I fail to do; but what I do is the wrong which is against my will; and if what I do is against my will, clearly it is no longer I who am the agent, but sin that has its lodging in me. I discover this principle then: that when I want to do the right, only the wrong is within my reach" (Rom. 7:18–21). The body has multiple relations and interdependencies with the world and enslaves it in the very sinfulness which, because of a perverted "heart," has taken hold of it. Somehow the body serves as instrumental means for the sinful outlook on the world around us (Rom. 1:14–32).

These strong expressions of St. Paul should not be interpreted as a devaluation of the body or of earthly realities. We have already indicated how Paul defends the resurrection-of-the-body reality (I Cor. 15) and the cosmic extension of Christ's redemption (Rom. 8:18 ff.). In his letter to the Ephesians (1:7–12), he refers to the mystery of the Father in terms of his design "that the universe, all in heaven and on earth, might be brought into a unity in Christ" (Eph. 1:10). In that to the Colossians, he asserts that Christ "is the image of the invisible God; his is the primacy over all created things. In him everything in heaven and on earth was created, not only things visible but also the invisible . . . the whole universe has been created through him and for him. And he exists before everything, and all things are held together in him" (Col. 1:15–17).

Thus, when Paul speaks of the "law of sin" in man and identifies it with the "law of the flesh," he wants to stress how the sin of the heart involves the body and the whole world of man, and how, once the body and the world have come under the dominion of sin, they constitute a sinful force holding man ever more in its clutch. If man wishes to open himself to the power of love, he must overcome that of sin in him and in the world; he must transform and subdue the self and the world, both of which are dominated by egotism and pride.

In speaking of flesh [sarx] in the pejorative sense as the setting and strength of sin, Paul never thinks of the body only or of the body as created by God. He presents the whole man: one who, in his body-soul totality, adopts or has adopted a selfish mode of existence by giving priority to his selfish ego over his brethren, his life environment, the whole cosmos and

God. The "law of the flesh" is nothing other than selfishness with all its usual consequences; the heart fixates on the ego as a mode of life. Self-centeredness then invades the whole personality and manifests itself as a potent deterrent against every invitation to love.

D. The World-Idol

When the Bible speaks of the pride of great nations, e.g., Babylonia or Egypt, it characterizes it as idolatrous. The greatness of a nation's own civilization and political power became the focal point of all preoccupations to the point where citizens (and more so the ruling class) forgot all about God and neighbor. The Bible regards such "pride" as an extension of the arrogant self-aggrandizement of men desirous of attaining a godlike power and sovereignty comparable to that symbolized by the tower of Babel episode (Gen. 11:1–9).

The golden calf which the Israelites constructed and worshiped in the desert is probably symbolic of the strength and power of the nation, victors over the Egyptians. Yahweh is "adored" as sign and source of the nation's strength. Even religion becomes a means of the self-enhancement of the nation. The Bible castigates the persons or nations that place their ultimate trust and supreme hope in themselves; they then become idolaters. When man no longer wholeheartedly entrusts himself to God in an adoring spirit, he is involved in setting up and using the world as an idol. He pairs terrestrial realities and earthly values as absolutes before which and for which he will sacrifice his true self and his neighbor. The man who no longer adores God loses the authentic sense and value of things including his own being; he becomes enslaved by lust, by his own realizations and earthly structures. The whole history of Israel bears tragic testimony to this truth which Paul, in the first chapter of his letter to the Romans, later explicitates and formulates in very clear terms as valid for the whole of sinful mankind.

In these contexts, Holy Scripture does not speak of secularization but of an idolized secularism or of a kind of pseudo-religion of man seeking his ultimate goal outside of God. For the inspired authors, such degeneration is not without diabolical influence, for the world thus alienated from God comes under the power of the Evil One. Insane in this idolatry, "secularized man," i.e., man who refuses to adore the true God, with his world becomes victim of the proud and lying spirits. No wonder, then, that the Gospel message remains veiled to these idolatrous men: "Their unbelieving minds are so blinded by the god of this age, that the gospel of the glory of Christ, who is the very image of God, cannot dawn upon them and bring them light" (II Cor. 4:4). The "wisdom of this world" which rejects the Gospel is very much related to the "princes of this world" (I Cor. 2:6; 3:19).

This does not mean that the created things, culture or the economic life are, by their very essence, the domain of devils. The world is not by itself the field or instrument of demonic power. When Scripture speaks in these terms, it wishes to underscore the profound repercussions of man's selfish attitudes. When man idolizes the world and earthly realities, they become fertile terrain for the devils' influence. By extending sin over the world, man gradually relinquishes it to the evil spirits, enabling them to assert their dominion over it. The devils are not necessarily extraterrestrial powers but rather represent the total embodiment of all the evil operating in man's history.

Thus are those statements of Scripture warning against every idolatrous attitude to be understood: "Then put to death those parts of you which belong to the earth—fornication, indecency, lust, foul cravings, and the ruthless greed which is nothing less than idolatry" (Col. 3:5). In other instances, there is reference to fornicators and the avaricious as idolaters (Eph. 5:5; I Tim. 6:10). They are all idol worshipers who render absolute either themselves or the world. In so doing, they spread sin to the earthly reality and allow Satan to expand his ruinous domain. The world is then transformed into a powerful and fascinating idol but one that proffers death.

The major danger lurking in modern secularism lies precisely in its negating or setting God aside, for it thus runs the risk of converting technology and the sciences into new and overpowering idols, oppressive to the dignity and freedom of man. It would then confirm with new terms and contents the idolatrous process against which so many prophets of the Old Testament committed themselves—a process which eventuates in enslaving men, especially the weak and defenseless.

In the past, one often found an idolatrous attitude in relation to socio-political and socio-religious structures. History bears witness to the many times the value of community service was lost to them; once structures had been made absolute, there was no hesitation to offer notable human sacrifices to them. It may help contemporary man to resort to historical flashback when judging the "anti-establishment" attitudes of today's youth. On the other hand, we need to pledge ourselves to the creation of new structures which would truly serve human dignity and solidarity, but structures flexible enough to meet our changing needs.

E. Ambivalence of This Contemporary Age

The present worldly reality is dramatically ambivalent. Its fundamental value, which arises from its being created by the Word of God in view of Christ, persists but it finds itself engulfed in a situation of profound alienation. The various cultural structures and social, political, economic or religious ordinances which together constitute the present world are strongly characterized by alienation and disjunction; consequently, they serve to estrange man from God.

When Scripture alludes to "this world," it often wants to designate the ambivalence of the cosmic-temporal reality and the strongly felt presence of sin in the human environment. Ambivalence should not be mistaken for an initial "indifference" which can later become good or evil depending on man's decision. *Ambivalence* here refers to a world already frustrated by man's sin; the positive elements for good are partially weighted down by the negative forces of sin.

Christ declares to Pilate: "My kingdom does not belong to this world" (Jn. 18:36). In the Cenacle, he warned his disciples: "If the world hates you, it hated me first, as you know well. If you belonged to the world, the world would love its own; but because you do not belong to the world, because I have chosen you out of the world, for that reason the world hates you" (Jn. 15:18–19). The person and kingdom of Christ do not come under the ambivalence of a world frustrated by the selfish pride of man. Christ comes to free man and his world. Once his disciples have accepted him in faith, they are liberated from the pride and selfishness of the world and no longer have any part of its ambivalence: "I pray thee, not to take them out of the world, as I am" (Jn. 17:15–16); so prays Christ in view of his death for the life of the world.

Scripture severely warns those "who are rich in this world's goods" (I Tim. 6:17; II Tim. 4:10), the "wise by the standards of this world" (I Cor. 3:18–20). However, there is no question of a radical judgment condemning the sciences, culture and the goods of the earth. On the contrary, it is a firm attitudinal stance against the pride and selfishness which would utilize creation to bind it to sin and lead men to idolatry. But it goes beyond a mere personal attitude. Biblical references also point to an investment or an incarnation of selfish idolatry in tradition, culture, public opinion and structures. Personal frustration originates from this false worship of structures and cultural artifacts, and each sin greatly affects and aggravates the situation.

"The concerns of the world [*sollicitudo saeculi huius*]" are ambivalent and therefore dangerous because of the deceitful glamor of wealth (Mt. 13:22). The hazard becomes greater whenever the religious perspective of grateful adoration of God in the service of neighbor is weakened. They are "worldly" people whoever selfishly avail themselves of earthly goods: "And so you are not to set your mind on food and drink; you are not to worry. For all these are things for the heathen to run after, but you have a Father who knows that you need them. No, set your mind upon his kingdom, and all the rest

will come to you as well" (Lk. 12:29–31). A believer's concern
for what he will eat or drink or use for dress ought to maintain
him openly confident in the Heavenly Father. It should never
suggest the proud assertion and haughty self-sufficiency of
idolaters but correspond to a spirit of adoration and brotherhood for whoever seeks the kingdom of God.

Earthly things, good in themselves and manifestations of
God's love, become dangerous only when they are no longer
seen in the light of God. Their quest entails risk if the search is
not integrated in the sincere pursuit of man's ultimate goal
(cf. Mt. 16:26); it then represents exploitation of the brethren
and an investment of egotism in the world where we must live.

In this context, Scripture never mentions secularization, but
it is not difficult to discover some of the main problems involved in secularism and in the whole process of today's secularization. At every step, there is a biblical reminder of how
man's secularity and the intrinsic value of the world are frustrated whenever they become radical assertions of man's autonomy and self-sufficiency. Oblivious of God, man then sets
himself and his self-actualization in his stead; but unavoida-
bly, then, he loses his own dignity and freedom by sacrificing
them to his new, self-made idols.

Scripture constantly reminds man of the absolute indispensability of vigilance and adoration. It is necessary to know how
to read the signs and to commit oneself in the present state of
ambivalence. Man lies forever exposed to the dangers of an
idolatrous secularism when the allurement of beauty and the
grandeur of the world, gift of God and work of his own hands,
lead him to ignore its Creator.

II. THE WORLD OF CHRIST

Christ stands at the very center of the biblical vision of man
and his world. Surely there is also the world, in a pejorative
sense, characterized by an adverse relationship to Christ, i.e.,
a closed-minded world in full opposition to him. However, the

positive evaluation prevails because both cosmos and man are created and redeemed in Christ.

It is imperative that today's theology return to a biblical Christocentrism. The Scotist current has always been strongly Christocentric; however, like all theological schools, it has sometimes yielded to abstractness and fallen into a "theology of possibles." Contrariwise, biblical Christocentrism founds a theology of reality, a theology of the real history, namely, that of existent humanity and the world in Christ. It is incumbent on theologians, in view of their authentic service in the Church today to return to such a vision.[2]

Christ stands as the Alpha and Omega of the evolution of both the world and humanity. "When all things began, the Word already was . . . through him all things came to be" (Jn. 1:1–2). All created things and the whole of human history assume value and meaning in him, the non-created Word of the Father and Word Incarnate in the fullness of time: "the whole universe has been created through him and for him. And he exists before everything, and all things are held together in him" (Col. 1:16–17). "Out of his full store we have all received grace upon grace" (Jn. 1:16).

Christ is not only the point Omega of the whole history of the world; he is also its *Redeemer*. "God loved the world so much that he gave his only Son, that everyone who has faith in him may not die but have eternal life. It was not to judge the world, but that through him the world might be saved" (Jn. 3:16–17). "We know that this is in truth the Savior of the world" (Jn. 4:42). John the Baptist points him out as "the

---

[2] See particularly:

Cerfaux, L., *Le Christ dans la théologie de S. Paul* (Paris, 1954).

———, *La théologie de l'Eglise suivant S. Paul*, 2d ed. (Paris, 1965).

Cullman, O., *Christ et le temps. Temps et histoire dans le Christianisme primitif* (Neuchâtel-Paris, 1947).

———, *Christologie du Nouveau Testament* (Neuchâtel-Paris, 1958).

Gogarten, F., *Jesus Christus Wende der Welt, Grundfragen zur Christologie* (Tübingen: Mohr, 1967).

Maloney, G., *The Cosmic Christ—From Paul to Teilhard* (New York, 1968).

Lamb of God; it is he who takes away the sin-solidarity [*ten hamartian*] of the world" (Jn. 1:29)—sin in the depth and complexity referred to earlier. Having come to save man, Christ redeems him in his personal totality and in the fullness of his fraternal and cosmic interdependencies. In Christ, human brotherhood returns once again to the solidarity of salvation and the world partakes of his victory over a sinful interdependency and death. A new solidarity is thus established.

The deleterious sin-death solidarity established within the whole of humanity, and gripping mankind and the cosmos, suffers defeat. Christ now sustains all in a community of salvation (the Church) and as a communion of the "redeemed" in him. Hence the full range of man's relations with God, neighbor, himself and the world are returned to their original value.

Christ is the light of the world (cf. Jn. 1:4 ff.; 3:19; 8:12; 9:5; 12:46). Whoever by faith shares the light of Christ as disciples become, in turn, light of the world (cf. Mt. 5:14–16; Eph. 5:8). Through the Gospel and their witness of faith and charity, the followers of Christ illumine the world, freeing it from the darkness of sin-solidarity (cf. Rom. 1:18).

Even in the most trying moments and in desperate situations, the Christian's faith-charity never ceases to radiate Christ in the immediate surroundings. Paul writes with regard to his imprisonment: "Friends, I want you to understand that the work of the Gospel has been helped on, rather than hindered, by this business of mine. My imprisonment in Christ's cause has become common knowledge to all at headquarters here, and indeed among the public at large; and it has given confidence to most of our fellow-Christians to speak the word of God fearlessly and with extraordinary courage" (Phil. 1: 12–14).

The category "light" is likewise found in the Qumran literature of the time of Christ but in a different perspective; there light is the privilege of a select group living cut off from the rest of the world, which is left in darkness. Christ, on the contrary, is the light that shines in the darkness; he becomes flesh to live among men as one of the brethren. If a Church keeps herself in contemptuous isolation, more concerned with safe-guarding her structures and institutions than with testifying to light in humble service to humanity, she is no longer faithful to Christ-Light.

Dietrich Bonhoeffer, while in his prison camp, underlined the necessity for Christian churches to die in Christ so as to be revived in him. He was scandalized by the Christian churches' failure to find courage to defend the weak, the poor and the persecuted because of fear for their institutional safety. Institutional egotism and a too worldly preoccupation for security had grown to the point where the Church's trust in the Holy Spirit and her commitment to justice and fraternal love were obscured. Christ remained, at all times, open, vulnerable and dedicated to the world. The Church must adopt the same attitude and exemplify it by being present in the world of the discriminated minorities, of the oppressed and the poor; there lies the choice of salvation.

Christ is the life of the world. His death and resurrection are intended for the life of the world. He gives himself to his disciples as "the living bread descended from heaven"; if one eats of him, he will live eternally (cf. Jn. 6:48 ff.). In the eucharistic celebration, the mystery of his death and resurrection is re-enacted in the anticipation of his glorious return. However, the words of Christ ought not to be limited to the sacramental-eucharistic sense. Christ is availability itself, the bread to be eaten by everyone; he is the Servant who gives himself selflessly for the life of the world. Likewise should Christians devote themselves wholeheartedly to the service of justice and charity and allow themselves to be "consumed" by their brethren.

Christ loves his own who remained in the world for not being of the world. He implores the Father to deliver them from evil but not to take them out of the world. He prays that they be sanctified—"in truth . . . may they all be one: as Thou, Father, art in me, and I in Thee, so also may they be in us, that the world may believe that thou didst send me" (Jn. 17:17–21). In this passage, the "world" comprises the totality of men in their life environment; thus the redemption of Christ proves true and valid also for all created things (cf. Rom. 8:21–24).

The resurrection of Christ serves as the surest pledge of the resurrection of the body (cf. I Cor. 15). It also marks the beginning of the liberation of the cosmos from the servitude of sin and death, and unfailingly presages the final liberation of created reality from the vanity of sin; it is a pledge of "the new heaven and the new earth." The redemption of Christ has a real cosmic dimension but always in view of mankind.

Christ is the prophet who comes into the world. In the Scriptures a prophet is a man who because of his experience of God takes a generous and genuine interest in his brethren, particularly the poor, the discriminated-against and the strangers. This commitment to his brethren is the criterion of true worship of God. Such a prophetic vein is not exclusively Judeo-Christian; through the grace of God, it is also found outside Israel and outside the churches and oftentimes as a wholesome reaction to aberrations from the veritable faith. In such instances, prophetism reveals an altruistic passion for a healthier and more brotherly world.

Christ courageously and unequivocally proves by his life that brotherhood is what determines the true value and meaning of the world and the use of worldly things. He forcefully denounces every form of idolatry and abuse of created things, especially the instrumental use of "religion" for self-enhancement and exploitation of one's neighbor: "Alas for you, lawyers and pharisees, hypocrites! You pay tithes of mint and dill and cummin, but you have overlooked the weightier demands of the law: justice, mercy, and good faith" (Mt. 23:23).

When the Pharisees protest that his disciples are not observing tradition, he responds by flinging into their face that they fail to respect the commandment of God. "You have made God's law null and void out of respect for your tradition" (Mt. 15:1–6). In Christ, then, we find the fulfillment of the generous prophetic tradition of Israel, one which, in Jeremiah, had tones of a courageous and vibrant protest; "Mend your ways and your doings, deal fairly with one another, do not oppress the alien, the orphan and the widow, shed no innocent blood in this place, do not run after other gods to your own ruin. Then I will let you live in this place . . . You gain nothing by putting your trust in this lie" (Jer. 7:5–8).

Redeeming and redeemed love gives sense and value to the world, to human history and to the use of all of God's gifts. Therefore, Christ can solemnly affirm on the eve of his passion: "I have conquered the world" (Jn. 16:33). He has vanquished the egotism and the pride that have rendered man's heart idolatrous, and introduced sin and death into the world (Rom. 5:12 ff.). The anguish and "absurdity" of death is nothing other than the fruit of sin. If Christ gives sense and value to death, it is by making of his own a manifestation of love and solidarity.

Christ is the judge of the world. The old man Simeon prophesied to Mary in the temple: "This child is destined to be a sign which men reject; and you too shall be pierced to the heart. Many in Israel will stand or fall because of him, and thus the secret thoughts of many will be laid bare" (Lk. 2:34–35). Christ is the salvific protest and scandal before whom men are compelled to take a stand. They are in the presence of the fullness of the Father's love and the manifestation of his redemptive plan, which strongly and urgently force men to take position. Christ comes among us as a light unmasking the darkness of the world, of all those who seek seclusion in a blindly proud egotism and thus prefer darkness to light.

As Christ concludes his discourse on the bread from heaven, many of his disciples exclaim: "This is more than we can stomach! Why listen to such talk?" And Jesus says: "Does this shock you? What if you see the Son of Man ascending to the place where he was before? The spirit alone gives life; the flesh is of no avail; the words which I have spoken to you are both spirit and life. And yet there are some of you who have no faith." John then comments: "For Jesus knew all along who were without faith and who was to betray him" (Jn. 6:60–64). The unambiguous words of Christ compel his disciples to manifest either faith or disbelief of the heart; they must decide intrepidly with no half measures allowed. As to the necessity and urgency of taking position, which his presence demands, Christ often comes back on the point: "No servant can be the slave of two masters; for either he will hate the first and love the second, or he will be devoted to the first and think nothing of the second. You cannot serve God and Money" (Lk. 16:13; and see Mt. 6:24 ff.).

The work of separation and judgment has begun with Christ's coming in the flesh: "It is for judgment that I have come into this world—to give sight to the sightless and to make blind those who see" (Jn. 9:30). Once risen, Christ continues his work through the Spirit whom he sends to his disciples: "When he comes, he will confute the world, and show where wrong and right and judgment lie. He will convict them to wrong, by their refusal to believe in me; he will convince them that right is on my side, by showing that I go to the Father when I pass from your sight; and he will convince them of divine judgment, by showing that the Prince of this world stands condemned" (Jn. 16:8–11). It follows that the judgment of the Church cannot be a triumphalistic verdict coming just from a "sacred institution" or one of orthodox abstraction devoid of charity; it is a humble testimony of love rendering present the Spirit which judges the world.

The work of judgment will be perfected with the return of Christ. He will then definitively separate those who have loved from those who have not overcome their own selfishness and pride (Mt. 25:31–46). However, even before the coming of Christ, religious faith constituted a presence of his grace and a judgment. That is why the whole history of Israel with all its vicissitudes was, through authentic faith in Yahweh, an efficacious sign of salvation and judgment, an appeal to other nations to decide for the true God. Israel's election and mission become condemnation instead of salvation for part of the elected nation because of its idolatrous pride; where Israel the servant is faithful, it is judgment only for those who reject its testimony; it is like Noah, who "by faith, was divinely warned about the unseen future . . . and made good his claim to the righteousness which comes of faith" (Heb. 11:7). "A faith operative in love" bears peace to the world and, at the same time, unmasks its idols and sin (cf. Gal. 5:6–23). "You must not think that I have come to bring peace to the earth; I have come to set a man against his father, a daughter against her mother. . . . By gaining his life a man will lose it; by losing his life for my sake, he will gain it" (Mt. 10:34–39).

Faith in Christ is victory over the world. "Every child of God is victor over the godless world. The victory that defeats the world is our faith" (I Jn. 5:4). The dominion of Christ over the godless world is manifested and actualized in faith and charity, which prepare for and participate in his final judgment and utmost victory. "The sovereignty of the world has passed to our Lord and his Christ, and he shall reign for ever and ever!" (Rev. 11:15). In the meantime, the faith which conquers the world finds expression in the proclamation, in word and deed, that Christ is the selfless love which triumphs over a loveless world. In faith there is no question of triumphalism; rather, it is a radical acceptance and testimony of Christ, the Servant.

Christ manifests and confirms his Messianic kingdom in the world by his love, the humbleness of his service and full submission to the Father's plan; he "made himself nothing, assuming the nature of a slave. Bearing the human likeness, revealed in human shape, he humbled himself, and in obedience accepted even death—death on a cross" (Phil. 2:7–8). He judges severely the type of messianic hope so common in Israel at the time of his coming, namely, a hope deeply contaminated by national pride, by the desire for power or careerism. He asserts that such a hope is not conducive to acceptance of salvation. In fact, it remains profoundly dominated by collective sinfulness, fruit of pride and selfishness, which Christ comes to conquer.

The devil shows him "all the kingdoms of the world in their glory," telling him: "All these, I will give to you, if you will only fall down and do me homage," but Jesus responds by: "Begone, Satan! You shall do homage to the Lord your God and worship him alone" (Mt. 4:8–10). The temptation midrash means not merely an episodic temptation; it is the moving expression of a profound and permanent reality in the whole life of Christ. He is constantly surrounded by such provocations in his own environment; throughout his life the Spirit carries Christ into the desert of humility and poverty, whereby he withstands this evil spirit of misuse and misunderstanding of religion.

When Peter shows himself unwilling to accept a Messiah for whom it would be necessary that "he go to Jerusalem and there suffer much from the elders, chief priests and doctors of the law, to be put to death," Christ dismisses him brusquely: "Away with you, Satan; you are a stumbling block to me. You think as men think, not as God thinks" (Mt. 15:21–23). Attention is called to the parallelism between the two passages of Matthew, both culminating in the same apostrophe to Satan.

Given time, Peter comes to believe and announces courageously: "Let all Israel then accept as certain that God has made this Jesus, whom you crucified, both Lord and Messiah" (Acts 2:36). "There is no salvation in anyone else, for there is no other name under heaven granted to men, by which we may receive salvation" (Acts 4:12). Thus will Peter be saved. Many priests, pharisees and scribes, on the contrary, remain unbelieving, closing their heart and repeating under the cross: "He saved others, but he cannot save himself. Let the Messiah, the king of Israel, come down now from the cross. If we see that, we shall believe" (Mk. 15:31–32). Before Christ's resurrection, the chief priests offered the soldiers a substantial bribe to have them say, "His disciples came by night and stole the body while we were asleep" (Mt. 28:12–13); when later the apostles begin to announce the death-resurrection of the Lord, "they are arrested and put in prison" (Acts 4:3). By closing themselves to Christ and taking position against him, the scribes and Pharisees reveal themselves and remain "the condemned world."

These biblical perspectives should serve to help us judge

theological trends (such as the Social Gospel and the *Kulturchristentum*) that reduce the meaning and value of the Gospel to a message uniquely or mainly capable of arousing a generous commitment for social and cultural development in this world. In the past, this kind of earthly messianism was almost always linked to a national or cultural superiority complex very similar to that of the Jewish priests and scribes who rejected Christ. Whoever thinks this way about faith ought to reflect critically on his position in the light of the decisive affirmations of Christ that his kingdom is not of this world (cf. Jn. 18:33–37). He should closely scrutinize his attitudes as to whether or not they are in the line of Satan's "temptation" in the desert or Peter's words on hearing of Christ's impending passion and death.

The Christian needs to take seriously into account his commitment to the salvation of the world; without it his faith is empty and lacking (cf. James 2:14–26). His socio-cultural commitment, however, should be totally different from a purely worldly mission; it should derive its inspiration, motivation and direction from faith in eternal life and be characterized by the love and humility of Christ. "Whoever, in obedience to Christ seeks first the kingdom of God will as a consequence receive a stronger and purer love for helping all his brothers and for perfecting the work of justice under the inspiration of charity" (GS, Art. 72).

III. THE WORLD OF RELIGION

A. *The Priestly-Religious Sphere of Worldliness*

Whoever reads the Gospel is immediately struck by the fact that the pejorative sense of "world" is applied frequently and with severity to the ecclesiastical world of the pharisees, the scribes and the priests. They constitute the condemned world: "You belong to this world below, I to the world above.

Your home is in this world, mine is not" (Jn. 8:23). They form a closed and immobile religious establishment, a socially privileged class committed to the protection of its own interests. They lack in the understanding of man and the living God. They are therefore insensitive to the "signs of the times." They seek signs and miracles primarily to demonstrate power and efficiency but have no interest in the great "miracle" of brotherly commitment. "It is a wicked generation that asks for a sign; and the only sign that will be given it is the sign of Jonah" (Mt. 16:2–4; Jn. 4:48; I Cor. 1:22).

The world of such sacred persons (scribes, pharisees, priests) perverts religion into an instrument for their own vanity and earthly advantage (cf. Mt. 6:1–5). They consequently close themselves ever more to Christ; their opposition against him grows to the point of deciding to kill him once they find an opportunity for seizing him without arousing the people (cf. Mt. 26:3–5). After the execution of the Master, their fierce antagonism persists against his disciples, according to Christ's prophecy: "They will ban you from the synagogue; indeed, the time is coming when anyone who kills you will suppose that he is performing a religious duty" (Jn. 16:2). The reason lies in the fact that the presence of the disciples also attests to the wickedness of their works (cf. Jn. 7:7).

The pseudo-religious world of the scribes and pharisees is neither capable of understanding nor of receiving the "Spirit of truth" which the Lord promises his disciples (cf. Jn. 14:16–17), so it remains under the dominion of "the spirit of the world." Contrariwise, Christians can joyously say with Paul: "This is the Spirit that we have received from God, and not the spirit of the world, so that we may know all that God, of his grace, has given us" (I Cor. 2:12).

By utilizing religion for the jealous defense of privileges, rights and honors of their social class (Mt. 23:5–7; Jn. 9:28 ff.), the Pharisees, scribes and priests seal themselves off from their brethren in need, and conceal the face of the Father, who is merciful and benevolent toward everyone (cf. Lk. 10:30–32). "Whitewashed tombs," they do not think of purity of heart in

charity but concern themselves only with man-made law: "So
it is with you: outside you look like honest men, but inside you
are brim-full of hypocrisy and crime" (Mt. 23:28). Alienated
from life and the needs of the brethren, they substitute for the
law of God their human traditions which oppress the weak
(cf. Mk. 7:11–13; Mt. 15:4–6). On the strength of tradition,
they can allow themselves to pull their donkey or ox out of
the ditch on the Sabbath but not to save the life of a brother
(cf. Jn. 9:16; Mt. 12:9ff.). Religion becomes reduced to an
excessive accumulation of human traditions through which,
says the Lord: "you shut the door of the kingdom of Heaven
in men's faces; you do not enter yourselves, and when others
are entering, you stop them" (Mt. 23:13).

Even in the primitive Church, there was no want of temptations for such a "worldly" religiosity. Paul fights against them
right along; he is conscious that his yielding would only block
the power and dynamism of the Gospel, enslaving it to this
world: "Allow no one therefore to take you to task about
what you eat or drink, or over the observance of festival, new
moon or sabbath. These are no more than a shadow of what
was to come; the solid reality is Christ. You are not to be
disqualified by the decision of people who go in for self-
mortification and angel-worship, and try to enter into some
vision of their own. Such people, bursting with the futile
conceit of worldly minds, lose hold upon the Head; yet it is
from the Head that the whole body, with all its joints and
ligaments, receives its supplies, and thus knit together grows
according to God's design" (Col. 2:16–19).

Paul then continues: "Did you not die with Christ and pass
beyond reach of the elemental spirits of the natural world?
Then why behave as though you were still living the life of the
world? Why let people dictate to you: 'Do not handle this,
do not taste that, do not touch the other'—all of them things
that must perish as soon as they are used? That is to follow
merely human injunctions and teaching. True, it has an air
of wisdom, with its forced piety, its self-mortification, and its
severity to the body, but it is of no use at all in combating

sensuality" (Col. 2:20–23). That which should be the preoccupation of the Christian is the wholehearted love of God and love of the other as oneself (cf. Mk. 12:29–31). Paul comments: "I may dole out all I possess, or even give my body to be burnt, but if I have no love, I am none the better" (I Cor. 13:3).

The Church becomes "world" when she loses prophetic courage for the sake of saving her institutions and privileges, when she manipulates revealed truth for socio-religious and politico-religious designs, when she makes of the Gospel an ideological domain or an abstract orthodoxy falling short of a wholehearted commitment to man's salvation. By keeping in mind these and other phenomena of unholy worldliness, which goes hand in hand with the unworldliness (alienation from life) of religious and ecclesiastical institutions, one can understand the deep significance of Karl Barth's and Dietrich Bonhoeffer's desire for a "religionless Christianity." In final analysis, it is a matter of Christianity radically refuting "mundanized" religion; it refers to a faith unhindered by a "worldly" deviation of religion, so that in faith and by the testimony of faith, Christ is truly Lord of the world created by him and for him.

The first epistle of John clearly counts among "the world of darkness" those Christians who do not live in charity: "My brothers, do not be surprised if the world hates you. We for our part have crossed over from death to life; this we know, because we love our brothers. The man who does not love is still in the realm of death" (I Jn. 3:13–15). He who does not believe in Christ with a faith that actualizes itself as generous and disinterested love of the brethren remains enslaved to the "world of sin" which Christ came to conquer. A faith which is concerned with a thousand and one legal or formalistic questions and an abstract orthodoxy alienated from reality and the concreteness of daily life or one deprived of a commitment to brotherly love, cannot liberate us from the Evil One and his worldly domain. It is not a faith that conquers the world.

B. The Impious World of Gnosticism

Toward the end of the apostolic age, Christianity was no longer pitted primarily against the Pharisaic-Judaic world but against a Gnostic world. There certainly remained difficulties of a pharisaic kind but there arose dilemmas of new urgency brought about by the Gnostic influence.

The Gnostics began with a radical depreciation of the human body and every other earthly or visible reality. Thus they rendered themselves incapable of understanding the Incarnation of Christ in its full reality, depth and salvific value. John so asserts: "Every spirit which acknowledges that Jesus Christ has come in the flesh is from God, and every spirit which does not thus acknowledge Jesus is not from God. This is what is meant by 'Anti-Christ'; yet you have been told that he was to come, and here he is, in the world already! . . . They are of that world, and so therefore is their teaching; that is why the world listens to them. But we belong to God, and a man who knows God listens to us, while he who does not belong to God refuses us a hearing" (I Jn. 4:2–6).

Unable to understand the meaning of Christ's Incarnation, the Gnostics considered faith as contemptuous of commitment for a better-ordained visible world and were therefore incapable and unwilling of meeting the exigencies of a true incarnate brotherhood of men in the fatherhood of God. "Faith" itself thus became a cause of alienation from the real world and consequently gave rise to secularism; such an attitude leaves the earthly realities for those who do not care for salvation. It bequeathes an economic, social and political world constructed without God and without that salvation which comes through faith in the Word Incarnate.

Faced by such an alienating faith and such religiosity, the reaction of John is strong: "That is the difference between the children of God and the children of the devil; no one who does not do right is God's child, nor is anyone who does not love his brother. For the message you have heard from the beginning is this: that we should love one another; unlike Cain, who was a child of the evil one and murdered his brother. . . . We for our part have crossed over from death to life" (I Jn. 3:10–14).

The love to which John refers is not purely idealistic but an active and operative love: "And we in turn are bound to lay down our lives for our brothers. But if a man has enough to live on, and yet when he sees his brother in need shuts up his heart against him, how can it be said that the divine love dwells in him? My children, love must not be a matter of words or talk; it must be genuine and show itself in action" (I Jn. 3:16–18).

Equally strong was the reaction of James against every vision of faith which did not lead to active justice and charity: "My brothers, what use is it for a man to say he has faith when he does nothing to show it? Can that faith save him? Suppose a brother or a sister is in rags with not enough food for the day, and one of you says, 'Good luck to you, keep yourselves warm, and have plenty to eat,' but does nothing to supply their bodily needs, what is the good of that? So with faith; if it does not lead to action, it is in itself a lifeless thing" (James 2:14–17).

The New Testament undeniably condemned with the same rigor those who are blinded by the goods of this earth or so selfishly possessive of them that they do not recognize Christ, and others who, while recognizing Christ, do not take seriously the visible world and the glorification of God in the body through an active and operative charity. To subtract oneself from commitment to a more humane and fraternal world is "worldliness" (or unholy unworldliness). The man who conceives religion as a "sacred egotism" leading to the narrow and petty confines of "sacred things" and "sacred rites" is responsible if others construe mankind and the world without God. This so-called religion becomes a cause of atheism and secularism.

Such a mentality is also found reflected in many manuals of moral theology of the last two centuries, particularly in the

treatment of "occasions of sin." In every activity and in every
new achievement of humanity, these moralists are concerned
primarily with singling out the dangers of sin. They wish to
create a "glass bell" that would insulate believers from every
risk, an attitude which keeps the faithful "outside" of the real
world. It is advocating withdrawal from the world, something
alien to Christ's prayer for his disciples (Jn. 17:15). At the
same time, a narrow concept of obedience toward authority
and the existing order discouraged prophetic protest and
efforts to build a better world.

Certainly, prudence is necessary but that of the Christian
cannot be a petty, individualistic calculation; it is the courage
of a heart that believes, loves and scrutinizes the signs of the
hour to discover the Father's will. The obligation to avoid
the occasions of sin is to be considered only within one's mission of being in the world so as to open it to Christ and his all-
embracing love. Confronted with new technical and scientific
achievements, one need concern himself above all with serving
humanity. If one looks solely or primarily for the occasions of
sin, one ends up depriving the world of the active and responsible presence of the believers; all new means and novel
achievements would then truly be perilous. These are ex-
tremely important points for a relevant catechesis and for
Christian formation today.

The temporary "flight" from the world in veritable Christian
contemplation differs totally from those forms proclaimed by
Buddhism and certain Gnostic or Manichean sects. It does not
consist in a depreciation of the world but in an intensified
effort to learn how to love the world in Christ, in full awareness
of the world's need of Christ for authentic progress. The
Christian contemplative seeks the depth and integration of a
live faith rendering him capable of becoming "light of the
world," "salt of the earth" without allowing himself to be as-
similated in the dispersion and egotism which still dominate
a great part of the world.

There is need to recognize, however, that a certain ascetical
literature has been and is still tainted by a too negative vision

of the world and of the human community. This kind of spirituality particularly characterizes the presentation and structuralization of the papal enclosure of nuns (decree *Venite seorsum*, 1969). It evinces a simplistic identification of the common life of people outside the enclosure with the "world" so strongly condemned by the Scriptures.[3] Such a misunderstanding does harm not only to the nuns but it manifests a danger of dichotomy threatening the Christian life of many.

C. This World and the Future World[4]

In the Scriptures, the "old aeon" and sometimes the "present aeon" are opposed to the new world which comes in Christ and which will be fully manifested and realized in the Parousia, when Christ "delivers up the kingdom of God the Father, after abolishing every kind of domination, authority and power . . . the last enemy to be abolished is death. . . . When all things are thus subject to him, then the Son himself will also be made subordinate to God who made all things subject to him, and thus God will be all in all" (I Cor. 15:24–28). The very fullness typical of the Parousia and the future world has already begun here below with the coming of Christ, his death and resurrection. The time of the Church, namely, the hour of grace between the first and the second coming of Christ, constitutes a valid opportunity for recognizing and actualizing the kingdom of God already present germinally.

Christ begins his apostolic activities preaching: "The time has come; the kingdom of God is upon you; be renewed and believe the Gospel" (Mk. 1:15). The "new aeon" is already dynamically present among us in the Messianic epoch of Christ and the Church. But "this age" and "this world," that is, the attitude and structures of a self-centered humanity, are an

---

[3] We shall return to these last themes in greater detail in Chapter 6. I only wish to mention them here.
[4] We refer particularly to J. Moltmann, *Perspektiven der Theologie* (Munich-Mainz: Kaiser Verlag-Grünewald, 1968).

attempt to obscure the dynamic presence of things to come: "The light shines on in the dark, and the darkness has never mastered it. . . . The real light which enlightens every man was even then coming into the world. He was in the world, but the world, though it owed its being to him, did not recognize him. He entered his own realm, and his own would not receive him" (Jn. 1:5–11).

"This aeon" and the "future aeon" are among men in tension and struggle. However, there are also points of continuity; the "present aeon" is the field in which the sons of the kingdom are scattered; the seed will grow and become a tree (Mt. 13:18–19). The kingdom of God is within the world of man as its leaven (Mt. 13:20–21). The mysterious, humble and real presence of the kingdom of God demands that in the midst of the world the faithful live "a life of temperance, honesty and godliness in the present age, looking forward to the happy fulfillment of our hope when the splendor of our great God and Savior Christ Jesus will appear" (Tit. 2:12–13).

Scripture insists as much on the fleetingness of the present age as on its density and on its urgency for the sons of God to bear fruit in justice and love for the life of the world. The present age is truly taken seriously: it is the time of salvation. However, it is not to be worshiped as if it were the full and definitive reality; we expect the fullness at the return of the Lord (I Cor. 7:29 ff.).

Christian hope is authentic only when it does not entail a depreciation of the earthly reality or a flight from social commitment in order to "avoid contamination." It expresses itself as a drive of fraternal charity, generous and vigilant, which seeks to bring home the earthly reality so as to put it ever more in the service of all mankind. When he returns, Christ will manifest and complete our commitment (Mt. 25).

The present time of favor (*kairos*) is one of continuous self-renewal for man "being constantly renewed in the image of its Creator" (Col. 3:10). This includes a creative and redemptive presence wherever the history of mankind can be shaped. The Lord, when he comes, "will transfigure the body belonging to our humble state, and give it a form like that of his own resplendent body, by the very power which enables him to make all things subject to himself" (Phil. 3:21).

Speaking of the world's destiny, Peter, in his second epistle, expresses himself in apocalyptic terms: "And the present heavens and earth . . . have been kept in store for burning; they are being reserved until the day of judgment when the godless will be destroyed. . . . But the Day of the Lord will come, unexpected as a thief. On that day the heavens will disappear with a great rushing sound, the elements will disintegrate in flames, and the earth with all that is in it will be laid bare" (II Pet. 3:7–10).[5] It is then a question of imagery common to the apocalyptic literary genre which expresses a severe judgment on all idols and on all that which is "world" (in the pejorative sense); the text underlines the transcendence of Christian hope. Notwithstanding, this does not allow us to neglect the hope testimony and hope commitment in this time of salvation.

Gaudium et Spes expresses itself similarly in modern language: "We do not know the time for the consummation of the earth and of humanity. Nor do we know how all things will be transformed. As deformed by sin, the shape of this world will pass away. But we are taught that God is preparing a new dwelling place and a new earth where justice will abide, and whose blessedness will answer and surpass all the longings for peace which spring up in the human heart. Then, with death overcome, the sons of God will be raised up in Christ. What was sown in weakness and corruption will be clothed with incorruptibility. While charity and its fruits endure, all that creation which God made on man's account will be unchained from the bondage of vanity" (GS, Art. 39).

The present commitment to justice, and all that is fruit of the Spirit, "love, joy, patience, kindness, goodness, fidelity, gentleness" (Gal. 5:22) are not doomed to destruction; they form the new man and the "new heaven and the new earth." At Christ's return, when human history comes to its fulfillment

[5] See also II Pet. 1:4; 2:5 ff.

in the complete freedom of the sons and daughters of God, all that has been done for the liberation of mankind from injustice and oppressive structures will be brought home forever, freed from the slag of imperfection found even in our best efforts. The present opportunities for optimal service to mankind will become abiding wealth for the world to come. Christ, who was, who is and who will come, gives us the guarantee that nothing will be lost which is done for him and with him.

CHAPTER 3

THE SACRED AND THE PROFANE

The overriding concern of our study lies in the assessment and growing understanding of today's secularization. If pursued in a spirit of serenity and loyalty, it will inspire believers to be a presence of living faith and to participate responsibly in the secularized contemporary culture. Through close scrutiny of the process of secularization, an attempt will be made to delineate the conduct expected of a committed Christian's presence in today's world. In other words, we intend to present the basic perspectives of a relevant moral theology for this day and age.

A just vision of the "sacred" and the "secular" demands that we explore the basis of the dichotomy that so often characterized the relationship between the "two realms."[1] It also requires that we speak, even if briefly, of the sacred-profane dia-

---

[1] Altizer, Thomas J., *Mircea Eliade and the Dialectic of the Sacred* (Philadelphia: Westminster Press, 1964).

Barry, E. R., *The Secular and the Supernatural* (London: SCM Press, 1969).

Brockway, A. R., *The Secular Saint* (Garden City, N.Y.: Doubleday, 1968).

Grand'maison, J., *Le monde et le sacré: I Le sacré* (Paris, 1966); II *Consecration et sécularisation* (Paris, 1968).

Ramsey, A. M., *Sacred and Secular* (New York: Harper & Row, 1967).

Taylor, M. J., ed., *The Sacred and the Secular* (Englewood Cliffs, N.J.: Prentice-Hall, 1968).

Tillich, Paul, *Christianity and the Encounter of the World Religions* (New York: Harper & Row, 1963).

Van Leeuwen, A. T., *Christentum in der Weltgeschichte—Das Heilige und die Säkularisation* (Stuttgart-Berlin, 1966).

lectics. In fact, an accurate perception of the sacred-profane link in its complex historical evolution is imperative for the understanding of secularity and today's secularization. It is above all essential to point out the difference between the concepts of "secular" and "profane."

Profane refers to that reality exclusive of the sacred. The *profane* defines itself by its negative relationship to the *sacred* and it follows that the sacred sphere and the cultic-priestly domain are seen as opposed to it. The *secular*, on the contrary, *can oppose itself* to the sacred but *it is not defined* as such. When it is not a matter of secularism—which is positively a-religious or anti-religious—the *secular* is not pitted against the sacred.

By itself, the secular underlines the value of the earthly reality and various human activities; it therefore stresses the autonomy which ought to characterize "the secular" when confronted by religion and, specifically, religious institutions and structures. The promotion of this autonomy does not necessarily imply an anti-religious thrust; instead, it attests to a search for a more humane posture and a more authentic organization of religion. It does not necessarily entail a proud desire to do away with God but indicates a determination to overcome all those institutions and forms of power which, by abusing God, offend man's dignity from the standpoint of responsibility and liberty.

Today's protest and refusal of faith-religion as presently conceived and experienced ought not be interpreted as a refusal of God as he revealed himself. More often than not, when sincere, they constitute an alternate route in the enthusiastic search for the true countenance of God through a commitment of fraternal love. It can therefore be a path toward God, who is Love.

In order to arrive at a better understanding of the foregoing, this chapter will probe the sacred-profane relationship. We shall follow the inspiring lines of its difficult and complex evolution by collecting the most significant data which emerge from the history of religions, from Holy Scriptures and from the history of the Church.

I. THE SACRED AND THE PROFANE IN THE HISTORY OF RELIGIONS

The historical development of the relationship between the sacred and the profane has long been the subject and the object of numerous studies and profound research. Already considered a classic is the work of Rudolf Otto[2]; another authoritative writer on the subject is Mircea Eliade.[3] There are notable differences between these two major studies; Otto seeks to specify the "sacred" by gathering the common data which emerge in analyses of the diverse sacred phenomena, while Eliade is committed above all to explicate the existing difference between the "sacred" and the "profane." Besides, Otto undertakes to research the relationship between the "sacred" and the "good" while insisting on their specific differences.[4] He shows that in the history of almost all religions, there is a definite cleavage between the sphere of the sacred and that of the good. Contrariwise, the New Testament and Christian faith are characterized particularly by the fact that both realize a living synthesis of the "sacred" and the "good," a synthesis which tears down all the walls erected between the two opposing concepts while clearly respecting their specificity.

Man's encounter with the "sacred" is characterized by a twofold spiritual movement: on the one part, there is fear, reverence and dread, while on the other there is attraction, joy and confidence. Both are necessary but when they are dissociated, one can no longer speak of a true encounter with the

[2] Rudolf Otto, *Das Heilige* (The Sacred) (Munich, 1963).

[3] Mircea Eliade, *The Sacred and the Profane* (New York: Harper Torchbooks, 1961).

[4] For the relationship between the sacred and morality, see my study *Das Heilige und das Gute* (Krailling, 1950).

"sacred." The sphere of the sacred, when authentic, is always marked by a *mysterium tremendum et fascinosum,* a harmony of contrasts or tensions of polar elements which remain in harmony (*Kontrastharmonie*).

Religion centers on a love that fears and a fear that loves; it is distinguished by a constant search for equilibrium; it is a vacillating quest because it never attains perfection. The religious history of humanity is an unending alternation of periods in which the fear-reverence sense prevails and periods in which love-confidence is predominant. In the first case, worship centers historically on bloody sacrifices (even human), while the prayer of praise and petition prevails in the second. Even one's personal religious history is marked by the quest for a fear-reverence and love-trust equilibrium.

When the prevalence of one spiritual movement precludes the other, we can no longer speak of religion. All the more perfect, then, are those attitudes and religious forms that succeed in synthesizing and equilibrating both. However, it is a question of balance and synthesis remaining forever fluid.

According to Otto, the "sacred" is designated as "irrational," i.e., supra-rational; the sacred is that which transcends human reason. The "numinous" is greater than man, beyond his possibilities and his capacities of acting and understanding. However, man is open and leaning toward the "sacred"; he has a sense of the sacred (*intentionales Gefühl*). Man reckons that the numinous is not a product of his fantasy or feelings; it is beyond him and above him. Man intuits the dynamic and established presence of the "totally other," i.e., that which is absolutely greater and by far more diverse than what he ordinarily sees and touches. Conversely, the profane is all that which remains enclosed in the categories of rationality, of causality or utility, whatever man can define, master or subdue.

In underscoring the supra-rational aspect of the sacred, Otto does not intend to negate human rationality in favor of sentiment; in no way does he pose as a protagonist of religious sentimentalism. That which Otto presses to emphasize is man's global propensity toward the sacred; man's whole being is open and tending toward the ever greater reality. To reduce religion to pure rationality would be to negate it as religion. Yet the danger is great. One need be aware that when the mystery is identified with the formula used to express it, the mystery is negated. There is always lurking in man that tendency to possess the mystery in rationality, but since possession is always a reduction, there is a constant danger of negation.

From these remarks, the reader should not conclude that we ought to abstain from reflection and every effort to better understand the "sacred" but even in our commitment to understanding, we ought to respect the mystery as mystery, i.e., we ought to overcome the temptation of "possessing it" or of "defining it." It is necessary to reflect but in the full awareness that whenever we attempt to reduce it to definitions, we deny the mystery.

In many religions, the "sacred" is experienced as a *powerful force* (mana, "wakonda," taboo) which threatens or saves the life of man. It can reside in persons, places, times, altars, amulets, formulas or songs. These are sacred, then, to the extent that they inspire fear-reverence and arouse love-trust. For example, the temple is circumscribed by enclosures (sanctuary, sanctum); it is the "terrifying" place which is not always accessible to everyone. A person's entrance is conditioned by the requirement to don particular vestments and undergo special purifications. However, the temple is also the place of salvation, being considered the pledge of salvation for the territory and for that nation in which it rose. Everything outside the temple enclosure is deemed profane; alone and together, men need the sacred strength which arises from it.

In cults of fecundity, sacredness was derived from whatever was directly related to the transmission of life. That is why the term "sacred" was applied to nature, which renews itself periodically, and to women, bearers of human life.

Very often the authority and the power of governors or

dynasties, the political or economic fortune of a nation, or the existing socio-political order become sacralized; they are set in direct contact and dependence on the "numinous" and are immediate depositories of its power. They are taboo, i.e., unapproachable and untouchable. The sacred destiny of a people or dynasty practically becomes a "sacralized egotism" which demands adoration and before which persons and nations cannot invoke human rights.

In almost all religions, a "sacred strength" is recognized as the appanage of the priests. All others (the profane and non-initiates) need the mediation of these sacred persons for an encounter with the powerful force on which everyone's life depends. By their special contact with the "sacred" and by disposing of it, the priests become sacred and taboo, not only in regard to their person but also in whatever is theirs: goods, food, clothing. Every attack on the priest's person or things is an assault against the "sacred force" itself; it is a *sacrilege*. This process of sacralization of things related to the priestly person occasionally reaches the point of absurdity; Max Weber has spoken of some extreme cases of "sacralization" of the excrements of sacred persons!

The priests of many religions constitute a closed caste who jealously guard sacred secrets and powers and transmit them from generation to generation. Whenever "profane" man fails to explain some phenomenon or cannot find its cause, he resorts to the priest-sorcerer. He even has recourse to him when he wishes the sacred power to be instrumental for some successful enterprise, most often to bring the sacred power to overwhelm his enemies. This recourse to the priest-sorcerer differs totally from prophetic prayer. The latter expresses faith in a personal God present in man's history and capable of intervening in it; prayer is an act of trust in the love of this God for man. Requesting others to pray for us presupposes faith in human brotherhood in the presence of a personal God. Recourse to the priest-sorcerer, on the contrary, is based on the conviction that he can dispose of the "numinous," that through rites and formulas known only to him, he can command the "sacred power" at pleasure.

In an era of sacralization there exists a neat distinction, then, between the priests and the profane people. The priests surround their rites with "mystery" or secrecy and celebrate them in a language unintelligible to the greater mass, hence the "sacred language"; they are conducted according to a ceremonial handed down to them with jealous precision even to the minutest detail. The priests view themselves as privileged, and those who are not members of their group are to be guarded against because they are unworthy of trust; they must keep away from the "profane." The priestly class is forever tempted to instrumentalize religion; if the priests defend religion so jealously, it is because of their many social privileges. In fact, encroachment on any of these privileges is proclaimed a sacrilege.[5]

The traditional manuals of moral theology and canonical legislation, as noted above, are still strongly influenced by such non-Christian conceptions when they refer to the sacredness of things, to sacrilege, and to the various ways of committing it. "Sacred persons" are "all the clerics and the religious and those to whom the Church has communicated special privileges."[6] A sacrilege is committed by disregarding or denying the privileges of sacred persons or arrogating material goods possessed by the Church.[7] Handling of the sacred vessels is prohibited for the layman save for sacristans and those who serve at the altar at the time of a service or celebration.[8]

The broader treatises of the history of religions disclose a constant in the separation of the "sacred" from the "good." Recourse to the "sacred," use of sacred things or words, and respect for sacred persons are not inferred or founded on the

---

[5] Cf. *Codex Juris Canonici*, Canons 1306, 1497.
[6] I. Aertnys, C. Damen, and I. Visser, *Theologia moralis, secundum doctrinam S. Alfonsi de Ligorio, Doctoris Ecclesiae*, 18th ed. (Torino, 1968), Vol. II, no. 35, p. 38.
[7] Ibid., no. 37, pp. 40–41.
[8] Ibid., Vol. III, no. 155, p. 160.

plane of the morality of life. They are divested of any inspiration or motivation which would open to mercy, justice, purity and sincerity of conscience. They are estranged from or indifferent to morality. Incessant reference to and use of the notion "sacred" remain within the confines of a closed ritualistic objectivism, having no bearing on commitment to a good life. Both parties are affected: he who knows and disposes of the "sacred" as well as he for whom the sacred rite is celebrated.

Contact with the "numinous" is often sought and realized through means totally opposed to the good. One of the most shocking examples comes from the phenomenon of "sacred prostitution" common to many cults of fecundity and found in many initiation rites. The encounter with the "sacred" is not one in which a man acts in full freedom and responsibility, but it is contingent on the physical union with a person, at which time the divinity becomes especially present because the partners are given to worshiping the sacred power. More tragic and absurd yet are the human sacrifices in honor of the divinity, the wars and sacred massacres which spare no one, not even the weak and most innocent.

Along the same line separating the "sacred" from the "good," religion typically structures itself more and more as a closed domain, completely isolated from the totality of personal and social life. Worship becomes all the more sterile; the people passively assist at rites without drawing from them a sense of commitment for growth in goodness. However, in spite of the fact that daily life is not vivified from within religion, it is not lived in a secular way; it becomes "sacralized" in a magical-fatalistic way through benedictions, exorcisms or amulets. Notwithstanding, it often remains "profane" in the strongest sense of the term; it fails to reveal a loving God who is accepting of all men.

II. THE SACRED AND THE PROFANE IN HOLY SCRIPTURES

A. *The Old Testament*

Initially, the conception of "sacred" was not too diversified in Israel. The oldest accounts of the Holy Writings reveal traces of a sacredness understood objectively and externally, devoid even of any explicit relation to Yahweh. There are also indications of a vision of the "sacred" cut off from the "good" and closed to it. The episode of Uzzah assumes meaning in this context.

During the transfer of the Ark from Baalath, with no evil intent on his part, Uzzah gives support to the Ark[9] and is immediately punished by Yahweh: "But when they came to a certain threshing-floor, the oxen stumbled, and Uzzah reached out to the Ark of God and took hold of it. The Lord was angry with Uzzah and struck him down there for his rash act. So he died there beside the Ark of God" (II Sam. 6:6–7). It was sufficient for Uzzah to touch the Ark for him to commit a sacrilege. There was no need of ill will; the question did not even arise as to whether he had acted through necessity so as not to let the Ark fall; the sacrilege was committed by the simple act of touching a sacred object.

The episode of Isaac's sacrifice on Mount Moriah (Gen. 22:1–8) expresses the change in conception of the "sacred" brought about by Israel's faith in Yahweh. It differed from that of Egypt and Babylonia in that there were frequent human sacrifices to the divinity in Canaan.[10] At first, Abraham sees

[9] In the Hebraic text, even "ark" is masculine in gender. It is therefore difficult to establish whether reference of danger applies to Uzzah or to the Ark itself. In both cases, the episode reveals the same vision of sacredness.

[10] References to such human sacrifices are not lacking even in the Bible (cf. Lev. 18:21 and 20:1–5; Deut. 12:31; II Kings 16:3 and 23:10). Of particular importance for an exact understanding of the sacrifice of Abra-

his relation to Yahweh in the light of the religious categories common to his environment; to express his own fidelity and his own devotion to Yahweh, Abraham comes to the point of sacrificing his son, who is also a gift of God, and one ever so dear to him. Abraham has retained a religious mentality by far too grossly sacralistic, but his faith in Yahweh opens new horizons and new perspectives to him; it frees him of the taboo-like sacralism.[11]

The whole prophetic history of Israel will later be scanned in the process of personalization of the sacred and the affirmation of a religiousness strictly linked to goodness of life and love of neighbor, a religiousness "knowledgeable about justice," of a people "who lay the law to heart" (Is. 51:7). The purification of the "sacred" and of religious forms is promoted by both priests and prophets. The priestly tradition and the prophetic, however, differ in emphases and concerns. The priests are committed, above all, to promote among the people an ever purer cult for a monotheistic faith in Yahweh. To this end, they multiply and make ever more detailed their prescribed rites; they expound on the purity needed for participation in them so as to exclude forms used by the polytheistic and naturalistic religions. The Leviticus is a marvelous testimony of the reform effort of the priests.

The worship promoted by the reformers of Israel is never separated from the sanctity of life. The priestly reforms, although aimed primarily at renewal of worship, tend also to encourage a greater sanctity of life. The cult of Israel is always that of God, who solemnly proclaims "You shall be holy to me, because I the Lord am holy." "I have made a clear separation between you and the heathen, that you may belong to me"

---

ham are "the foundation sacrifices" common in Canaan at the time of the patriarchs; the first-born were sacrificed in the foundation of the home or city, because it would assure the protection of the gods for it. Cf. R. De Vaux, *Le istituzione dell'Antico Testamento* (Torino, 1964), pp. 430–32.

[11] Cf. M. Buber, "Le sacrifice d'Isaac," *Dieu Vivant*, no. 22, pp. 69–75; C. Schedl, *Storia del Vecchio Testamento* (Roma, 1959), pp. 286–87.

(Lev. 20:26; cf. 19:1). The "code of sanctity" teaches fraternal love, justice, truth and mercy together with worship (cf. Lev. 19:9–18).

There always remains, in the great mass of Israel as in its "priestly class," the temptation to emphasize in an extravagant and unilateral way, the temple, the rites and sacred things. At times, the temptation grows stronger and it is then that prophets arise. They do not pit themselves against worship or the temple or against the ideals of priestly reform; in fact, some of them belong to the priestly caste. The prophets are primarily concerned with encouraging the people to a holy life as a response to the revelation of love of the infinitely holy, just and merciful God.

The prophets shift the emphasis from external worship to goodness of life for the honor of God. They proclaim that the true worship of Yahweh does not consist so much in that which is rendered him in the temple as of justice in one's life. The salvation granted by Yahweh to Israel is not a function of a specific number of sacrifices of animals or things but it is contingent on goodness of life and love of neighbor. So Ezekiel writes: "You say that the Lord acts without principle? Listen, you Israelites, it is you who act without principle, not I. If a righteous man turns from his righteousness, takes to evil ways and dies, it is because of these evil ways that he dies. Again, if a wicked man turns from his wicked ways and does what is just and right, he will save his life. If he sees his offences as they are and turns his back on them all, then he shall live; he shall not die" (Ez. 18:25–28).

The prophets particularly contrapose all forms of mechanical and ritualistic worship that brings about no change of heart. "Your countless sacrifices, what are they to me? says the Lord. I am sated with whole-offerings of rams and the fat of buffaloes; I have no desire for the blood of bulls, of sheep and of he-goats. . . . The offer of your gifts is useless, the reek of sacrifice is abhorrent to me. New moons and sabbaths, and assemblies, sacred seasons . . . I can put up with them no longer. When you lift up your hands outspread in prayer, I will hide my eyes from you. Though you offer countless prayers, I will not listen. There is blood on your hands; wash yourselves and be clean. Put away the evil of your deeds, away out of my sight. Cease to do evil and learn to do right" (Is. 1:11–17).[12]

In the prophetic tradition, sin against fellowman is the real profanity. The sinful man whose proud heart has made him indurate is profane. Most lively and ironic is the expression of Amos: "Listen to this, you cows of Bashan who live on the hill of Samaria, you who oppress the poor and crush the destitute, who say to your lords 'Bring us drink'" (Amos 4:1). The distance between the "sacred" (the infinitely holy God) and the "profane" (sin against love and justice) then appears in its full depth and dynamism. In the light of the revelation of the all-holy God, man not only recognizes his own imperfection as creature, but also his own sin, the one and true profanity. "For well I know my misdeeds—cries out the psalmist—and my sins confront me all the day long. Against thee, thee only, I have sinned and done what displeases thee, so that thou mayest be proved right in thy charge and just in passing sentence" (Ps. 51:3–4).

Man is not so much confronted by "sacred things" as by God's perfect holiness. It is a communitarian confrontation, yet fully personal. The encounter with Yahweh is terrible in that it touches man in his innermost being and reveals him to be a sinner and deserving therefore of God's wrath. However, it also opens man's heart to trust because Yahweh is merciful and the source of a more holy and more brotherly life. "In the year of king Uzziah's death, I saw the Lord seated on a throne, high and exalted. . . . I cried, Woe is me! I am lost, for I am a man of unclean lips; your iniquity is removed, and your sin is wiped away. Then I heard the Lord saying, Whom shall I send? Who will go for me? and I answered: Here am I; send me!" (Is. 6:1–9).

The prophets are constantly on the lookout for those deviations which the religiosity and sacralism of the neighboring

[12] Cf. Amos 5:21–26; Hos. 6:6 and 8:12 ff.; Jer. 7:21 ff.; Ps. 50:7–13.

people would want to establish in Israel: "You shall not say
'too hard' of everything that this people calls hard; you shall
neither dread nor fear that which they fear. It is the Lord of
Hosts whom you must count 'hard'; he it is whom you must
fear and dread" (Is. 8:12–13). Their action is generous; they
neither hesitate nor stop when faced by danger and threats.
Jeremiah risks his life more than once without ceasing to
preach that salvation bears no connection with the material
edifice of the temple; salvation is related to the goodness and
justice of one's life. "These are the words of the Lord of Hosts,
the God of Israel: mend your ways and your doings that I may
let you live in this place. You keep saying, 'This place is the
temple of the Lord, the temple of the Lord, the temple of the
Lord!'[13] . . . You gain nothing by putting your trust in this
lie. You steal, you murder, you commit adultery and perjury,
you burn sacrifices to Baal, you run after other gods whom you
have not known, then you come and stand before me in this
house, which bears my name, and say, 'We are safe'; safe, you
think, to indulge in all these abominations" (Jer. 7:3–11).

In the historical and prophetic books of the Old Testament,
the "sacred" is not delimited to the narrow confines of worship
and sacred things. The whole world and the history of nations
belong to Yahweh; through them he sanctifies his name and
manifests his power and glory. The marvels operated in favor
of Israel do not reveal his holiness for Israel only but for all
people. So does Yahweh speak in Isaiah: "I will say to the
north, 'Give them up,' and to the south, 'Do not hold them
back.' Bring my sons and daughters from afar, bring them
from the ends of the earth; bring everyone who is called by my
name, all whom I have created, whom I have formed. . . .
My witnesses . . . are you, my servants, you whom I have
chosen . . . You are my witnesses, says the Lord. I am God;
from this very day I am He. What my hand holds, none can
snatch away; what I do, none can undo" (Is. 43:6–13).

[13] It is evidently a matter of a "sacred formula" particularly common.
Noteworthy is the irony and the depreciation of the passage for every
sacred formula and for those who use them.

The entire history of Israel is in the hands of Yahweh; it is nothing other than successive disclosures of the merciful love of God, who, even when punishing evil, does so in order to forgive. The history of Israel abounds with renewals of infidelity and Yahweh's unremitting love and forgiveness. God punishes the sinful people but he reconciles a contrite people. Such was the situation at the time of Jephthah: "But the Israelites said to the Lord, 'We have sinned. Deal with us as thou wilt; only save us this day, we implore thee.' They banished the foreign gods and worshiped the Lord; and he could endure no longer to see the plight of Israel" (Judges 10:15–16). Yahweh confirms true religiousness and worship according to the exigencies of his faithful love. "How can I give you up, Ephraim, how surrender you, Israel? . . . I will not let loose my fury . . . for I am God, and not a man, the Holy One in your midst" (Hos. 11:8–9).

The transcendence and holiness of God appear with increasing clarity in relation to his merciful love, which, in Messianic times, will bring salvation and saving judgment for all men: "My servants shall eat but you shall starve . . . My servants shall shout in triumph in the gladness of their hearts, but you shall cry from sorrow and wail from anguish of spirit" (Is. 65:13–14). Yahweh's holiness and love emerge in an ever more universal perspective: Yahweh is the Savior of all nations. "Was it not I the Lord? There is no God but me; there is no God other than I, victorious and able to save. Look to me and be saved, you peoples from all corners of the earth; for I am God, there is no other" (Is. 45:21–22). The work of the prophets decisively introduced a phase of purification and authentication of the "sacred." After stripping things, places and holy words of their alleged "sacredness," there remains to do away with the monopolizing concept of "holy people." The whole world is Yahweh's for he is the unique Savior of all. If Israel is "holy," it is only in view of all nations.

Prophetism has never been the exclusive prerogative of Israel. Other religions have produced "prophets," usually men and women of humble origin who commit themselves generously to an authentic service of the brethren in justice and love. It would be fraudulent to set up the prophetism and priesthood typical of Israel as diametrically opposed to the religious genius of other cultures. While being fully aware of the uniqueness of depth, continuity, sincerity and constancy of the prophetic history in Israel, we must nevertheless appreciate the many signs of hope that God has continually given to other nations with diversity in emphases, perspectives and generosity. Christ will be the perfection of both: the priesthood and prophetism. He is the prophet who, by opposing priestly decay and false sacralization, opens the era of adoration of God "in Spirit and in truth."

B. The New Testament

In spite of their generous commitment, the prophets did not succeed in uprooting the conception of a partially sacralized Yahweh. Tension remained in Israel, at times dramatic, between a vision of faith and worship centered in the sacred power of priests and in the temple as place of Yahweh's glory, and that prophetic vision centered in God's holiness which does not want victims but a contrite spirit and humble heart (Ps. 51:16–17). Christ it is who completes the process of purification and personification of the "sacred" and of "sanctity." In the New Testament, the "sacred" is manifested not in things or holy places but in the Spirit of God, who anoints Christ (cf. Mk. 1:24; Lk. 4:34). Christ is the revelation and presence of the Holy God, whom "no one has ever seen"; he "is nearest to the Father's heart, he has made him known" (Jn. 1:18). Revealing the Father as infinite love, he prophetically centers holiness in love; one is holy if he remains in love. "As the Father has loved me, so I have loved you. Dwell in my love" (Jn. 15:9).

By revealing the face of God, Christ also exposes the true features of the "profane": sin, pride, as well as the egotism of individuals and communities who refuse or are opposed to the love of the Father. They decide to remain in darkness by closing themselves to the brightness of light (Jn. 1:4 ff.). Thus the profane are all those who turn a deaf ear to the salvific gift of the Father's love in Christ. The pagan sense of the profane yields its place to the sense of sin conceived in a personal, communitarian and universal way. "He called the crowd and said to them: Listen to me, and understand this: a man is not defiled by what goes into his mouth, but by what comes out of it" (Mt. 15:10–11).[14]

God's revelation of love and holiness is dynamic; he arouses us to a saintly life in fraternal love: "I have delivered thy word to them . . ." prays Christ in the Cenacle, "Consecrate them by the truth; thy word is truth. As thou hast sent me into the world, I have sent them into the world, and for their sake, I now consecrate myself, that they too may be consecrated by the truth" (Jn. 17:14–19). God sanctifies man by realizing a new relationship with him. Through Christ, man enters into a filial relationship with God, one characterized by fear and love (cf. Jn. 15:15 ff.), joy (Jn. 15:11) and adoring faith (Lk. 12:22 ff.). But all this remains empty talk unless it flows also into a new relationship with one's neighbor, the whole human community and the world (I Jn. 4:7–21).

Even in the New Testament, the "sacred" or the holiness of God that sanctifies his sons transcends the "good." Adoration and faith in God and his Christ remain central. Paul never tires of repeating: "For to us, our hope of attaining that righteousness which we eagerly await is the work of the Spirit through faith. If we are in union with Christ Jesus, circumcision makes no difference at all, nor does the want of it; the only thing that counts is faith active in love" (Gal. 5:5–6).[15]

---

[14] The language of the whole passage is very prophetic; the irony is lashing. We are faced by a radical demythologization of sacred things and traditions in view of exposing the very core of true sacredness, of the revelation of the Holy God.

[15] Continuing the discourse of Paul, we ought to have the courage to assert fully that the sacramental rites by themselves are of no avail but only the faith-charity to which Christ is given. The sacraments are signs of faith-charity; they are to signify the gift of himself to us and that of ourselves to Christ. The *"opus operatum"* cannot mean that Christ does

Religion is infinitely more than a simple, humanistic morality; it consists of a new relationship to God but one which inherently leads to a complete "metanoia," i.e., to a radical and total transformation of the whole of life. Paul writes to the Romans: "But God be thanked, you who once were slaves of sin, have yielded whole-hearted obedience to the pattern of teaching to which you were made subject, and emancipated from sin, have become servants of righteousness" (Rom. 6:17–18). Wherever God's love enters there is no more profanity or sin; injustice toward God and the brethren, falsehood, darkness and fraud are driven out (cf. Acts 11:5 ff.).

Man does not possess holiness objectively as a quality or a secret which he can transmit to others at will. "Holiness" belongs only to God. Man is gratuitously and liberally sanctified by God through faith and the signs of faith by which he enters in communion with him through Christ (Eph. 1:4 ff.; Rom. 3:24–26). After Christ's coming, it is no longer possible to think of the sacred or holy sphere without centering it in the living, dynamic and sanctifying presence of God and without its being profoundly characterized by gratitude for his grace.

Holiness cannot be transferred mechanically through rites and formulas. The holiness of those sanctified by God in Christ can never be separated from truthfulness (Rev. 3:7), from justice and mercy (Mk. 6:20; Acts 3:14; I Cor. 13:1–13) or from a life which is pleasing to God because founded on his reign of love (Eph. 1:14 and 5:7; Col. 1:22). Christians are called holy only insofar as through Christ they belong to God and are therefore redeemed from the proud and egotistical world (Jn. 17:6). Man's single and generous effort, even to the point of giving his own life for his brethren, cannot grant holi-

---

not require our faith-charity for the gift of himself to us; it would then fail to be a personal encounter and be a magical ritual. The initiative of the gift always belongs to God; it is not something of which we are deserving. It is God's gift but a gift which he offers to him who believes and loves. The grace of God is a presence of love which attracts and saves, but in a commitment-response of love; it cannot be reduced to a dead capital deposited in the soul or "the bank of the Holy Spirit."

ness if man positively persists in resisting grace, in refusing the
gift of the Father in Christ. Holiness is above all *grace:* gracious gift of the Father in Christ through the Spirit. Grace is a
powerful gift, an appeal to a commitment for a new life in
brotherhood, freedom and more generous solidarity. "Graced"
men are gracious, gentle and generous.

In the writings of the New Testament, little or no importance
is attached to the temple and sacred places. It is true that
Christ purifies the temple of Jerusalem by driving away the
vendors and money changers, shouting: "My house shall be
called a house of prayer" (Mt. 21:12–13). But he does not
bind prayer to the temple: "But when you pray, go into a
room by yourself, shut the door, and pray to your Father who
is there in the secret place; and your Father who sees what is
secret will reward you" (Mt. 6:6). He himself retreats to pray,
going "up the hill-side to pray alone" (Mt. 14:23). Before the
supreme moment, he goes to the Garden of Gethsemane to
pray with his disciples: "My Father, if it is possible, let this
cup pass me by. Yet, not as I will, but as thou wilt" (Mt.
26:39).

Therefore, there is no longer any reason to quarrel about
places of worship. "Believe me," said Jesus to the Samaritan
woman, "the time is coming when you will worship the Father
neither on this mountain, nor in Jerusalem. . . . But the time
approaches, indeed it is already here, when those who are real
worshippers will worship the Father in spirit and in truth"
(Jn. 4:20–26). The destruction of the "holy city" and of the
temple facilitated considerably the primitive church's transi-
tion to prayer "in spirit and in truth," freeing her from every
bond of place and temple. Christ also abolishes the priesthood
understood as a privileged class that alone knows and disposes
of the "sacred power"; he abolishes the hereditary priesthood
of the Old Testament.

His apostles are assigned the mission of proclaiming his
death and resurrection; "Go forth therefore and make all nations my disciples; baptize men everywhere in the name of the
Father and the Son and the Holy Spirit, and teach them to ob-

serve all that I have commanded you. And be assured, I am with you always, to the end of time" (Mt. 28:19–20). The worship to which Paul devotes his effort is "preaching the Gospel of his Son" (Rom. 1:9).

The apostles reveal themselves as witnesses by what they do: "What I say to you in the dark you must repeat in broad daylight; what you hear whispered you must shout from the housetops" (Mt. 10:27; Lk. 12:3). So as to ensure their witness' being faithful and courageous, even in the most difficult situations, Christ sends them the Spirit after his death-resurrection (Lk. 12:4–12). The apostles are called upon to continue Christ's work of reconciliation and peace but with the same humility as Christ, by being like him the servant of all: "Then if I, your Lord and Master, have washed your feet, you also ought to wash one another's feet. I have set you an example: you are to do as I have done for you" (Jn. 13:14–15). It is the only way they can "confirm" the brothers (Lk. 22:31–32). The priestly and apostolic credibility lies with those who, like Christ and through his grace, give their life for the brethren; they spend it in the proclamation of the Gospel of peace and reconciliation.

With their charity and fraternal unity, Christ's apostles insert themselves in the world as "salt" and "leaven" (Mt. 5:13–14), consuming themselves in service. By their charity and unity, they are in the world as a sign of living faith; before leaving the Cenacle, Christ prays: "may they all be one: as thou, Father, art in me, and I in thee, so also may they be in us, that the world may believe that thou didst send me" (Jn. 17:21).

Thus the sacraments of the New Covenant, of which the apostles are ministers, are not so much "sacred things" as acts of Christ, a message of salvation in the name of Christ, a powerful word of God, who invites man's response. They are "signs of faith" with no mechanical ritualism possible.[16] To use the sacraments or the apostolic mission itself as instruments for

[16] For the complex sacramental problematic of today, see my book *Vita Cristiana nella luce dei sacramenti.*

personal egotism or for class privileges is, in the fullest sense of the term, a sacrilege. When speaking of those to whom are entrusted the mysteries for proclamation to all, the New Testament avoids the term *"hiereús"* as used for the priests before the coming of Christ. It is not a casual omission; it ought to be reflected upon with courage.

In a most shocking way Christ "desacralizes" the priestly class, particularly in the parable of the merciful Samaritan (Lk. 10:30–37). The higher clergy comes and sees the poor man who has been robbed and gravely wounded; "when he saw him, he went past on the other side"; so did the lower clergy. Contrariwise, the Samaritan, member of an adjudged "schismatic and heretical nation," was moved by compassion and looked after him. He is the truly "holy man." The clergy observed laws of ritual purity. The Samaritan observed the law of mercy and love in dealing with a man of a hostile nation; he thus honored the name of the one God, Father of all men.

No longer is there a holy nation or a holy race. "God has no favorites" (Rom. 2:11). "For through faith you are all sons of God in union with Christ Jesus. Baptized into union with him, you have all put on Christ as a garment. There is no such thing as . . . slave and freeman, male and female; you are all one person in Christ Jesus" (Gal. 3:26–28). All the disciples of Christ, gathered from all the nations, are "a chosen race, a royal priesthood, a dedicated nation, and a people claimed by God for his own, to proclaim the triumphs of him who has called you out of darkness into his marvellous light" (I Pet. 2:9).

More than any other, Paul untiringly combats every form of "sacralism" of things: temples, Hebraic or pagan customs. He writes to the Galatians: "I am astonished to find you turning so quickly away from him who called you by grace, and following a different Gospel. Not that it is in fact another gospel; only there are persons who unsettle your minds by trying to distort the gospel of Christ. But if anyone, if we ourselves or an angel from heaven, should preach a gospel at variance with the gospel we preached to you, he shall be held outcast. I now repeat what I have said before: If anyone preaches a gospel at variance with the gospel which you received, let him be outcast" (Gal. 1:6–9). All that which hinders the universal acceptance of the Gospel and unity of all men, whatever tends to create distinctions or privileges in the name of the "sacred" is sinful; it is profane in the deepest and most radical sense of the term.

III. THE SACRED AND THE PROFANE IN CHURCH HISTORY[17]

The first centuries of Christianity are characterized by a generous commitment to overcome Judaic ritualism and that of various pagan cults. The liturgy is of extraordinary simplicity and sobriety. In the liturgical celebrations as much as in the other forms of prayer, there is concern to safeguard spontaneity even when initial tendencies for stifling are there.[18] Reflection on and study of the Word of God are not the patrimony of a few experts. Theology is not yet restricted to a very select few or an elite group; anybody and everybody can be fully "initiated."

There exists no "sacred language" unintelligible to the great mass of early Christians; both for the written tradition of truth as well as for the liturgy, the common language is used. The believers lack almost completely in buildings serving uniquely for prayer and worship; the liturgy is celebrated in private houses; it is a living expression of faith and hope and a commitment to fraternal solidarity.

It is not long before the martyrs begin to receive a particular remembrance and veneration. For the celebration of the Eu-

[17] See particularly the studies contained in *Concilium*, V (1969), no. 7.
[18] Already Paul spoke of the dispositions with respect to the Christian assembly; for example, on the eucharistic celebration (I Cor. 10–11), on the use of charisms (I Cor. 12–14). They only tend to avoid inconveniences and do not yet create rigidly uniform celebrations. The diverse traditions on the eucharistic institution are a splendid testimony of the absence of rigid uniformity.

charist, the early Christians now prefer to congregate at those places where their relics are kept, especially to mark the anniversary of their martyrdom. During the persecutions, their tombs become places of fraternal encounter and prayer while serving as a summons, a pledge and support for a courageous witness. Initially, holy bishops would receive no cult unless they had sealed their mission with martyrdom. Later on, the veneration of the holy virgins was also added to that of the martyrs. With the abating of persecutions, particular recognition was given to "confessors," i.e., to those who had given testimony to Christ with a particularly holy life even without ever suffering martyrdom. All these developments occurred along the lines of ethical prophetism.

The Constantinian era witnessed the spreading of a climate of sacredness and sacralism throughout all levels of Christianity. The person of the emperor became sacred and untouchable even for Christians. This sacralization of the person of the emperor was soon to be followed by the "Sacred Roman Empire of that Germanic nation." Grandiose churches were constructed to compete with and cast a shadow on the pagan temples. The clergy turned into a socially privileged class; the bishops assumed dignity and took on princely tasks for the emperor; the priests were gorged with benefits and exemptions far in excess of those accorded pagan clergymen, and all this was surrounded by an atmosphere of sacredness.

Between the clergy and the rest of the people came a cleavage, a distinction or separation ever more pronounced; the term "layman" came to connote "profanity" and "worldliness." Laymen were no longer allowed to touch the sacred vases and vestments. The liturgy of the East and even of the West graduated to an "imperial style" and a particular new emphasis bore on "the awe-inspiring mystery," thus keeping the people at a distance. The churches began to set aside an area reserved for the celebration of the eucharistic sacrifice; only the priests and their attendants could approach the altar and the space immediately surrounding it. Barriers of different types (iconostases, balustrades) were created between the "presbytery" and the rest of the church. While initially the opposition was between the Church and the pagan world, the polarity was now found within the Church itself; the clergy constituted the "holy" segment of the Christian population whereas the laity were the "profane."

The conversion of the Germanic princes brought an end to the evolutionary process introduced by Constantine and his immediate successors; Christianity then became the "Church of the nation" (*Volkskirche*). The confused religious sentiment and sense of the sacred so commonly found in the masses flocking into the Church at this period persisted even after their conversion to Christianity since it was not preceded by sufficient preparation.

The missions of the Celtic-Germanic world preserved many religious customs, places and times of prayer, giving them new significance and value. The same methods utilized by the primitive Church were now adopted for the Christianization of the Greco-Roman world; evangelization centered on the acceptance, purification and integration of the values and positive strengths of the Germanic peoples. However, such a process was not always profound enough. At times, it was nothing other than a mere ritual for a new sacralization of that which previously existed. In practice, then, there was evidence of a sacralistic syncretism, even in theological reflection. The prohibition of servile works on festive days originated from an elaborate casuistry relative to the days and types of work permitted in which the influence of the Judaic and pagan sacralism were very evident.[19]

The cult of the saints (martyrs, virgins, confessors and bishops) here assumes great importance in popular piety and worship. Their relics were carefully kept because of the thaumaturgic power attributed to them. Churches were constructed over the tombs of saints and they immediately became shrines attracting numerous pilgrims. In moments of need, the saints' help was implored. Patron saints were multipled and given assignments over settlements, dioceses and diverse activi-

[19] See H. Huber, *Spirito e lettera del riposo domenicale* (Roma, 1961).

ties. Where all these developments could have had a positive significance, they often reverted to the magic categories of the pre-Christian "sacred."

The demons and angels now assumed prominence. They not only became substitutes for the diverse pagan gods but their interventions were interpreted in analogy to these gods. Belief was strong in benedictions and exorcisms for persons as much as for things and places. Great attention was paid to the exactness of the formula in the performance of these rites.

Following the Iconoclast crisis, the cult of sacred images was further developed, attributing to all pictures and statues an intimate connection with heavenly truth and power. The veneration of relics reached a peak at the time of the Crusades. They clearly testified to the centrality which Christianity would subsequently give to sacred places and things. The fact that western Christianity was committed to the point of sacrificing numerous human lives for the conquest of Palestine should lead us to reflect on the depth of the sacralization process within medieval society. The progressive sacralization of things and places could certainly not be the unique cause of the complex social and religious phenomenon of the Crusades, though, admittedly, it was not a minor influence; it did foster a further decay of religion in this direction.

It was the time in history, then, when all the trades, associations and cities had their own patron in honor of whom processions were organized, churches built and pilgrimages undertaken. Many religious orders gave meticulous attention to the external form of their habit, asserting that they had received it through a direct revelation of the Virgin or from saints. Indulgences assumed ever greater importance. Holy places and privileged altars were multiplied, devotions and good works were enriched by indulgences. To gain them, it was required to fulfill the stated meticulous conditions literally. After the Pope's exile in Avignon, the official administration of indulgences, blessings and devotional practices was complicated to the point of becoming a sacred bureaucracy of its own. It was strongly linked to the financial needs of the Curia and privileged priestly careers.

The Protestant reform of the sixteenth century reacted against this complex sacralistic system. However, it failed to liberate itself completely from the diffuse sacralistic atmosphere; there still prevailed an excessive demonology and numerous superstitious beliefs. Only when the influence of humanism and of the Enlightenment (*Aufklärung*) became relevant to the people did the process of desacralization expand to include new possibilities in the sense of ethical prophetism; it often entailed great dangers, however, for the religious sense.

The Council of Trent was very intent on educating Christians to sobriety of faith through a just vision of the sacraments and their celebration, a greater integration of devotions and a rethinking of the practice of blessings, indulgences and the like. However, the liturgy still maintained the use of a language no longer understood by the great mass of believers, and which was fast becoming the privilege of a few. Besides, a good portion of the best conciliar directives never passed into practice because they were blocked by the still powerful current of sacralism-clericalism which jealously defended clerical privileges as well as the sundry practices of blessings and indulgences.

So it came that the world of worship and the realm of the sacred were cut off from the daily life of believers. With the advent of scientism in the last two centuries came the assertion of a more positive, empirical and rational mentality which not only widened the gap between religion and life but made it more strongly felt. In spite of the courageous efforts of the many saints and prophets of that era, the process of alienating sacralization continued.

Only in the wake of secularization does a profound change of mentality become evident. The believers of today are not about to be misled in thinking that the true sanctification of the world can be realized by blessings and exorcisms; they are convinced that Christians will be saved by the testimony of justice and service to the needy. The true holiness of the world depends on the generous and disinterested commitment of believers for an authentic brotherhood among all men, a fraternal unity inspired by faith.

Discussion on the validity of orders, for example, and reform of the canonical legislation on marriage are unfolding today in a climate totally different from that found in traditional manuals of theology. Moralists of the past dedicated much space and spent considerable energy questioning (often in the abstract only) the validity and non-validity of constitutive blessings. They gave rise to scruples of the sacralistic type relative to the validity of sacraments and sacramentals when involuntary flaws crept into the celebration of the rite; all in all, it failed to lead to justice and truthfulness, to simplicity and adoration of God in spirit and truth. It seems that Christianity needed "shock therapy" to overcome this kind of alienating sacralization.

If accepted in love and with a critical sense inspired by faith, today's secularization can be a valid help not only for ecumenical dialogue but also for the very renewal of both the liturgy and personal-popular piety. Today we have a pressing need to renew the expressions and forms of Christian worship in such a way that they are true testimonies of a living faith, one which tends to build up a brotherly world to the glory of God the Father; in all this, secularization can be of invaluable help. For the world as well as for secular man, it is important to witness firmly to the holiness which a Christian seeks to realize: sanctity of life springing from an effective justice and charity, inspired and directed by gratitude and by adoration of the one God, Father of all, and his Christ, sent to be the servant of the world.

We have already noted earlier how the process of secularization did not come about at the same rhythm in all cultures and even within the same culture. Besides, the tones, nuances and emphases are very varied. It would therefore be mistaken to impose a new style of worship on all. A pluralism in worship and spirituality would seem absolutely necessary today; we must be wary not to fall into new ritualistic fixedness or into secularized styles of celebration that do not respond to the need of people of diverse cultures and subcultures.

I believe that even in a secularized world, part of the traditions concerning worship and religious custom can still be a source of piety and fraternal commitment. Above all, pastoral discernment is needed. In each case an intelligent catechesis is indispensable which would give a just vision of the forms of traditional piety, would purify them, link them to liturgical worship (cf. SC, Art. 12, 13), and score them as encounter with God, source of witness and fraternal commitment.[20]

The encounter of religion and life can no longer be entrusted predominantly to blessings and to propitiatory processions. Today, these are often reduced to pure folklorish manifestations incapable of expressing or nourishing the faith of the participants; they remain incomprehensible if not scandalous for many of our contemporaries. The genuine synthesis between religion and daily life is the fruit of a mature, convinced faith capable of expressing itself in forms and attitudes perceptible and meaningful to the men of today—a faith which, in overcoming the traditional hiatus between worship and life, becomes a source of responsibility in generous and sincere brotherhood.

The conceptualization of the *sacred* and *profane* inherited from antiquity and medieval times should be overcome in a loyal encounter of faith with the world of today in keeping with the spirit of *Gaudium et Spes*. The witness of faith ought to find a language and forms which are not opposed to and do not offend the autonomy, freedom and responsibility of the earthly city. Faith ought to share the sufferings, commitment for the good and victories of humanity.[21]

It would be an absurdity and a scandal today to pray, "From pestilence, famine and war, deliver us, O Lord," while failing to make efforts in this very sense. What would it mean to pray for peace if those who thus pray make no sin-

[20] Bernard Häring, *The Law of Christ*, 6th edition (Westminster, Md.: Newman Press, 1963), Vol. II, pp. 139–98.
[21] See particularly *Gaudium et Spes*, Part I, Chapter IV.

cere commitment for sensitizing public opinion by word and example, for mobilizing all the forces of science-technology and generosity for a change of attitudes in view of a more equitable socio-economic organization for overcoming the social evils which still afflict humanity? This affirmation does not intimate that prayer no longer serves any purpose; we exclude from the unique dignity of prayer only the evasive, alienating prayers which fail to create in man a determination to place all his talents in the service of others and to capitalize on today's possibilities for good. It would not truly be "prayer" but a mere repetition of empty words and "sacred lies," which can only serve to weaken the credibility of our faith. Sincere prayer opens us to the needs of others and prepares us to do what is in our power to assist our brothers in need. Genuine prayer for peace and unity transforms us into instruments of peace and unity.[22]

This new awareness likewise changes our discourse on divine and natural law. Our contemporaries no longer tolerate a "taboo" mentality; they are searching incessantly for better ways and means of promoting man in his dignity, freedom, responsibility, spontaneity, creativity and fraternity. If we speak to them of a "sacred" and immutable natural law identified with yesterday's formulation, without manifesting an updated knowledge about man and today's possibilities, we will stand accused of abstractionism, apriorism and alienation. A concept of a "sacred" natural law devoid of an acceptable explanation and alien to the shared experience and co-reflection of humanity today can only make the teachers of these "sacred laws" look like the pagan priests of the past who judged all the non-initiates as being "profane." There is a major difference, however, in that these teachers and not the others will be living a marginal existence. They will be pitied by those who are truly initiated in the behavioral sciences and all the efforts of the men come of age to know more about mankind's common quest for ultimate meaning.

[22] See Chapter 7 on the renewal of prayer in a secular age.

CHAPTER 4

RELIGION AND CULTURE

Sociologism reduces religion to mere reflection or to a super-structure of the complex social, economic and cultural situation. The strongest and most humbling expression of such valuation is that of Karl Marx, who sees religion as a huge overlay of economic disorder begetting all forms of alienation. Marx's promise of an "ultra-worldly" happiness, namely, a classless society without further dialectic tensions, is the uttermost alienation of the "homo faber": a promise and hope contradicting the basic structure of life as Marx himself described it.

Whether personally or community-wise, man is characterized by his activity in the economic, cultural and social field as well as by his faith and religious expressions. Prior to modern secularization, cultural and social life was totally and strongly impregnated by religion. In the complex sphere of life, there was no field eluding the influence of religion and/or its official representatives. Man's participation in the economic, cultural, social and political life unequivocally reflected the influence of religion. For the individual, social interaction implied fellowship in religion and religious expressions. As member of a culture marked by religion, everyone wittingly or not found himself to be both a citizen and a religious man.

The situation today is very different, even from the religious standpoint; the social climate has changed considerably. Many of our contemporaries seem to have lost all sense of religion, living as they are without any interest or participation in worship and in a life of faith. Some boldly declare they have no need of religious faith or any form of worship, whereas for others, participation in the cultic celebration stands devoid of meaning and value. Such a situation compels believers to re-examine the significance of this obscured religious sense with greater discernment and it bids them to trace the problem to its roots.

The more critical thinkers will examine the religious posture of our culture to assess its maturity, or, alternatively, the in-quiry could bear on whether there was ever maturity of the religious sense in the earlier stages of human history and, if so, what were its indicators? Could it be that our culture and the modern world have rendered man incapable of arriving at that level of human maturity needed to approach the prob-lem of religion, or, rather, is the present crisis a function of man's maturation forcing him to be critical when confronted by specific forms of the sacred? Is contemporary man incapa-ble of sensing the need of the sacred-religious in modalities similar to those which informed and expressed it in the past? Were the explications and concretizations of the sacred more a response to earlier cultures than to the contemporary situation? Could it be that the new culture presents a wholesome chal-lenge to reach out for a more mature expression of faith?

It is imperative that the problem of the interdependence of religion and culture be envisaged boldly. Classical sociology confronts it on the phenomenological plane. One of its fore-most representatives, Max Weber, sets in relief the multifarious reciprocal influences while abstaining from any judgmental valuation of them.[1]

One cannot penetrate realistically the great expressions of man, be they cultural, social, economical or religious, while prescinding them from the complex totality of the person in community. A human fact can never be isolated and consid-ered as separate from the others; a human experience finds verification in manifold interdependencies and through the relative strength of interactions. We cannot be scandalized,

[1] Max Weber, *The Protestant Ethic and the Spirit of Capitalism* (New York: Scribner, 1958).

then, if we constantly behold an interpenetration and inter-dependence of the religious phenomenon with life, the family and the cultural, political, economic and social structures. A sober reflection on the facts and their meaning prevents us from concluding simplistically in favor of social-economic-cultural reductionism of religion. "Pure" religion is an abstraction which can no more be verified in reality than "pure" economics or "pure" politics. Every human phenomenon bears an invest-ment of the complexity of the person in human community. It is of utmost importance, then, to study with great care the religious phenomenon itself in its relationship to the main ex-pressions of human life; otherwise man himself and his religion may lose his identity and unconsciously be reduced to a mere superstructure of the existing culture.

To this end, we now undertake to study the problem of the reciprocal incidence and dependence of religious phenomena and socio-cultural phenomena. Assuming a strictly sociological research, we shall also approach the problem from the philo-sophical-theological level but with a definite pastoral intent, remaining ever mindful, however, of the exigencies of an age of secularization.[2]

I. SALT OF THE EARTH, LIGHT OF THE WORLD

The conciliar constitution *Gaudium et Spes* speaks of "the earthly and heavenly city penetrating each other" as a fact

[2] Benson, P. H., *Religion in Contemporary Culture: a Study of Religion Through Social Science* (New York: Harper, 1960).

Berger, P. L., *The Social Construction of Reality* (New York: Double-day, 1967).

——, *A Rumor of Angels. Modern Society and the Rediscovery of the Supernatural* (New York: Doubleday, 1970).

Miller, S. H., *Religion in a Technical Age* (Cambridge, Mass.: Harvard University Press, 1968).

Radhakrishnan, S., *Religion in a Changing World* (London: Allen, G., 1967).

Wright, John H., *Religion and Change* (New York: Harper, 1969).

Yinger, J. M., *Religion, Society and Individual. An Introduction to the Sociology of Religion* (New York: Macmillan, 1968).

which, in the depth of its salvific meaning, is accessible to faith alone (GS, Art. 40). The presence of the Church in the world cannot possibly be conceived on the model of a mission to be accomplished without explicitly positing a vital exchange with those to whom it is sent. The Church is truly fulfilling a mission in the world: she is entrusted to announce the Gospel to all peoples in their own language (cf. Mt. 26:18–20; Heb. 13:14).

w/
Dialogue!

The Church lives in the world, consistently expressing her interdependence with the exigencies and conditions of life for those to whom she is sent, and she has to do so consciously if she is to fulfill her apostolic mandate. The path chosen by the Word Incarnate for the presentation and realization of salvation in the world always stands as the "norm" for the Church. Her mission cannot be characterized by indifference, lack of interest or a superficial relationship with the socio-cultural contemporary world, but depends on her incarnation in it.

The perspectives and method of approach to today's world are presently the object of numerous discussions. The Second Vatican Council, in its very early phase, warned of the urgency of reconsidering and redefining the relation of the Church to the world, but it was not yet fully capable of coming to grips with the problem. Unfortunately, the Council's decree *Inter Mirifica*, while evincing concern for how the modern media of social communications could be used in the apostolate of the Church, did not show a real awareness that the Church is now living among new generations of men who must be addressed in totally new terms. The very inadequacy of this decree, however, proved to be a blessing in that it occasioned more serious reflection on the problem.

The press, the cinema, radio and television have in fact created a new type of mentality different by far from that which existed prior to their discovery and diffusion. The Church's self-questioning should bear, first of all, on whether she is conscious of this change, and whether or not she is ready to pledge herself to renewal insofar as her mission is involved, i.e., announcing the Gospel in a way that would enable her to enter into dialogue with and be understood by contemporary man. How can she help man to realize himself in this new culture permeated by the mass media? Not until she has weighed the answers to this basic question can she expect to avail herself intelligently of the modern communications media for the explicit purpose of announcing the message of the kingdom of God, and helping man to grow toward maturity in faith as in his life. The problem can be exemplified dramatically by a desire of so many churchmen to operate according to an older model of "secrecy" which hurts modern man in his relationship to a hoped-for "open" Church.[3]

Our present historical moment is pregnant with grave problems and attendant responsibilities. The Church would gain by loyally asking herself what can be done to help man preserve and develop his own personal and communitarian integrity, his own capacity to reflect and to decide responsibly, overcoming the dangers of "massification" lurking in the use of the mass communications media. The Council justly noted: "The Church recognizes that if these instruments are rightly used, they bring solid nourishment to the human race . . . but the Church is also aware that men can use these gifts against the mind of the divine Benefactor, and abuse them to their own undoing" (IM, Art. 2). However, merely pointing to the dangers falls short of her mission; it is necessary to contribute generously and constructively in surmounting the obstacles by capitalizing on the tremendous positive potentials.

Confronted by the increasing and controlling influence of public opinion, the Church has to gain a full awareness of these new problems and search for their value and significance; consequently, her concern will focus on the initiatives she can and ought to promote. Believers and all men of good will manifest a growing commitment "to form and to voice worthy views on public affairs" (IM, Art. 8).

[3] The pastoral instruction *Communicatio et Progressus* of Pope Paul VI (1971) is an enormous progress in comparison to *Inter Mirifica*. It shows direct concern for man's own growth by using optimally the new opportunities. The vision of evangelization is more realistically related to the understanding of this new phase of history.

The prominent role of public opinion today does not so much set itself as a force for the Church's self-questioning as for how it can be directed authentically for greater service to all. Of course, it also poses ethical, dogmatic and structural problems within the Church. The rediscovery of the *"sensus fidei"* of all the faithful is also due to the modern revaluation of public opinion; in the moral domain, it divulges the urgency of a morality no longer elaborated *"in vitro"* (experimentally, cut off from the flow of life), but developed as a result of dialogue involving every committed member of the Church and the whole of humanity. This openness and awareness is necessary for fruitful collaboration with experts in the use of the media of social communications. The task is of utmost importance, demanding that the believers be prepared to seek a dialogue characterized by mutual trust and respect of everyone's competence and responsibility.

We pause here to exemplify, so as to underline, the complexity of the problems faced by the Church in her search for an authentic presence in today's world. A true response will be possible only if she reflects attentively on the interdependence of the "earthly city" and the "heavenly" one. Our faith would be very differently objectified and become formally sacralized were it to serve the sole purpose of placing the light "under the bushel" (Mt. 5:15), but it would very soon extinguish the flame itself.

In final analysis, every religion finds actualization as a community of men who feel profoundly united before God and solidary with one another. Therefore, religion is strictly bound with the social dimension of man and consequently cannot ignore the forms, social perspective and ordering in which the social nature and vocation of man became concretely conceived and expressed at various epochs. Christianity, more than any other religion, has to be more aware of this fact, viewing it as a reflection of the salvific economy of the Word Incarnate. In the dynamism of its mission, the socio-religious component of Christianity assumes the value of "sacrament," i.e., a sign which testifies to the presence of salvation in the world and one through which salvation is to be realized. The Church cannot be a "sacrament of union with God" without being a "sacrament of the unity of all mankind" (LG, Art. 1).

The incarnate character or salvific interpenetration of faith with the socio-cultural reality should not be misunderstood. It cannot be interpreted in the sense that Christianity is the mere result of socio-cultural applications and powers. Where the Church is vigilant and faithful to the Gospel she will not suffer a passive molding by the dynamism of the earthly city. The Church's identity transcends historical data but it remains profoundly related to it; the Church gives to the world and receives from it. No longer can the Church and the secular world be radically opposed to one another, for the Christian vision of the world ascribes an original sacred value to it which, though frustrated by sin, always stands created by and redeemed in Christ.

The divine plan on the world assigns to faith the special task and important role of being a unifying force for man. Faith summons a response from the whole man granting him and demanding of him the integration of all his experiences and various worldly callings into a uniquely great perspective. The fullness of revelation and the perfect man are epitomized in Christ, the plenitude of value-significance of God's bounties for man and the whole of human history. The economic and socio-cultural realities are intended for man, who, as a faithful steward, returns them to God in Christ (I Cor. 3:22–23). Assumed in faith and expressed in redeemed love and justice, they become expressions of faith incarnate. The whole cosmic and human reality comes from God in Christ; in the hands of the truly religious man, it progressively becomes more perfect as a response to God in fraternity and generous solidarity.

A true religion is always prophetic; it can never be uninterested in man's total salvation and well-being. It cannot be indifferent or recusant before a commitment for more humane conditions of life. Because the community and message of salvation in Christ transcend earthly reality, they can never obscure whatever comes from God for the benefit of mankind. Man's actualization of his talents to the benefit of all men becomes a thanksgiving and glorification of the Father in heaven.

Man's unity is very complex; his sense of integrity is very strong, making repulsive to him whatever is perceived as threatening it. However, our contemporary civilization imperils personal and communitarian integrity and integration through its fragmentation; the more sensitive men of today (as person or as community) are therefore more keenly desirous and willing to be integrally and authentically themselves.

The religious man and the community of believers cannot ignore this new conflict and self-awareness. Faith is presently confronted by the following alternatives: either to insert itself as a leaven in the social, cultural and economic life with a strong integrative capacity and discernible example of wholeness *or* accept to disappear by allowing itself to be molded passively by forces which spell renunciation to integrity and integration. Disintegration and inertia signify decay and represent the real "profanity." In fact, when the social and cultural realities are found in a state of disintegration, lacking the enlightened discernment of faith-charity, they become "profane," that is, alienated from their highest finality, from their true meaning and value; they stand inimical to man's dignity and total vocation.

History and sociology attest to the shrewdness and truth of Lord Acton's observation: "religion is the key of history." The remark is equally valid for that part of our world which is not only secular but also secularistic and atheistic. "For, taken as whole, atheism is not a spontaneous development but stems from a variety of causes, including a critical reaction against religious beliefs, and in some places, against the Christian religion in particular" (GS, Art. 19). All this can be understood only by courageously accepting the reciprocal interdependence and interpenetration of religion and the earthly city. Again I insist on reiterating that religion cannot exist in a vacuum; it must insert itself and be enmeshed concretely in the life of our times. When this reciprocal enrichment fails to be negotiated, the consequences cannot be other than disastrous for both religion and the social-cultural reality.

Salvation and sin affect man in his totality; salvation leads to wholeness and integration whereas sin sinks the roots of disintegration. We ought not only to be aware but to realize and recognize critically how often religious expressions, forms and structures, including socio-cultural and economic phenomena, are somehow falsified by the presence of sin. The interdependence and interpenetration of the one by the other can then be disturbing and dangerous.

Against these dangers, Karl Barth cautions through his insistence on a faith without a man-made religion, or a "religionless Christianity." Faith comprises a total submission of man to the Word of God and his grace. In its light, every sacralistic religious attitude is a profane element. Through faith in the Word of God, the believer receives the capacity to discern the salvific plan of God in the earthly reality; faith by itself gives an integrated and integrating perspective of man and sheds its light on the whole of reality. However, it must be remembered that Karl Barth in the first decades of his theological activity failed to heed sufficiently the necessary interpenetration of a faith lived and expressed in a community of believers, a faith rooted in the totality of the human condition. Only later, in dialogue with men like Dietrich Bonhoeffer, did he interpret and develop differently the encounter of faith and culture.

When the expressions of religion are worked out without adequately taking into account the social and cultural components of our way of thinking, dialoguing and living, they not only become an alienation from life for its adherents but also leave believers defenseless before the numerous and varied negative influences coming from their workaday world and the broader social context. Whenever theology, liturgy and Church structures fail to confront consciously, loyally and in redemptive solidarity the totality of the world in which we live, they then exercise a negative influence and fascination; in fact, they backfire.

A good example can be cited in the aristocratic tendency of Dom Guéranger's spirituality of more than a century ago as well as in the whole mentality that led up to the "Una voce" of today. Both trends of thought despise the living language of the common people and ignore the desire of youth to worship with spontaneity and creativity. While claiming pure concern for the sacredness of worship and the orthodoxy of formulas, in reality they are championing social-cultural values linked to the prerogatives of the upper bourgeois class. These values are marginal to the contemporaneous evolution of culture and are even more strikingly opposed to genuine Christian values. Guéranger destroyed whatever still existed of the old liturgical tradition in favor of Roman uniformity. He protested against any effort to prepare liturgical texts for the simple people for he saw in this a sacrilegious attack on the "sacred" prerogatives of the monks and priests. While claiming to fight for an "objective" and unchangeable conception of faith, the traditionalist identifies his religion with concern for higher social status and pits himself against evolution. He is led to fear that faith which would commit him to a total change of heart and life.

Such phenomena are often found and seem more pronounced outside of Christendom than within it. Was it not the case of the monk of the Hinayana Buddhism who had committed himself to saving his soul through a radical separation from society? His decision to become a monk had been strongly influenced by the aristocratic caste to which he belonged, including his motivational pattern and his very mode of alms-seeking.

II. DIVINE MESSAGE IN HUMAN WORDS

God speaks to us in all his works since everything is created in the Word: "and through him all things came to be; no single thing was created without him" (Jn. 1:3), "all things are held together in him" (Col. 1:17). Everything save sin is a gift of

God, his word, his message and his call. The gratuitous nature and free character of God's bounty shine forth very particularly in the gift of salvation in Christ. In him and through the Spirit, the Father offers us communion to the dynamism of his trinitarian love. The fact that all God's gifts are to be received in gratitude and with a view to solidarity is underscored by the doctrine of the gratuitousness of salvation.

The God-Redeemer presence in us is conceptually distinguished from that of the God-Creator in all his works but cannot be dissociated. The same love with which God creates the universe and man makes us sons through his Word, and the same word of God by which all is created and sustained in existence grants us sonship. In the light of this truth, it is necessary to study the interaction of the Gospel message and its expressions throughout history; the mode of expression is always marked by the culture and historical period. But if faith has deep roots and if the community of believers is vigilant to the opportunities and needs of the times, the message preserves its identity. God works in and through all cultures; no culture and no theology is thus allowed a monopoly.

In view of the strong temptations arising from ideologies such as sociologism, it is necessary to repeat untiringly that the message of salvation and the essential mission of the Church are simply a gratuitous and free gift of God; neither is a human phenomenon stemming only from social, economic and cultural causes. The Christian faith transcends all the historical factors of culture and civilization. Paul's expression remains ever valid: "Jews call for miracles, Greeks look for wisdom; but we proclaim Christ—yes, Christ nailed to the cross, though this is a stumbling block to Jews and folly to Greeks" (I Cor. 1:22–23).

Not only does salvation revealed and realized in Christ surpass all that man can imagine and attain by himself but it projects beyond the present human and cosmic history: "Christ was raised to life, the firstfruits of the harvest of the dead. For since it was man who brought death into the world, a man also brought resurrection of the dead" (I Cor. 15:20–22).

This message is proclaimed courageously but it should not be allowed to interfere with our perception and testimony to the other aspect of salvation, namely, its incarnation dimension. When transcendence or incarnation receives unilateral emphasis, we no longer announce the full Gospel of salvation and fall short of the plan of the Father (cf. I Jn. 5:1 and 4:7–8).

The Word took flesh in the world and history; "he came to dwell among us" (Jn. 1:14). Christ inserts himself in a redemptive way in the dynamics of human history so as to bear the full burden of it and reshape everything in a new spirit. The words and actions of Christ, so dense in symbolic value, and those of the apostles reflect the language, culture, social and religious structures of the Israelites in the period of Roman domination and, particularly, the ambience and dialects of their fellowmen.

The divine message enters history in human words. The conciliar constitution *Dei Verbum* in reporting a text of St. John Chrysostom speaks of the "condescension of eternal wisdom. . . . For the words of God, expressed in human language, have been made like human discourse" (DV, Art. 8). The interaction of the message and its expression in human language should inspire gratitude on our part. In fact, the dynamic interaction continually renews itself and staves off any attempt to obstruct the proclamation of salvation by means of static formulas or a "sacred language." The sacralization of a language and stereotyped formulas destroys the interplay intended by God, Lord of history, and negates the reality of Christ's incarnation.

Language is a social phenomenon; not only do we express ourselves orally but the concept of language also includes nonverbal cultural symbols. Language pertains to the whole culture insofar as it stands for its "objective spirit," i.e., as an expression and communication of all that which the human spirit has succeeded in understanding and achieving. In fact, the spoken-written language is only a part of the complex phenomenon of economic, cultural and social communication; all human phenomena or humanized acquisitions are imparted through communication skills and symbolic language.

Language is the customary vehicle for communicating thought, emotions and perceptions to others, but it is also an instrument of thought. The structure of a language reveals and conditions the mental structure of a given culture. Whenever we speak and think in a specific language, we thereby become debtors of a culture that finds expression in it and from which it derives its structure; we share equally in its values and its limitations.[4]

It is peculiar to man to preserve the documents of his history in museums and archives. We read with interest, even after centuries, the works of outstanding thinkers and artists, but whenever we approach works and documents of the past, we immediately experience difficulty in grasping and decoding their language. Effort must be expended to decipher the expressions of these eminent thinkers in the total context of their culture so as to understand the thought and facts. It proves that language as a means of communication and reflection is never static; it evolves constantly. Language development constitutes an integral part of the total development of humanity; it accompanies its evolution and conditions its rhythm. Therefore, any attempt to sacralize a specific language signifies not only an anachronistic effort and an erroneous preservation of the treasures of tradition but most of all, it constitutes a flight from life. In final analysis, a sacralized language in either liturgy or doctrinal communication serves no other purpose than alienation from a commitment to sanctify life. Despite its diverse and assiduous contacts with the treasures of the past, language purports to realize continuity in newness.

Every thought statically closing in on itself is destined to death. Neither religious thought nor its expressions can elude this law; refusal to move at a pace equal to that of the culture

[4] Macquarrie, John, *God-Talk: An Examination of the Language and Logic of Theology* (New York: Harper & Row, 1967).
———, *God and Secularity* (Philadelphia: Westminster Press, 1967).
Moore, S., *God Is a New Language* (London, 1967).

and its language brings loss of vitality and incapability to influence life, which, in the meantime, continues to grow and develop. A static religion plunges into a "heterodox orthodoxy."

Initially, the interaction of the Gospel message with the Hebrew language and culture was a necessity and in full accord with the plan of God's condescension. In the course of his apostolic work, Christ himself asserted it: "I was sent to the lost sheep of the house of Israel, and to them alone" (Mt. 15:24). At the Last Supper, however, he solemnly proclaims that his blood is "the blood of the covenant shed for many" (Mt. 14:24) and before ascending into heaven, he sends his apostles to evangelize and baptize all nations (Mt. 28:19–20). The initial interaction with the Judaic world, however, cannot be interpreted as condemning the message of salvation to suffocation in the culture of this one people. The Gospel is a leaven, a dynamo of life and truth; every historical-cultural identification with it and every attempt to fixate it must be energetically protested and rejected.

The history of the primitive Church is most significant in this respect. Believers among the Greeks protested against a certain monopoly on the part of their brethren of the Hebraic culture; the apostles then laid their hands on seven Greek deacons chosen from the whole assembly (Acts 6:1–5). The openness of Peter to the Gentile cultures was contested (Acts 10:34–43; Gal. 2:12) by the traditionalist element of the Judeo-Christian group (Acts 11:1–17; Gal. 2:11–13). Paul, nevertheless, reacted energetically and continued to combat generously the danger of burying the Gospel of Christ in the Judaic culture (Gal. 2:14).

The diffusion of Christianity in the Hellenistic world proceeded at a pace equal to its assumption of and incarnation in the thought, language, symbols and structures of this culture and consequent liberation from those of Judaic origin. This historic necessity was inspired by the dynamism of Christ's incarnation. Nevertheless, not all the Fathers understood equally the importance and indispensability of such a process; some, like Tatian, lined up against it.

Of itself good and necessary, the Christianization of the Hellenistic world and the partial Hellenization of the Gospel message constituted a danger for the Gospel, especially after the initial fervor, when Hellenization met with a period of stagnation and resulted in a status quo. The peril grew all the stronger when the churches of the Hellenistic world came in arrogant confrontation with those of other cultures. Because the Greeks were wanting in commitment to discernment, dialogue and uninterrupted renewal, the cultural influences prevailed over the genuineness of faith. The social-cultural factors had not been consciously challenged in the light of the Incarnation.

The same dynamics came into play in the process of Romanization and Latinization. The Church was destined to accomplish her mission in a certain period of history and within a definite sector of humanity, but it was not spared the attendant risks and dangers. If faithfulness to the Roman Church should imply fidelity to the language, categories of thought, symbols and juridical structures of the Roman culture, such "fidelity" would betray the Gospel and the Church of the Word Incarnate, and discredit the ministry of unity of the successor of Peter. As was the case for Paul, protest then becomes a necessity: the Gospel and the Church are neither Roman, nor Greek, nor bear the monopolistic label of any culture. The Second Vatican Council attentively singled out the cultural elements for the purpose of overcoming the perils of a false "Romanic" loyalty. This strong awareness and determination are encountered at every step (cf. LG, Art. 13; AG, Chapter 1). Sustained efforts in this direction demand courage, humility and prayer.

The social dimension of the person simultaneously involves an active and passive insertion into existing social structures. A society exists before the person and this constitutes an inevitable fact. The structures, however, are affected by persons; a member of society accepts them responsibly when he commits himself to their evolution or transformation in keeping with the best interests of all concerned. This discourse applies equally for believers whether they are considered as individuals or as community. The Church fulfills her mission in the world by adopting the contemporaneous socio-cultural forms and by inserting herself in social environments as a leaven of love, truth and justice.

Christ had chosen twelve apostles to symbolize the twelve tribes of Israel. After the treason of Judas, the primitive community felt compelled to bring the number up to its original; they came to choose Matthias, "who was then assigned a place among the twelve apostles" (Acts 1:26). It was one of the first acts of the Church after the resurrection and ascension of Christ. Paul, on the contrary, although recognized as Apostle by the whole Church (cf. Gal. 2:7ff.) was never counted among the twelve. He thus stood as a living symbol of the transcendence of the Gospel over the tribes of Israel; to this testimony, he consecrated his whole life.

The first Christian community adopted various elements of ordering and customs of the synagogue (e.g., the elders, the presbyterium) as well as the patriarchal structure common to the agricultural society of that period. In the evangelization of the Mediterranean world, it assumed new elements; the center and fulcrum of missionary action came to be the great urban centers. The structural evolution of the episcopate and authority of the Patriarchs is partially due to this fact. It certainly represents an authentic and necessary development; however, it cannot be considered definitive or immutable.

The haughty totalitarianism of the oriental emperors and their culture was opposed by a similar arrogance of their occidental counterparts; the lack of discernment by the Church of Constantinople and that of Rome became a source of great tension. It finally resulted in a schism destructive of the unity of Christ's Church. Then followed monopolistic pretexts, triumphalism and refusal to accept, with constancy and loyalty, the called-for criticisms and protests. This fission diminished the vitality of the Churches, oriental as well as occidental, and eventuated in obscuring the message of salvation itself.

In the Roman Catholic realm, obfuscation of Christ's message is exemplified in the extended discussions on Chinese and

Indian rites. The decision to impose on all nations and all cultures the rite, formulations, categories of Latin theological thought has compromised for centuries the worldwide mission of the Church. It certainly has been a grave obstacle to the diffusion of the Gospel in spite of all the generous efforts of missionaries. It was not only a mistake on the policy level but an error of genuine self-understanding on the part of the Church; it was basically a too restricted and too static vision of the message of salvation.

Vatican II succeeded in committing the "Latin" Church to overcome the monopolistic ritualism, formalism and centralism which constituted a source of immobilism and alienation for so long. In the decree on ecumenism, one reads, for example: "What has already been said about legitimate variety we are pleased to apply to differences in theological expressions of doctrine. In the investigation of revealed truth, East and West have used different methods and approaches in understanding and proclaiming divine things. It is hardly surprising, then, if sometimes one tradition has come nearer than the other to an apt appreciation of certain aspects of a revealed mystery, or has expressed them in a clearer manner. As a result, these various theological formulations are often to be considered as complementary rather than conflicting" (UR, Art. 17).

The day has come for challenging and re-examining courageously all the catholic forms (in the original sense of the term of catholic=all-embracing) of presenting the Good News by studying the historical-social components which have determined them. This procedure will enable us to perceive the just complementarity as well as the limits of the various adaptations. Such a study is necessary for its ecumenical and missionary aspect, but also for arriving at a better understanding of the nature and value of dogmatic-moral expressions. It would then be easier to avoid excessive socio-cultural conditioning; faith would then be the leaven of the world always and everywhere. In meeting the African, Asian and Latin-American cultures we are still far from genuine appreciation of them; in spite of so much good will, there is more ethical and cultural colonialism than we are ready to acknowledge.[5]

III. RELATIONSHIP OF RELIGION TO SOCIAL CLASS

Sociological study of the great cultures of different historical periods cannot suffice; one must further know how to detect specific influences coming from the diverse subcultures which developed within every one of them. There is need of an analytic study of the way and the extent to which the various social classes have had an impact on the formulations of thought and religious expressions.[6] The analysis is here restricted to those social classes having subcultures of their own, especially in static and closed societies.

Reference has already been made to the consequences for religion and religious ethics of priests being considered as and organized into a privileged class. The natural solidarity and alliance, more or less explicit, between the priestly and other privileged classes have had remarkable repercussions in Church matters. One example would be the relative underdevelopment of the universal priesthood of the People of God in Catholic theology and Church life. An important angle for studying the influence of the various social classes lies in the investigation of the source of priestly vocations. Whenever there is found a predominance, numerical or qualitative, of one specific class, then its mentality and customs usually bear a strong influence on all the expressions of religion and on the religious thought and ethics of the period.

In the poorer and less educated social strata, emotionality and spontaneity are greatly diffused; they tend to be less self-conscious, less reflective, more prone to admiration and amazement. Their faith is often simpler and more humble, but stands

[5] See the chapter "Missionary Dimensions of Protest" in my book *A Theology of Protest* (New York: Farrar, Straus & Giroux, 1970).
[6] Bernard Häring, *Introduzione alla sociologia religiosa e pastorale*, 2d ed. (Roma, Ed. paoline, 1963), pp. 178–211.

more exposed to the dangers of sacralistic objectivism and
superstition. These less sophisticated persons lean toward the
sacred and are sensitive to its experiences. However, they
lack in necessary discernment and attach themselves too
strongly to places, formulas and rites, exhibiting a propensity
for external sacralization of life.

The poorer, simpler classes are particularly open to an eschatological vision of life, to a hope vividly presented to them.
Burdened by numerous daily problems and worries, the poor
are more disposed to hope in a final liberation. Continually
smitten by the injustice and egotism of the more powerful, they
have a keener sense of sin (in its totality) and feel strongly
the need of deliverance. They more readily understand the
communitarian aspect of religion, of hope and of morality
itself.

The poor man is aware that solidarity with the other poor
represents his only chance to survive and to assert his rights.
His preoccupations center on remaining united to others. He
feels deeply the suffering of those who, like him, are exploited
and in misery. His whole morality is marked by the communitarian dimension to the point that whatever assails or
destroys the solidarity of the poor is, in his eyes, the gravest
of sins.

The religion and religious ethics of the middle class differ in
many respects from those of the simpler folk. In fact, it is in
the middle class that ideas of liberty are developed (often
with clear accents of egocentric individualism), as well as
concepts of a socio-economic order centered in the respect
and defense of private property, freedom and the rights of
the individual. Besides, it is the stratum of society that em-
phasizes commutative justice while playing down its social
aspect. For middle-class members, the sense of solidarity is
oftentimes minimal.

The middle socio-economic class likewise sets the religious
problem in a predominantly personal key; most of the time,
personal sufferings give rise to self-questioning on God. At
every step, the "sacred" risks remaining encapsulated in con-

cepts of merit and individual retribution; it then assumes dimensions and expressions of a quasi-commercial character. People pray only when they need God or because of the hope of future retribution. They do not rise to the level of authentic praise, joy and thanksgiving.

The religion of the middle class is readily enclosed within the narrow limits of a "God and my soul" relationship, *Deus et anima*. When religiosity remains on a more or less superficial level, it takes on the character of a purely cultural and social embellishment of life in which one indulges primarily for the sake of greater prestige. Religion is reserved for Sunday, bearing no dynamic relationship whatsoever to the daily economic, social or cultural life.

Personal salvation stands at dead center in this middle-class perspective. The one religious question of interest is: am I counted among the predestined to eternal life? Interest in the social and cosmic aspects of salvation is consequently minimal. Fraternal charity as commitment to the redemption of the world is non-existent; it is reduced to occasional almsgiving. Even on the level of moral reflection, there is preoccupation with delimiting the "superfluous" and specifying precisely where the grave obligation to give to the poor begins.[7] Happiness for the singular soul in heaven is dissociated from the expectation of God's all-embracing kingdom on earth, a characteristic of the hope of the poor. It is in this context that problems are posed to theology, like the already classical question relative to the nature of eternal bliss: does it consist principally in the satisfaction of the intellect or that of the will?

The man of the middle class is generally conscious of his own rights and freedom and exhibits little inclination to the communitarian, and somewhat emotional, religious expressions of the poor. Middle-class believers tend increasingly to stress the doctrinal elements bound in a static formulation that gives

[7] An example would be I. Aertnys, C. Damen, and I. Visser, *Theologia moralis, secundum doctrinam S. Alfonsi de Ligorio, Doctoris Ecclesiae,* 17th ed. (Torino, 1956), Vol. II, pp. 345 ff.

a feeling of security. Religion then becomes a *quasi*-ideology.[8] This process of abstraction and objectification of concepts and formulas not only bears on the sentimental aspect but attains vital dimensions of faith and religion; its highly individual-istic ethics is practically irreligious, bearing no direct relation to faith-piety ideally expressed and lived within the social dimension. A morality of duty and commandments cut off from the law of grace and brotherhood is a typical product of the middle class.[9]

One cannot overgeneralize, however, ascribing to all middle-class believers the same vision of morality and religion. In fact, the heterogeneous composition of the middle class ac-counts for differences in origin and activities. Therefore, a variety of emphases, angles and socio-cultural perspectives can be expected within it. These diversities naturally influence religious outlook, religiosity and ethics.

In no way is the foregoing intended to negate or protest the importance of free decision and spontaneous development of personality, for without them, there would be no morality, in the true sense. But moral values are sham when devoid of fraternal solidarity and co-responsibility. Attention is called to the way class mentality gives an altogether particular stamp to values, accentuating or exaggerating some while diminish-ing and negating others. Such a phenomenon is even encoun-tered in the Sacred Scriptures, although in a more balanced form. For example, the many non-Israelite sages of the Old Testament often reflect somehow the middle-class milieu and way of thinking. As a matter of fact, mere comparison of the

[8] For the study of this dynamism within the Protestant churches in the United States, a classical work is that of H. R. Niebuhr, *The Social Sources of Denominationalism* (New York, 1929).

[9] An illustration of this phenomenon is the mentality of the "godly" peo-ple of the Dutch Reformed Church in South Africa, where this author lectured while doing the final editing of this book. The all too "good con-science" of this higher middle class in relation to the immense suffering and moral damage wrought by their apartheid politics is a classical ex-ample.

trends of knowledge with the prophetic current alerts to the striking diversity of outlook.

The culture and mentality of the middle class strongly influenced the history of the Church. The reformed Churches single out a significant historical constant: whenever the mentality and culture of the middle class no longer leaves room for the piety of the poor, the latter detach themselves from the more aristocratic group and come into being as new churches more fitted to the life style of the simple people. However, as the years come to transform deeply these splinter groups along the lines of social ascent of their members (now middle-class), the phenomenon is repeated.

In the Catholic Church, the abstractionism of catechisms and theology manuals can be attributed mainly to the influences of the middle class and aristocracy. So also can be explained the dichotomy between dogmatic and moral theology, liturgical form and language; the popular reaction has been numerous extra-liturgical devotions. To the influence of this middle class can be traced the elaboration of a type of morality unilaterally concerned with the self-fulfillment of the individual, with a vision of justice centered on commutative aspects with little or no sensitivity or concern for the social. It eventuated in a gradual alienation of the working class and the modern proletariat.

One should not conclude prematurely that the influence of the predominant social class on religion and ethics is a phenomenon specific to Christianity or Judaism; it has also been recorded and was perhaps more strongly marked outside these confines. In the Hellenistic culture, for example, the aristocratic tendencies were noticeable before they ever came to influence early Christianity, at least in certain manifestations of religious groupings and some philosophical-ethical schools. The Stoic ethics is a clear example.

In India, the Brahman movement is also typically aristocratic. The Brahmans belong to the most well-to-do classes and dispose of power and culture. In the religious sphere, they therefore ascribe great importance to knowledge by asserting its indispensability for salvation; such an affirmation is typical of an aristocratic religion that scorns the unlearned mass. Even Buddha is a member of the high nobility; he thereby gives to classical Buddhism a distinctively aristocratic stamp. The monk of the Hinayana radically cuts himself off from the sufferings, joys and hopes of the simple people because he is so fully and uniquely engrossed with self-liberation for eternal life. However, Buddhism was profoundly altered later as it met with other classes and different cultures.

Awareness of all these phenomena poses grave problems for the Church on the level of theological reflection, proclamation of the Gospel message, worship and structures. She ought to realize unity in diversity and diversity in unity. Surely it is a difficult task to harmonize pluralism with the call to unity in one faith. The Church's universal mission demands a type of pluralism that confesses faith in one God and in the one Spirit who, through his manifold gifts, calls mankind to oneness in faith and thus in justice, peace and solidarity among themselves. Pluralism, in the true sense, means incarnation of the Gospel in all cultures and helps people of the various cultures and social classes to understand the identical message of salvation. It requires much vigilance and discernment for the Church to insert herself constantly anew in society and human history without becoming fixed or fractionated, continuing always to be the one Church of Christ for all men salvifically bound within a brotherhood open to the Father. Sensitivity and openness to the value system of other cultures and subcultures is a necessary remedy against the dangers of narrow-mindedness and the trend of absolutizing one kind of religious experience.

IV. INTERPENETRATION AND AUTONOMY IN *GAUDIUM ET SPES*

The Pastoral Constitution on *the Church in the Modern World* has intrepidly confronted the problem of dialogue with the contemporary world. It soon became apparent in the course of Council discussions that it was impossible to approach such a dialogue in the perspective of a dualism of two totally separated "realms." The Church is certainly not identified with the earthly city; in her mission she is distinct from it and there are times when she ought to state it pointedly in order to respect the autonomy of the secular city. But the Church cannot arrive at self-definition by pitting herself against the earthly city or by seeking her identity through an absolute separation from culture, the economic and social life. The Church received a mission from Christ to make his love visible in the world and for the world. Besides, a believer is inevitably a member of the social-economic-cultural world: each of the faithful belongs to a specific nation and to a well-defined social class, sharing its mentality, successes and failures.

The Church-world interdependence and interpenetration pose formidable questions and give rise to complex pastoral and theological questions. When believers are not conscious or remain oblivious of these interdependencies, failing to arrive at a just vision and serene evaluation of the situation, strong polarities arise. It is important that the Church experience the tensions and meet the challenge if she is to unveil her true face to the world. In fact, it is necessary that the Church find a life style and language appropriate for her making clearly evident to the man of today her understanding of being "in the world"; she should likewise spell out her relations with the secular city.

A. The Church Gives to and Receives from the World

A fruitful dialogue demands as a first and indispensable step a loyal presentation of the interlocutors in their true identity. The second condition, equally vital, is the thoroughly sincere belief that everyone has something to give and to receive from the other. In this respect, *Gaudium et Spes* overcomes the strong theological current of the past whereby the Church thought only of giving to the world without receiving anything from it, the underlying reason being that she was self-sufficient and thought that she had all she needed to serve her purpose and life. According to the Council, the Church stands truly in need of the world and its help; she can and ought to learn from the world. God also works in the secular world and through it.

Once it had recognized that the Catholic Church was indebted to the other Christian Churches, the Council added: "At the same time, she is firmly convinced that she can be abundantly and variously helped by the world in the matter of preparing the ground for the Gospel. This help she gains from the talents and industry of individuals and from human society as a whole" (GS, Art. 40). Then follows a whole paragraph which the Constitution devoted to "the help which the Church receives from the modern world" (GS, Art. 44). When theology unreservedly makes its own the perspectives of the history of salvation, it sees the secular city, whether secularized or not, primarily as a presence of the power of the Creator and Redeemer, not merely as an object of mission or a danger.

The world in its actual form witnesses to the multiple contributions of the diverse religions and particularly of Christianity. In many respects, it shows the power of grace in redeemed human behavior. All this should be acknowledged in gratitude even if vigilance is called for because of confrontation by the complex mingling of good and evil in man's pilgrim situation.

Throughout its history, the Church has continually received from the world even if her relations with it have not always been friendly and respectful of its autonomy and dignity. For example, a profound knowledge of man and natural law which makes of the Church a community of experts within humanity is the result of dialogue, interaction and exchange with the various human cultures. "Thanks to the experience of past ages, the progress of the sciences and the treasures hidden in the various forms of human culture, the nature of man himself is more clearly revealed and new roads to truth are opened.

These benefits profit the Church also, for from the beginning of her history, she has learned to express the message of Christ with the help of the ideas and terminology of various peoples, and has tried to clarify it with the wisdom of philosophers, too" (GS, Art. 44).

In this respect, it is worth noticing how the Church did not take only words or abstract concepts. She has made hers the genius of the language and of the whole culture, even the mental structure itself, in such a way that it has become her mode of thinking and her way of perceiving the realities of faith. In the Syrian Church, for example, the images and symbols have a much greater role to play in theology than in the Greco-Roman world.

The Church has always made use of philosophical categories for her proclamation of and reflection on revealed truth. Philosophy presents a more or less existential reflection on human experience but in a way that is an integral part of the mentality of a specific culture in a definite epoch. By adopting philosophical categories and availing herself of them, the Church places herself in deep rapport with the secular city, i.e., with the concrete culture both as a giver and as a receiver.

Historically, the encounter with the religiosity peculiar to the various peoples before the proclamation of the Gospel is noteworthy. It has greatly contributed to the tangible attainments of the Church in her structures and in her expressions of faith and charity. As mentioned earlier, secularization is, in part, a phenomenon of Christian inspiration. Today, its influence assumes new emphases and new forms; it is mandatory that the Church open herself with discernment and love to such newness and accept all that is worthy of elaboration. However, receiving and learning from the world cannot be viewed apart from the total reality of the Church-world interpenetration; they form part of the dynamics of mutual exchange and reciprocal enrichment (GS, Art. 44).

On this point, the Council draws a very important conclusion: a Church conceived and realized according to overly clerical criteria is incapable of promoting such an exchange or of enriching herself through it. "To promote such an exchange, the Church requires special help, particularly in our day, when things are changing very rapidly and ways of thinking are exceedingly various. She must rely on those who live in the world, are versed in different institutions and specialities, and grasp their innermost significance" (GS, Art. 44).

God also manifests his will to us through the secular world. The necessity of listening to the world so as to better announce the Gospel of salvation or even perceive more clearly its dynamism was not emphasized sufficiently in the past. Therefore, the Council reminds us: "With the help of the Holy Spirit, it is the task of the entire People of God, especially pastors and theologians, to hear, distinguish, and interpret the many voices of our age. . . . In this way, revealed truth can always be more deeply penetrated, better understood, and set forth to greater advantage" (GS, Art. 44).

The Council Fathers did not categorize theology and theologians simply as mediators between the Magisterium, believers and the world by their interpretation of official doctrine. Theologians must simultaneously assume the task of helping the Church in the difficult but indispensable task of listening to and understanding the world; they must keep themselves in continuous and attentive contact with life and human culture, enriching themselves from it so as to be better able to bring to it the message of salvation; it is also incumbent on them to form hypotheses bearing on the most fitting ways of interpreting the "signs of the times," of announcing the message and of testifying to it.

The help which the Church receives from the world is not restricted to thought and language but extends to its very structures. In fact, the Church as sacrament of Christ has a certain visibility; she is a communion incarnated in reality. The concrete physiognomy which she acquires historically in fidelity to Christ owes much to the structures of specific eras and distinct cultures; the Church assimilates from the human environment in which she must actualize herself, the manner and forms for realizing and testifying to the original pastoral-sacramental structure intended by Christ.

Whoever, therefore, commits himself to the promotion of the human family in view of international solidarity also lends a helping hand to the Church. She is thereby led to rethink her own structuralization and moves to renew herself and to witness more authentically to the Lord. The vision and forms of authority remain closely related to those of the contemporary civil society; they depend greatly on the direct personal experience which churchmen (especially members of the hierarchy) have had in their family and the social milieu from which they emanated.

Today's secularization prophetically summons the Church to an indispensable historical evolution of her structures, especially with regard to forms and style of authority. Institutional flexibility complemented by depth of discernment and prophetic courage should be essential features of her renewed structures. At all levels, the Church must be wary of the mighty temptation to sacralize falsely the now obsolete structures and forms of authority which she had assumed earlier in the course of progressive interpenetration of secular modes of government.

In judging her structures and forms, the Church should not invoke the cliché "until now, it was done this way"; she would gain by displaying more concern for a criterion like "do these structures reveal to the man of today the loving design of Christ?" That which is dysfunctional, which no longer responds to the present needs or poses an obstacle to such a goal should be revamped. A readiness for self-renewal is fundamental for the Church's fidelity to Christ, for the validity of her proclamation as well as for the coming to faith of those who listen to her words and behold her countenance.

The authority crisis to which the Church addresses herself today and which constitutes a source of unrest stems from the interdependence of forms of authority and the historical evolution of humanity. Her failure to sense and to attend to the "authority problem" earlier produced considerable confusion as to the mode of exercising authority.[10] The Church "can and ought to be enriched by the development of human social life. The reason is not that the constitution given her by Christ is defective, but so that she may understand it more penetratingly, express it better, and adjust it more successfully to our times" (GS, Art. 44).

The structure of the Church cannot be reduced to any of the calculating forms of the secular city. The Church should not be tied up with any political regime, be it imperial or democratic. In the past, she adopted a style of governance similar to that of the existing aristocratic or monarchical society. Her specific duty today lies in the adoption of new forms respectful of subsidiarity and collegiality, forms which are congruent with the just desires of modern man to bear his share of the responsibilities for today's social and cultural life. If he were to find in the Church only obsolete notions of authority, how could he believe in the proclamation of the love of Christ for the man of today? Those structures of the Church which obscure the Gospel message constitute a genuine obstacle to the choice and commitment of faith for today's believer instead of being a helpful testimony.

While striving hard at self-reform, the Church should not lack the prophetic courage that makes her protest all the glaring injustices of the existing political, social and economic structures. In no way should she be identified with contemporary regimes. She needs to pay attention to prophetic voices, to every well-grounded criticism of her. Even the Church's enemies can be of help to her: "Indeed, the Church admits that she has greatly profited and still profits from the antagonism of those who oppose or persecute her" (GS, Art. 44). If the Church is to be serious in accepting to examine her organizational structures, style of authority, doctrinal and moral expressions and formulations in the face of protests from her enemies (at times partially unjust or excessive), it is obvious that

[10] Cf. Häring, A Theology of Protest. One chapter bears on "authority crisis."

she must be all the more ready to heed the criticism and loud
prophetic protest of the many who love her passionately.

B. Interpenetration and Autonomy

The salvific mission entrusted to the Church concerns man
in the full integrity of his dignity and vocation. The Church is
the servant who proclaims the absolute rights of God, the uni-
versality of his kingship and his salvific design for the whole
world. She has the task of announcing and witnessing by her
life and ministry to that man who is trustee of the created
world.

The Gospel's heralding of the liberty and dignity of the
sons of God implies and demands absolute respect for conscience. "It is one of the major tenets of Catholic doctrine that
man's response to God in faith must be free. Therefore no one
is to be forced to embrace the Christian faith against his own
will. . . . It is therefore completely in accord with the nature
of faith that in matters religious every manner of coercion on
the part of men should be excluded" (DH, Art. 10).

One can easily intuit, however, how the emphasis and perspectives of such respect for conscience likewise depend on the
society and secular culture of the day. The progress of the secular city renders us capable of understanding better how the
Gospel "has a sacred reverence for the dignity of conscience
and its freedom of choice" (GS, Art. 41). On the other hand,
by virtue of the Gospel, the Church is the leaven of sincerity
and source of prophetic commitment for the rights of the person. The Second Vatican Council returns ever anew to the interdependence of the Church and the secular city: "By virtue
of the gospel committed to her, the Church proclaims the
rights of man. She acknowledges and greatly esteems the dynamic movements of today by which these rights are everywhere fostered" (GS, Art. 41).

At a time when authoritarian and paternalistic societies
elaborated a concept of absolute allegiance and unconditional
obedience to rulers and absorbed so much of man's whole life

that this approach partially obscured the dignity of conscience, the Church herself failed to testify clearly and dis-
tinctly to the respect due to conscience. The general social
climate has now changed; full recognition of the dignity and
freedom of conscience on the part of the Church is now facilitated by the strong awareness of these values which she is
called to assert in the secular city. That is why when the
Church fails to witness or to stimulate prophetically to such respect through her proclamation of the Gospel, her life and her
structures, she erects a wall between herself and the contemporary world.

On the other hand, the firm determination of our modern
culture to defend and valorize conscience is not without ambivalence and dangers. In fact, secularism depletes conscience
because it disengages itself "from every requirement of divine
law" (GS, Art. 41). Conscience then often becomes synonymous with arbitrariness, superficiality and egotism; it loses its
fundamental value.

The Church ought to reject prophetically any arbitrariness
that tends proudly to set itself up as autonomous before God
and as supreme in its own right. In fact, when man allows such
pride to rule him, he is then enslaved to his own egotism, personal realizations and whims. He creates new idols, becomes
an idol-worshiper and loses that freedom which wants to assert itself; this freedom-pride combination erodes brotherhood.
The Church must be prophetic in reacting against such dangers by testifying to the true dignity of conscience and to the
unadulterated freedom of God's sons and daughters.

Such testimony can only be credible when accompanied by
sincere respect for the rightful autonomy of the culture and
science, and by subduing every desire for ecclesiastical-politi-
cal power. If the presence of the Church in the world is to be
authentic, it must be a service of love and salvation. Humility
should be the fundamental character of her insertion in the
world; without it, she is unfaithful to her Lord: "For the force
which the Church can inject into the modern society of man

consists in that faith and charity put into vital practice, not in any external dominion exercised by merely human means" (GS, Art. 42).

C. The Church: Quasi-Sacrament of Unity for the Whole of Mankind

The Gospel of the one Creator and Redeemer of all reality is a dynamic power calling all men to unity and solidarity. Christ "is himself our peace. Gentiles and Jews, he has made the two one, and in his own body of flesh and blood has broken down the enmity which stood like a dividing wall between them, for he annulled the law with its rules and regulations, so as to create out of the two a single new humanity in himself, thereby making peace. This was his purpose, to reconcile the two in a single body to God through the cross, on which he killed the enmity. So he came and proclaimed the good news: peace to you who were far off, and peace to those who were nearby" (Eph. 2:14–17).

The Church contributes to the unity and solidarity of mankind to the extent that she becomes a visible and convincing sign of the oneness of humanity before God, of a unity alien to rigid uniformity. The Church advocates a unity based on gratitude in love for a rightful diversity (cf. LG, Art. 13; GS, Art. 42). In saying that the Church is a sacrament of unity for the whole of humanity, the emphasis rests on the *sacred:* she can lead to the unifying and pacifying strength coming from Christ and she expresses it in her faith, hope and love. She is "sacrament" only to the extent that she lives and makes visible her faith active in love. Paul writes: "There is one body and one Spirit, as there is also one hope held out in God's call to you; one Lord, one faith . . . But each of us has been given his gift, his due portion of Christ's bounty" (Eph. 4:4–7).

Christ renews man in his totality. The faith, hope and charity which he places in our hearts are dynamics of unity prompting respect and acceptance of the variety of gifts through the presence of the Spirit. The epoch in which we live constitutes an experience and a very particular call to unity for humanity. With every new day, we become more conscious that the future of the world and that of man depends on the defeat of group or national egotism and rests on peaceful co-operation at all levels.

Christianity participates in such an experience and grows in awareness, all the while learning from it. The Christians of today recognize more readily that unity stands at the very heart of their vocation. This consciousness will not so much direct them to create Christian organizations in the secular world for the promotion of the unity of peoples as arouse them to a more sincere effort for realizing unity and solidarity in the life of the Church. Thus energies will be expended in the direction of forming a mentality and creating a strong desire for unity in every believer so as to make him an "instrument of peace" in the Church and the world. The Church has to aim at that experience of unity in faith and hope which makes everyone of her members a "leaven" in the secular world. Further ecumenical commitment is fundamental for the testimony which the Church must render to the mission of Christ, who came so that "all in heaven and on earth might be brought into a unity in Christ" (Eph. 1:10). However, ecumenism would be meaningless were it to dissociate itself from the thrust found in the secular world toward new forms of solidarity and collaboration among all men.

The Church "recognizes that worthy elements are found in today's social movements, especially an evolution toward unity, a process of wholesome socialization and of association in civic and economic realms" (GS, Art. 42). If she is to accept this dynamism toward the unification of the modern world, to incarnate herself in it and contribute responsibly to it, the Church must adapt her own structures and internal organization so as to align them with the style of authority and communitarian life style proper to this historical period. This calls for a more sincere respect for diversity. The upshot of contempt for the pluralism of cultures is divisive and in turn leads to experiences of painful conflict. These indispensable first steps for a prophetic presence of the Church in the world of the twentieth century merit serious consideration.

D. A New and Vital Synthesis of Faith

Certainly, the problem of Church-state relations is still relevant today although it assumes different forms. In a period of history witnessing all types of institutional crises, the Church-state questions fall into second place. The constitution *Gaudium et Spes* has given it relatively little attention. Thus, the image of the Church delineated by the Council differs sharply from the medieval concept which placed the problem of Church-state relationships primarily on the institutional plane. The diplomatic corps of the Vatican is still a remnant of that outdated approach.

The primary concern of *Gaudium et Spes* lies in the search for a living and dynamic synthesis of faith which will permit the believer to function fully and freely as a member of the Church and a citizen of the secular world. These coincident roles are essential for a truly Christian faith; in fact, this ought necessarily to be reflected and provide a thrust for the totality of life. Therefore, the Council notes: "The split between the faith which many profess and their daily lives deserves to be counted among the more serious errors of our age. Long since, the prophets of the Old Testament fought vehemently against this scandal and even more so did Jesus Christ Himself in the New Testament threaten it with grave punishments" (GS, Art. 43).

Such a religion-and-life split has a number of historical, social, ecclesiastical and personal roots. First, there was a notable lack of awareness and attention on the part of the hierarchy and theologians relative to the indispensable interpenetration of religion and the totality of life, both social and individual. For too long the hierarchy was convinced that preserving the purity and integrity of the faith signified separating the two, keeping the religious elite aloof from the earthly city or totally cut off from it. Not enough attention was given to the urgency of continuously "translating" the proclamation of faith and the life of faith into a living language and forms befitting the diversity of cultures and the variety of social classes. There were times when the prophets of such renewal were opposed and many of them constrained to silence.

The eschatological hope of Christians does not allow us to ignore our social responsibilities and earthly tasks. As a matter of fact, hope reveals its fullness and its goals in the light of all the works of God covering the continuum of time: past, present and future. Christian hope means trust in the full and integral salvation of man, which remains connected always to that of the whole of creation (cf. Rom. 8).

"Therefore, let there be no false opposition between professional and social activities on the one part, and religious life on the other" (GS, Art. 43). This clear admonition of *Gaudium et Spes* would be nothing less than pure and simple moralism were it not to express and respect a sincere effort of the Church to renew herself in such a way as to serve more effectively the reintegration of the whole of life in faith. The purpose is to "gather their humane, domestic, professional, social and technical enterprises into one vital synthesis with religious values, under whose supreme direction all things are harmonized unto God's glory" (GS, Art. 43).

When the Church succeeds in finding and testifying to a synthesis respectful of the new conditions of life in fidelity to Christ, it then becomes easier for the individual believer to realize his own personal synthesis. This specific task befalls every faithful and it is facilitated and sustained by whatever the Church succeeds in realizing at the level of structures, worship and proclamation of the Gospel. All elements must concur for a continuous renewal of the faith-life synthesis of the Church.

When we speak of the Church, we refer to the whole people of God and not only to the hierarchy. Alone, the latter can never confront and resolve the new problems in a tangible and definitive way: "Let the layman not imagine that his pastors are always such experts, that to every problem which arises, however complicated, they can readily give him a concrete solution, or that such is their mission. Rather, enlightened by Christian wisdom, and giving close attention to the teaching authority of the Church, let the layman take on his own distinctive role" (GS, Art. 43).

Above all, in an era of profound transformations, a just, live and vivifying interpenetration of religion and life would be impossible without creative freedom, spontaneity and the courage to dare or risk. The Second Vatican Council was conscious of the fact that the process of interpenetration often demands pluralism even within the Church; it recognized it and adjudged it positively: "Often enough the Christian view of things will itself suggest some specific solution in certain circumstances. Yet it happens rather frequently, and legitimately so, that with equal sincerity some of the faithful will disagree with others on a given matter" (GS, Art. 43). However, the Council reminds that in these cases no one can "vindicate exclusively" the Gospel or the Magisterium, but that "they should always try to enlighten one another through honest discussion, preserving mutual charity and caring above all for the common good" (GS, Art. 43).

Until recently, such statements would not have been uttered; we were most convinced that an assiduous religious control and direction was necessary to guarantee the material uniformity of solutions. Suffice it to recall the numerous discussions on Christian trade unions and Catholic labor unions at the beginning of the century. Yet even then, the climate of the secular city was yielding gradually to pluralism.

The process of interpenetration of Church and world is a continuous and gradual one. Of course such a dynamic process implies difficulties and calls for the courage to take risks. A static understanding of interaction is an absurdity. However, churchmen whose whole formation was marked by a rather static vision of life are still tempted to apply mainly static categories to this very interaction. No wonder, then, if sometimes they act like guardians not only of an established church order but also of a relationship with the secular world determined once for ever. Especially in our dynamic age we remind ourselves that every new event, new success or failure calls for new considerations and new ways: "The Church also realizes that in working out her relationship with the world, she always has great need of the ripening which comes with the experience of the centuries" (GS, Art. 43). This process of maturation includes the necessity of conversion for the individual person and for various groups: "It does not escape the Church how great a distance lies between the message she offers and the human failings of those to whom the Gospel is entrusted. Whatever be the judgment of history on these defects, we ought to be conscious of them, and struggle against them energetically" (GS, Art. 43).

Consequently, there is need for a continuous renewal of structures, an impossibility without a spirit of humility. Equally important is the willingness to atone for past errors in the exercise of authority, in her structuralization and in the mode of relationships established with the secular society, especially those repeated attempts against its freedom and autonomy.

E. Religion and the Promotion of Culture: New Styles of Life

Gaudium et Spes dedicates the introductory chapter and Chapter II of its second part to the problems of culture. It reveals the Church's sincere effort to understand the newness of modern culture while seeking a relevant modality for the insertion of faith in it.

The Church is cognizant of the fact that "the living conditions of modern man have been so profoundly changed in their social and cultural dimensions that we can speak of a new age in human history" (GS, Art. 54). The new ways and novel possibilities have unveiled the wherewithal for perfecting and diffusing culture more broadly. Altogether, the enigmatic situation which has arisen for the faith and the life of the Church makes it urgent for all believers to respond to these challenges if the Gospel is to be the leaven of brotherhood in Christ for modern man.

The Council takes a phenomenological approach to the novelty of modern culture and endeavors to identify the positive elements in view of constructive interaction with it and eventual interpenetration. Accepting the newness of modern culture without apriority or moralistic biases makes way for an objective understanding of it. The Church has to refrain from deciding first how "it ought to be." That is why the Church would gain by valuing the findings and critically realistic sense of the modern social sciences, for she has much to learn from them.

By placing herself without apriority before reality, the Church will succeed in understanding the deep transformations of culture and its link to "the so-called exact sciences [which] sharpen critical judgment to a very fine edge. Recent psychological research explains human activity more profoundly . . ." (GS, Art. 54). "Advances in biology, psychology, and the social sciences not only bring men hope of improved self-knowledge. In conjunction with technical methods, they are also helping men to exert direct influence on the life of social groups" (GS, Art. 5).

Yet the biological, genetic and psychological sciences allow interventions on human "nature" itself; we are entering upon an era of genetic engineering. "Thus, the human race has passed from a rather static concept of reality to a more dynamic, evolutionary one. In consequence, there has arisen a new series of problems as important as can be, calling for new efforts of analysis and synthesis" (GS, Art. 5). It is clear that such a mentality radically contraposes all forms of religion centered in the sacralization of things or resting in a statically conceived order of things.

Teilhard de Chardin has already asserted how today we feel God's creative presence in evolution, in progress and in history. The progressive change in mentality and structures calls into question the value of some of our religious traditions. If the Church insists on "divine tradition" in matters of purely human and cultural customs or of religious practices influenced by past socio-cultural situations, then she risks fomenting loss of faith and of the religious sense. It is particularly difficult to speak of tradition today, since in the past "tradition" and "traditions" were not clearly differentiated. The confounding of terms explains why there was so little concern for making Christian tradition live and dynamic, i.e., for specifying how it could be the life of a pilgrim community.

"Young people . . . have grown impatient on more than one occasion, and indeed become rebels in their distress" (GS, Art. 7); they react forcefully against static concepts which reflect the mentality and structures of other eras. In the religious field, more often than not, they appreciate the "sacred" from the prophetic standpoint but protest every false sacralization of the past, its structures and its way of thinking. However, the imminent danger in their reaction is that they will lump together values and forms, rejecting both indiscriminately. The hazard is all the greater when official representatives of the Church fail to distinguish faith from human traditions even at the institutional level.

"Finally, these new conditions have their impact on religion. On the one hand a more critical ability to distinguish religion from a magical view of the world and from the superstitions which still circulate purifies religion and exacts day by day a more personal and explicit adherence to faith. As a result, many persons are achieving a more vivid sense of God. On the other hand, growing numbers of people are abandoning religion in practice" (GS, Art. 7). This dismissal of religion compels us to reflect on the situation and solicits a more intense and generous apostolic commitment. The point should be made clear that separation from the great religions or from the Church itself does not always necessarily mean separation from God or absence of a religious sense. At times, the alienation from life of the official representatives of religion or of those who describe themselves as "believing and practicing" causes severance of critical people from the institutional Church. It can have an authentic value for persons searching for more genuine and live religious forms outside the Church, even if we cannot consider it the objectively right response.

A period of deep transformation is inconceivable without perturbation of mind, without some sort of disequilibrium which, *Gaudium et Spes* notes, "are linked with that more basic imbalance rooted in the heart of man. For in man himself many elements wrestle with one another" (GS, Art. 10). It is inevitable that the relationships of modern man with religion and the Church reflect these imbalances. It is important to form honest and loyal hearts in our quest for new solutions if we are to inform life with a climate of fraternal dialogue. In this way, the imbalances will neither frustrate nor scandalize us; they will be an integral part of the communitarian search for truth.

The elements mentioned so far provide ample evidence of the importance for theology to study our contemporary culture attentively, especially in that which is specifically new. A fruitful investigation requires that it be accompanied by research, consideration of the theological thought and achievements of the past, and pursued in the light of anthropology and history. Such an in-depth study will succeed in identifying the sociocultural presuppositions serving as basis for the theology and religious forms of yesterday; it will create an awareness and also facilitate the acceptance of today's cultural assumptions.

We are witnessing today the birth and affirmation of a new humanism characterized by a scientific study of the human phenomenon and by an awareness of the possibility of dominating and disposing of nature, including that of man. Faith has no alternative but to accept its values, enrich itself in it and promote it; in no other way can faith preserve and develop its own vitality. The necessity looms especially great for moral theology, called as it is to respond to new problems; the task is impossible without assuming fundamentally new perspectives in which to think and dialogue.

Particularly crucial is the problem: "how is the independence which culture claims for itself to be recognized as legitimate without the promotion of a humanism which is merely earth-bound, and even contrary to religion itself?" (GS, Art. 56). The question is of paramount importance for the future of faith. Discernment is needed as well as the courage and confidence to attempt new ways and new forms without shirking responsibilities or desisting when faced by inevitable failures.

Man is a cultural being; he is molded by culture and is called to shape culture. This cultural vocation bears a close relationship to his integral calling and therefore ties in with his religious vocation. "For when, by the work of his hands . . . man develops the earth so that it can bear fruit and become a dwelling worthy of the whole human family, and when he consciously takes part in the life of social groups, he carries out the design of God. Manifested at the beginning of time, the divine plan is that man should subdue the earth, bring creation to perfection, and develop himself. When a man so acts, he simultaneously obeys the great Christian commandment that he place himself at the service of his brother men" (GS, Art. 57). On the moral plane, these words of the Council are particularly important; in fact, they are addressed to the new perspectives which moral theology is to assume if it wishes to remain faithful to its mission of proclaiming love in a realistic way.

In the past, the "profane" sciences were considered more as "handmaids of theology [*ancillae theologiae*]." Today, they are viewed in their intrinsic autonomy as a reflection of the "marvelous wisdom which was with God from all eternity, arranging all things with Him." Progress frees man from the servitude of things and allows him to subdue them for the benefit of mankind in general; it also enables man to "be more easily drawn to the worship and contemplation of the Creator" (GS, Art. 57).

A cultural commitment, when inspired by faith and redeemed love, is a form of pre-evangelization. Culture is forever in need of the purifying and renewing power of faith and the Gospel. Most of all, the "interior freedom" which is the fruit of grace inspiring the action of believers can be of great help for the development of modern culture, especially in that which concerns overcoming the most treacherous imbalances.

The psychologically mature religious man, even in the grips of ineluctable tensions, will be able to influence the process of cultural evolution in a way which goes beyond the exclusively spiritual dimension of the person, "in such a way that there results a growth in its ability to wonder, to understand, to contemplate, to make personal judgments, and to develop a religious, moral and social sense" (GS, Art. 59).

The Council posits respect and promotion of a rightful freedom as an indispensable condition for a normal development of culture: "Because it flows immediately from man's spiritual and social nature, culture has constant need of a just freedom if it is to develop. It also needs the legitimate possibility of exercising its independence according to its own principles. . . . It demands respect and enjoys a certain inviolability, at least as long as the rights of the individual and of the community, whether particular or universal, are preserved within the context of the common good" (GS, Art. 59).

In the same context, the Council mentions the freedom to which theology is entitled in view of fulfilling its own task. We have already underlined how theology has a distinctive role to play in the dialogue with the contemporary world, a task to which the whole Church is committed. It is particularly theology's responsibility to help overcome the hiatus between culture and faith, between daily life and worship. But if the just freedom needed for research, the freedom of expression and freedom to dialogue is not granted, the situation will certainly not foster a climate of serenity and trust which is mandatory for a possible encounter of the Church with the secular city.

It would be pharisaical to preach freedom for culture in the secular city if it is not first realized within the Church. If one is mindful of the complex interpenetration of religion and culture, one immediately understands how lack of freedom in the one field or the other disturbs both, but mostly their mutual relationships. "Because of circumstances, it is sometimes difficult to harmonize culture and Christian teaching" (GS, Art. 62). But these tensions can become a stimulant for a more serious and more profound search as well as a source of genuine progress. The Lord of history does not allow man to be satisfied with what has been achieved up to now; he expects and demands further growth in grateful response for his bounties.

V. POLITICAL THEOLOGY

Over the past few years, "political theology" has become a fashionable slogan, at times abused, but one that grasps well some of the most urgent exigencies and tasks of theology today.[11] The most influential spokesman of the new school of "political theology" is Johann B. Metz.[12] Passionate discussions followed the publication of some of his works on the subject, all of which served to clarify the fundamental goals, concepts and perspectives of this new breed of theologians.[13]

If this school of theology labels itself "political," it intends the term in its etymological meaning and not in its modern technical sense; "political" refers to whatever constitutes a philosophical or theological discourse on the "polis," on the dynamism of life in society. It wishes to score critically the influence it exercises on religion and on the Church, and con-

[11] I have confronted such problems as "political theology," interdependence of political life and religion (including theology) in several chapters of my book, *Macht und Ohnmacht der Religion, Religionssoziologie als Anruf* (Salzburg: Otto Müller Verlag, 1956).

[12] J. B. Metz, "Aspekte einer neuen 'politischen Theologie'" in Metz, Moltmann, Oelmüller, *Kirche in Prozess der Aufklärung* (Munich: Kaiser, 1970); "Political Theology," *Sacramentum mundi*, V (New York-London), pp. 34–38 (almost identical is his article in *Concilium*, 16 [1968], pp. 3–11), *Theology of the World* (New York, 1969).

[13] Coste, R., "Religion and Politics" in *Convergence*, 1 (1971), pp. 7–11. Paupert, J. M., *Perspective de théologie politique* (Toulouse, 1969). Peukert, H., ed., *Diskussion zur "politischen Theologie"* (Mainz-Munich, 1970). Stimma St., "Religion and Politics in a Socialist Society" in *Convergence*, 1 (1971), pp. 32–34. Zizola, G., "The End of the 'Sacred' Neutrality" in *Convergence*, 1 (1971) pp. 3–6.

versely, that which it constantly receives from religion, theology and the whole reality of the Church. Political theology is not and least of all does it want to be a modern and "clean" form of clericalism; on the contrary, it positively guards against every clerical and theocratic temptation. Political theology represents an attentive reflection on the concrete applications of the great intuition of John: "If he does not love the brother whom he has seen, it cannot be that he loves God whom he has not seen. And indeed this command comes from Christ himself: that he who loves God must also love his brother" (I Jn. 4:20–21). Consideration of the basic tenets of political theology should reveal its import.

(a) Every religious expression and formulation, inclusive of the very image of God, is deeply rooted in political experience (understood in a broad sense).

Hence, in the patriarchal family, the authority of God is conceived according to the fundamentals of *potestas patris familias;* in the monarchical type of society, God is seen as the all-powerful King or Emperor; in a militaristic society, God becomes the great Leader, victorious in battles. Very significant in this respect is the development of the concept of Yahweh in Israel; there is always a parallelism and a profound interdependence with the social and political situation.

The same relevance is likewise found for models according to which the Church, throughout its history, has internally exercised authority. In a social and political context of the monarchical type, she has taught, with great security, the monarchy of ministry of the successors of Peter and the other apostles. In the New Testament, on the contrary, there cannot be found any monarchical presentation of the pastoral service in spite of the fact that the historical-cultural and socio-religious situation offered remarkable possibilities in this sense. Her too great security arose from a lack of awareness of the actual interdependence of political and religious experience, of political reflection and theology.

In reality, theology can never be independent of the global

experience of humanity because the Lord it proclaims is the Lord of history who encounters and saves man in ongoing history. It is important that believers be made aware of this fact so as to live their history in an authentic way. Otherwise, they run the risk of falsifying the very proclamation of salvation. Insight and explicit reflection on these facts are especially urgent today because of the social and political revolution of the last years; otherwise, the *aggiornamento* (updating) and the renewal of the Church would be greatly jeopardized.

(b) At their own time, all the religious formulations, expressions and structures have political implications.

Official religious pronouncements and practices invariably exercise an influence on the life of the earthly city. Every decision taken by the Church (and even every decision not taken by her) has repercussions in the political field. The religious concepts bound in taboos of different types are a grave hindrance to the progress of humanity. The Karma of Hinduism, for example, is partially responsible for the permanence of a socially discriminatory mentality in the Indian culture.

History bears testimony that Christianity is not without periods when it exerted a negative influence on the earthly city. One can think, for example, of the inflexible position of theology when confronted by the positive sciences at the inception of the modern scientific epoch. The last centuries have seen a religiosity set in a very individualistic key and with profound repercussions in the social field, namely, promotion of an attitude concerned solely with saving one's soul and tending "not to soil itself" in politics; together with other causes, this has resulted in the birth of modern secularism and atheism, but it also lies at the root of innumerable social injustices.

Conservatism in rituals and a concept of dogmas which failed to evince a significant dynamism toward individual and social conversion made the Church an ally of conservatism in the cultural, economic, social and political life. A good example of how man-made "religious" doctrine reflects a certain type of society and confirms it can be found in the doctrine on *limbo*. According to Augustinian and scholastic tradition, *limbo* is the sad place where all children who died without baptism rest eternally cut off from God. This theory which condemned to eternal underdevelopment a great majority of human beings afforded a terribly good conscience for the cultural and political elite who kept the great masses of people in a striking underdevelopment. Revelation has not the slightest indication of this doctrine. It could never have come up in a Church and society which provided equal and real chances of development to all human persons. Our commitment to peace, social justice and opportunity for progress of all nations and all social classes obliges us to unmask the paltry political background of such a "doctrine."

(c) A mutual dependence of religion and politics is positive to the extent that it emanates from a sincere and responsible effort of sensitization and reflection.

The more consciously and responsibly believers reflect on the depth and breadth of these interdependencies, the better will be the fruits for the earthly city and the community of believers. This is the end-goal of political theology.

On the one hand, political theology wishes to eschew a social-political dependence that could be so strong as to falsify both social life and the reflection of the community of faith. On the other hand, it also wants to preclude the existence of strictly political intentions in the formulation of faith, in the religious decisions of the believers and especially in the decisions of the hierarchy. Political theology wants to steer faith clear of any attempt against the true secularity of the earthly city which could involuntarily become a cause of atheism or secularism. In summary, it wishes to guide believers to a generous commitment to the progress of the earthly city and keep themselves free from any pretext or desires to domineer.

Today it is particularly important that the Church be mindful of the extent to which her structures, formulations, language and moral imperatives bear the influence of forms already discarded by more promising present political structures and mentality. Such an effort is particularly important because of the long period of history when the whole life of the Church was affected by the synthesis (or confusion) of roles in the very person of the Pope as Successor of Peter and king of the churchly state. The dual role was decisive, for example, in the elaboration of concepts of ecclesiastical authority and Christian obedience; the latter unduly became the cornerstone for the whole of morality. We should be apprised of how all our daily ecclesiastical realizations depend on and influence the contemporaneous social and political climate. The concept of collegiality itself depends on the overall social and political evolution, and its implementation will not be without resonance in the political and economic life.

The teaching of the Church is never without repercussion on the national and international political life. Think only of the impact of *Humanae Vitae*. If the Church were to teach rigidly one means of regulating births without showing concern about the accessibility of this method for all classes and for all cultures, its teaching would have a striking echo in the life of the earthly city. On the other hand, were the Pope to approve of the "pill," he would have to shoulder grave responsibilities relative to the future of humanity. By an authoritative pronouncement on the medical acceptability of certain "pills," the Pope would have negated the autonomy, competence and responsibility of the medical sciences. The Church ought to recognize and admit to her incompetence with regard to the therapeutic value of various drugs, but even more ought she to be conscious that every one of her decisions carries weight in the life of the secular city. She should also be mindful that her refusal to speak out on tangible problems bears serious political implications.

(d) Political theology insists on a more humble image of the Church, one that will make more transparent the face of Christ, servant of God and of brethren.

This brings to light the particular risks, dangers and defects of an ecclesiology based on the identification of the Church with the hierarchy. It brings out how a notion of authority depends on and inserts itself in a particular social-political climate, such as that in which Louis XIV could assert: *"L'état, c'est moi!"* Certainly, such is not the climate today.

In no way does political theology wish to attack the original structure of the Church intended by Christ, but it does seek to free her from overidentification with outdated forms of wielding authority. The urgency of such a purification arises mostly from the thought that a paternalistic hierarchy today would likely lead to alienation and eventually to atheism or secularism. In underlining the implications of perspective and language, political theology seeks a clear perception of the Church-servant. It sets itself against those bishops and theologians who, in the name of God, are politicians; it attests to and proves historically the incompetence of the successors of the apostles in the political realm.

The political incompetence of theologians and canonists is a fact as historically sure and proven as in the case of bishops and cardinals. Discrimination in favor of the theologians would be unfair, for the disqualification is theirs as well as the bishops'. Careful scrutiny of such ineptness should, however, result in loyal collaboration of the hierarchy, theologians and laymen in discerning the political import of eventual decisions, or their failing to take position on the most urgent problems. Most of all, one should not listen one-sidedly to the powerful; there is need for vigilance relative to the dangers befalling the politically interested.

The Magisterium of the Pope and bishops along with the work of theologians should illumine the conscience of all their brethren on the necessary interdependence of Christian life and political responsibility, a pledge of fraternal love and a political commitment. To be underscored is the fundament that no one can adore the one God, Father of all, without zealously working for the solidarity and brotherhood of the whole human race. However, asserting principles is not sufficient; it is mandatory to seek sincerely those modalities which make their realization possible in the various historical and cul-

tural situations. For the implementation of such concrete
possibilities, a loyal dialogue among pastors, theologians and
laymen, among believers and experts in the sciences and technology becomes impelling.

(e) We are living in a pluralistic society; even the Church
is opening herself to a more or less marked pluralism.
Therefore, a fundamental question is raised: who speaks
in the name of the Church?

The voice of a bishop can no longer be considered the
unique, true and valid voice of the Church, especially when
the matter pertains to decisions having direct bearing on the
life of the earthly city. Especially in such cases should there
be a just pluralism of opinions in the interior of the Church;
it will be all the more positive when most of the believers commit themselves loyally to search for valid answers to the new
questions. The new situation imposes on the ecclesial Magisterium a certain restraint in not giving officially *one* answer if
the problems have not yet been sufficiently studied in depth.
It is clear that the pastors would sin by presumption and would
not speak in the name of the Church were they to propose a
unique solution when, in the community of believers, there is
a just pluralism of positions; it would create dangers of schism
even at the practical level.

Instead, pastors ought to pledge themselves to illumine
consciences and to foster in all believers a greater commitment
to the search for constructive answers. On the other hand, it is
not right for the faithful to stand there gaping, waiting for the
hierarchy to shoulder alone the whole responsibility and give
ready-made solutions. There is need for all the faithful to col-
laborate with the hierarchy in the common search for solutions
to contemporary problems. Unjustifiable would be the accusation of "insecurity complex" or an allegation of "fear of committing itself" when the hierarchy does not speak out officially
because it is not yet prepared to do so with clear insight and
sufficient information. Meanwhile, attention to the various pro-

phetic voices coupled with concern to solicit a common effort of careful study would likely serve the interests of all the faithful.

At times, conditions are such that the problems have attained sufficient depth, the responsibilities are so grave and urgent as to compel the Church to speak out through the Successor of Peter and/or all the successors of the apostles. It would seem to me that on the contemporary scene, such would be the case for problems of racism, the massacre of the innocent, violence, outright injustice against minority groups, suppression of human rights and the like. It is fundamental that the Church take a strong position against slavery of any form.

The pastors of the Church owe it to their fellow-Christians to follow attentively the development of socio-political events; however, they ought to be of help to all segments of the people of God. The converse is also true; finding a valid solution to a human problem becomes all the more difficult when the study remains closed to hierarchical collaboration or divorced from theological considerations. Valid answers are the fruit of the common quest and prayer of the whole Church. The responsibilities weigh on the whole Church. During the period of search and study, we should never discount the prophetic voices which recall to all believers their grave responsibilities before God and the world. It would be an irreparable damage if prophets would either be lacking in the Church or if they were not heard.

It is therefore necessary that believers be courageous in promoting initiatives of their own so as to respond to the novel situations and new exigencies. For example, I would list among developments of great actuality today, the rise of groups of believers committed to the ideals of non-violence and actively searching for practical means to implement these ideals. The particular importance of such initiatives arises from the new waves of violence which now rock the whole world. It would be pharisaical to stand there, gazing into space, under the pretext of awaiting a solemn pronouncement from the hierarchy on this issue.[14]

In summary, political theology ought to sensitize all believers to the indispensability of a generous commitment to the life of the earthly city. It wants to convince them that salvation is not attained by remaining uninterested in the neighbor; general apathy would only negate the love of God and become a cause of practical if not of theoretical atheism. At the same time, political theology ought to commit itself to delineate a viable type of presence of the Church in the earthly city, one characterized by loyalty in collaboration, respect for the autonomy of created reality, and a testimony of faith in God, who is Love, in Christ, who is our Peace and saving Protest.

[14] See Häring, *A Theology of Protest.*

CHAPTER 5

"FAITH ALONE" IN AN ECUMENICAL AND SECULAR AGE

In his discourse on "the bread from heaven," Christ admonishes the grumbling Jews: "Stop murmuring among yourselves. No man can come to me unless he is drawn by the Father who sent me; I will raise him up on the last day" (Jn. 6:43–44). This attraction-revelation of the Father calls for man's response in faith: "The obedience of faith must be given to God who reveals, an obedience by which man entrusts his whole self freely to God who reveals, and freely assenting to the truth revealed by Him" (DV, Art. 5).

In the sixteenth century crisis, "faith alone," "grace alone" and "Scriptures alone" were the slogans by which Martin Luther characterized his protest and his reforming action. While opposing itself globally to Luther's vision, the Council of Trent shared its fundamental inspiration with regard to faith. Faith is a gift of God, one without which it would be impossible to be accepted by God.[1] It is the gift *par excellence*, the most precious and gratuitous, on which our whole salvation depends, the fundament and root of all justification.

The Church has always considered faith as foundation and center of the whole of Christian life. However, in the course of her history, she has had to announce such truth and testify to it with varying emphases and nuances so as to adapt it, in a redemptive way, to the various epochs and socio-cultural situations. A fair appraisal of this historical dynamism requires that we keep in mind what we have said earlier relative to the interdependence of religion and the earthly city.

[1] Council of Trent, Sess. VI, C. 8; Denzinger-Schönmetzer, No. 1532.

Awareness of the diverse mentalities and historical-cultural influences on the enunciation of principles bearing on the centrality of faith is important in a search for the value and significance of singular formulations. It becomes indispensable the moment one seeks to delineate or suggest expressions adapted to the newness of today. To tease out the "essential" in complex past formulations is certainly a difficult but necessary process if one wishes to vivify the present in a Christian way.

The post-Tridentine theology was the fruit of a Church maintaining a prevalently self-defensive attitude in the world; it was internally structured along a hierarchical system in a closed and static manner. Besides, it reflected the existing climate of the various Christian churches where theology was predominantly apologetic and resorted to polemics when questioned about the intent of reforms. On the other hand, the social context in which it developed was still stagnant and strongly paternalistic. The principle which made of religion a "state act" emphasized the corresponding polemic attitude of the Churches. Culture was still conceived as homogeneously Christian to the point that even politics were sacralized, at least in the vision of theologians and ranking churchmen. Today, much of the socio-religious and ecumenical situation is very different.

I. NEW ASSUMPTIONS OF THEOLOGY

Classical moral theology was founded on the presupposition of a homogeneously Catholic or at least Christian world. It not only accepted the particular socio-religious ambience in which it was initially elaborated, but for lack of critical historical reflection, it assumed it to be the normal human situation, that is, simply according to the nature of man. The social context of these centuries was permeated and profoundly affected by faith, and, in Catholic nations, by the teachings of the Magisterium. All public and private spheres of activity were remarkably bound and influenced by the "sacred," including art, politics and economics; for culture, the process of desacralization was in the initial stage only.

In such a socio-religious environment, the concerns of moral theology turned almost exclusively to details. In the Catholic domain, the polemic reaction to the "freedom of conscience" advocated by the reformers evinced excessive tutelage on the part of the Magisterium with strong direction of the laity by the clergy. Therefore, moral reflection centered on the solution of "cases"; the search for a typical response to the various situations was such that the faithful could do nothing other than translate this response into practice by adapting it to analogous situations.

Prior to the Enlightenment, theologians felt no compulsion to clarify in an explicit way the concepts, fundaments and central perspectives of Christian morality. One should not be astonished by this state of affairs since the theologians were living in a fundamentally homogeneous world molded by the "sacred"; the society was culturally Christian. The manuals of moral theology displayed little concern for the global vision of faith, for the bearing of faith on morality or for relating faith to life; all was assumed as an evident datum.

On the social plane as much as on the religious, the world of today is characterized by a pluralism which slowly affirms itself even within the Church; her unity is not so much uniformity-homogeneity as unity-solidarity which accepts socio-religious diversities in Christ. Among the various churches, "there flourishes such an admirable brotherhood that this variety within the Church in no way harms her unity, but rather manifests it. For it is the mind of the Catholic Church that each individual Church or rite retain its traditions whole and entire, while adjusting its way of life to the various needs of time and place" (OE, Art. 2). It is hoped that such a pluralism is also asserting itself in the new canonical legislation. Adhering to the norms elaborated for liturgical reform there are, for example, provisions characterized by respect for a healthy pluralism in the last legislation on mixed marriages. Nevertheless, there still remains a long way to go.

The Church's acceptance of pluralism does not necessarily signify its accepting it or restricting it only for geographical-cultural levels. The plurality of the contemporary world goes beyond the international fact; it begins within specific human groups. There is an honored pluralism within the local Church communities, a diversity determined by the formation and experience of individual believers who have been more or less strongly tinted by the process of secularization. Rationalism, Marxism, the various reactions to them, and a typically laicized bourgeois mentality strongly typify most of today's believers. In every local community, close to the deeply convinced believers live others whose faith is in infancy and some in whom the socio-cultural influences are so intense as to leave little room for an authentic Christian faith.

On the moral plane, however, each group manifests attitudes differing in kind and emphasis from those assumed by classical moral theology. The scientific sophistication of today renders us distrustful of an ethical system conceived prior to any empirical-anthropological research on the conditions, processes, interdependencies and possible opportunities. Earlier, the acceptance of an ethical system was a matter of course. Not only within the Catholic camp but even among proponents of a secularistic rationalism, schemata of thought were proposed in the form of complete systems with little or no attention given to the methodological exigencies which sociology, psychology and other anthropological sciences deem basic today.

Contemporary moral theology ought to be aware that it becomes hazardous for the faith to structure itself as a closed ethical system that nods to concreteness and historicity only with systematic-casuistic considerations. In fact, modern man would immediately be informed of the gap between the system and casuistic reflections; it would consequently lead him to reject radically the whole ethical system. By training, modern man begins from critical observation and significant experience; he tends to disbelieve all apriorities. In his reaction or overreaction to systems, the risk entails faith itself.

The primary question posed today relates to the fundamental

import of moral theology. Is it better to start from a global vision of faith and later rise to the exigencies of faith in this twentieth century? Or is it more advantageous to start from existential moral experiences and gradually expose them to the light of faith? Or should we attempt a combination of the two methods? Finding a valid response to these questions cannot prescind from an awareness of the fact that not all persons effectively arrive by faith to moral convictions; some get a glimpse at the horizon of religion and faith only through the most urgent and fundamental ethical problems such as the value and sense of conscience, the dignity of the person, freedom, solidarity and the like. The relevance and importance of moral theology solicit careful consideration of the socio-religious presuppositions.

The desacralization of culture and traditions compounding the powerful experience of historicity generates difficult problems of hermeneutics as much for the moral message of Holy Scriptures as for the various pronouncements of the Magisterium in ethical matters. The historical-sociological dimension so fundamental to the modern mentality compels the man of today to question insistently the essentials of salvation truth, the principal unchanging moral exigencies of faith and the criteria for distinguishing forms alterable through the centuries for the sake of incarnation or expression in different historical and sociological contexts.

In the fundamentally static society of yesteryear, the knowledge of the elders, sacred and human traditions, religious authority and its pronouncements were all accepted unquestioningly as a "matter of faith," so to speak. The now universal tendency to question all traditions and structures was hardly perceptible then. The religious sanctions imposed differentially according to the gravity of transgressions of a specific precept were equally accepted in the aggregate of "sacred" respect for the established order. This tendency to fully accept aprioristically has completely disappeared today. Man has become critically pragmatic in the sense that he accepts that which is proposed only if a just use and functionality seem clear to him either for the personal or social good. If these qualities are lacking, the proposal will be rejected inexorably even if it is borne on the shoulders of a more or less long and glorious past. Today's wave of protests (not always sufficiently self-critical and often violent) can be curbed only by recognizing and promoting a firm commitment to healthy discernment.

It is worthwhile to consider the method by which the manuals of traditional moral theology appealed to the Magisterium; the words of the Magisterium were quoted literally without any consideration for the concrete situations in which they were uttered and they were applied rigorously to other situations and other eras. Today, moral theology acknowledges the urgency of a careful historical-theological hermeneutics which lifts from context the message which the Magisterium sought to convey. One then seeks those instances scored by the Magisterium as being part of the revealed deposit of faith and bearing the fruit of its incarnation in contingent historical situations. Finally, today's theology asks itself how it can express the evangelical message in the present situation.[2]

Contemporary moral theology is expected to give a response of salvation to the new situation in full awareness of the earlier presuppositions so that even the doctrine of "faith alone" can be thought of in a way different from that of the Reformation and Counter-Reformation without diminishing the main concern.[3] Because of the totally dissimilar socio-historical con-

[2] Cf. *Magistero e morale: Atti del 3° congresso nazionale dei moralisti.* (Bologna, 1970).

[3] Bennett, J. C., *Storm Over Ethics* (Philadelphia: United Church Press, 1967).

Berton, P., *The Comfortable Pew* (Philadelphia: Lippincott, 1965).

Häring, B., *Morality Is for Persons* (New York: Farrar, Straus & Giroux, 1971).

——, *This Time of Salvation* (New York: Herder & Herder, 1964).

MacIntyre, A., *Secularization and Moral Change* (New York: Oxford University Press, 1967).

Mitchell, B., *Law, Morality and Religion in a Secular Society* (London: Oxford University Press, 1967).

Robinson, J. A. T., *Honest to God* (London: SCM Press, 1963; Westminster [paperback], 1963).

text, the emphases and fundamental perspectives should also be different.[4]

This chapter will now examine how Christian faith can remain the basis, the fundament and crown of the whole of Christian morality. In fact, a serene and constructive confrontation with today's mentality demands no diminution of the centrality of faith; rather, it supposes that a more radical and full existential dimension be given to it.

II. FROM PAUL TO LUTHER

Paul's presentation of the doctrine of justification "in virtue of faith" (Gal. 3:8; Rom. 5:1; Eph. 2:8) is fundamentally "good news" in the sense of being an essential part of the kerygma, but it is formulated in a polemic way.[5] To the legalistic pride of the Jews as later to the proud knowledge of the pagans, Paul opposes faith: "What room then is left for human pride? It is excluded. And on what principle? The keeping of the law would not exclude it, but faith does. For our argument is that a man is justified by faith . . . if it be true that God is one. And he will therefore justify both the circumcised in view

---

————, *Christian Morals Today* (London, SCM Press, 1963; Westminster [paperback], 1964).

————, *Christian Freedom in a Permissive Society* (London: SCM Press, 1970; Westminster [paperback], 1971).

[4] Danielou, J., *La foi de toujours et l'homme d'aujourd'hui* (Paris, 1969).

Dewart, L., *The Future of Belief* (New York: Herder & Herder, 1967).

————, *The Foundations of Belief* (New York: Herder & Herder, 1969).

Galloway, A., *Faith in a Changing Culture* (New York: Humanities Press, 1968).

Lehmann, P. L., *Ethics in a Christian Context* (New York: Harper, 1963).

Lunn, A., and Leon, G. *The New Morality* (London: Blandford, 1968).

Thurian, M., *La foi en crise* (Taizé, 1968).

Williams, C., *Faith in a Secular Age* (New York: Harper & Row, 1966).

[5] See particularly Gal. 3–5.

of their faith, and the uncircumcised through their faith" (Rom. 3:27–30; cf. I Cor. 1:18–31).

Paul's preaching on faith also reflects the profound experience of his encounter with Christ at Damascus. Saul had placed his confidence in the most faithful observance of the law and in the "sacred" privileges of Israel; for this reason, his mind was closed to the Gospel of Christ. He had accepted as final criterion of truth and of goodness, even before the Good News, an absolute fidelity to the "sacred" law and to the "sacred" traditions of a Judaism conceived in a monopolistic perspective. Thus had law and traditions deprived Saul of true freedom until the onset of blindness when he was confronted by the light of Christ. Through the forceful coming of grace, faith liberates him from blindness and servitude; salvation and justification are gratuitously given to him in Christ and not because of the workings of the law (Gal. 1:13–17).

The truth which Paul sets at the center of his missionary undertaking is that of faith. It is through faith only that we find salvation; faith repudiates every reality which becomes an obstacle to the realization of the unity of humanity and cosmos in Christ. It overthrows every particularity and tradition (even the "sacred") that does not favor unity in Christ: "For through faith you are all sons of God in union with Christ Jesus. Baptized into union with him, you have all put on Christ as a garment. There is no such thing as Jew and Greek, slave and freeman, male and female; for you are all one person in Christ Jesus" (Gal. 3:26–28).[6] "For to us, our hope of attaining that righteousness which we eagerly await is the work of the Spirit through faith. If we are in union with Christ Jesus circumcision makes no difference at all, nor does the want of it; the only

---

[6] Our more beautiful affirmations on the intrinsic equality of every person before God lose all their credibility if they are not accompanied by a generous commitment to conquer all racial and social discrimination. The whole life of the Church ought to proclaim that "God has no favorites" (Eph. 6:9; Rom. 2:11; Col. 3:25). It is also necessary that believers commit themselves to the secular city for the realization of a socio-economic order structured along the exigencies of the fundamental equality and dignity of every person.

thing that counts is faith active in love" (Gal. 5:5–6). The personal "metanoia" of Paul and his mission as Apostle of the Gentiles thus form a wonderful synthesis.

In such a personal and historical context, it is clear that morality for Paul is not to be considered as the primary and central reality. Christ does not exist for a morality understood in its socio-religious context in which "law" and "tradition" are so "sacred" that they become an obstacle to the unity of all men in Christ. On the contrary, law and morality are for Christ, and glorify the Father in him; rightly understood, they lead to him: "thus the law was a kind of tutor in charge of us until Christ came when we would be justified through faith" (Gal. 3:24). Tradition (even if "sacred") forever remains subordinated to a living faith in Christ. Religion and morality thus undergo the most radical personalization.

However, morality as seen by Paul prior to his being called to faith, was neither the path to salvation nor to the unity of mankind in Christ through the Spirit. After his conversion Paul's fundamental problem was: given that we cannot accede to Christ along the legal path or that of traditions binding us in a proud self-sufficiency, it is vital that we cut short with legalism.

The courageous apostolic commitment of the Apostle Paul tends to unmask and confute the false sacredness of laws and traditions: "But all such assets I have written off because of Christ. I would say more: I count everything sheer loss, because all is far outweighed by the gain of knowing Christ Jesus my Lord, for whose sake I did in fact lose everything. I count it so much garbage, for the sake of gaining Christ and finding myself incorporate in him, with no righteousness of my own, no legal rectitude, but the righteousness which comes from faith in Christ" (Phil. 3:7–9). To know Christ in the full surrender of oneself to him through a living faith is, however, a new life: a life in Christ and with Christ, according to "the life-giving law of the Spirit" (Rom. 8:2), "in growing conformity with his death, if only I may finally arrive at the resurrection from the dead" (Phil. 3:10–11).

Paul was equally severe with the Hellenistic attempt to accept or reject the Gospel only to the extent that it stood as another precious gem in its treasury of self-sufficient human wisdom, little disposed to submit totally to the judgment of the mystery of Christ. He writes to the Corinthians: "God . . . chose to save those who have faith by the folly of the Gospel. Jews call for miracles, Greeks look for wisdom; but we proclaim Christ—yes, Christ nailed to the cross; and though it is a stumbling-block to Jews and folly to Greeks, yet to those who have heard his call, Jews and Greeks alike, he is the power of God and the wisdom of God. Divine folly is wiser than the wisdom of man, and divine weakness stronger than man's strength" (I Cor. 1:21-25).

All in all, Paul enthusiastically defends the uniqueness of revelation and salvation in Christ against every false anthropocentric vision, whatever be the basis of its selfish confidence: trust in deeds, in the law, in wisdom, in a "sacred" people or in a religious tradition. That only which saves is faith bearing fruit in charity, leading to the unity of mankind and cosmos in Christ.

The overall situation in which Martin Luther found himself was similar in some respects yet very different from that of Paul. Luther had to contend with (1) a monastic asceticism which excessively and sacralistically stressed norms and works to the point that it partially concealed the law of grace; (2) an immobile institutionalism, closed and resistive to renewal and conversion; (3) a legalism which did not allow morality to insert itself into the vivifying dynamism of faith; (4) a clamorous commerce of indulgences which unreasonably accentuated the precise and minute fulfillment of prayers or well-specified works as indispensable conditions for obtaining forgiveness; (5) a ritualism and a cumulation of unenlightened devotions in which faith shone through with difficulty. Those who engaged in these practices hardly understood faith as a humble and full acceptance of Christ in total surrender to him in the service of the brethren.

All this explains Luther's enthusiastic interest in Paul's

preaching on faith and his condemnation of trust in the works of the law. For Luther, as for Paul, it was not a matter of any opposition between faith and morality considered in themselves but rather the conflict between "faith" in an existential sense and a concrete type of "works" within a real historical situation.

Paul opposes trust in the Jewish law because it separates Jews and Gentiles, while genuine faith in Christ tears down all man-made barriers. Luther's protest is directed as much against a faith presented in abstract formulas, with no impact on personal life, as against a meticulous asceticism and ritualism, against the economy of indulgences and the numerous forms of traditionalism and institutionalism which cannot arise from or lead to the testimony of a saving faith.

The other main component of Luther's experience, namely his passionate rejection of the proud humanism of the Renaissance, meets Paul's fight against the trust of the Greek in human wisdom. In addition, Luther had a strong aversion to those rationalistic tendencies of a certain scholastic theology which so often concealed the mystery of the ever greater God and the uniqueness of faith which is man's total response to the Gospel. In fact, a part of scholastic theology under the influence of the new trends of the Renaissance movement placed faith in a singularly intellectual perspective. In these schools, faith had become almost uniquely a rational adherence to well-defined propositions and concepts. To this reductionism there also concurred a strong sense of trust in reason and human concepts along with a "blind obedience" to ecclesiastical authority modeled on the contemporary socio-political obedience.

In the light of this complex historical background, it is no wonder that Luther refers to human reason as a "prostitute." For Luther, an "adulterer" (in the biblical sense) refers to whoever places his trust in human wisdom over the living and vivifying Word of Christ; he does not look more favorably on the wisdom of theologians who obscured the mystery and

dampened interest in reform than on the humanists of a secularist stamp.

All this is true, but one needs to acknowledge that whoever
directly scorns the human intellect, a great gift of God, is also
contemptuous of God himself. The cynicism of Luther is evidently not directed at the human intellect as gift of God, but
only to its proud use, in a culturally and religiously anthropocentric context of thought and of life. It is not unusual for a
polemic theology to dangerously shift the emphases especially
when it is partially motivated by religious trauma. Besides, in
many aspects, the historical context of Luther is very different from that of Paul. The relationship of the monk of Wittenberg with the bishop of Rome did not mirror too well that of
Peter and Paul on the occasion of the dispute of Antioch, and
much less that developing between Christianity and the synagogue during Paul's missionary life.

Likewise, the fundamentally individualistic formation and
mentality of Luther were not consonant with those of Paul.
While the question "How can I find a merciful God for myself?" was a basic anguished concern of the whole theology of
the Reformation of Wittenberg, the Judaic education of Paul
led him, instead, to emphasize the aspect of "people of God,"
the importance and extension of the solidarity of Israel before
God. Once overcome by the light of faith, he decisively insists
on the solidarity and unity of the whole human race in Christ.

According to Paul, faith is a total openness to God and a life
response and commitment of the human person in community;
any individualistic deviation is radically excluded. Such faith,
by inborn necessity, will bear fruit in love and justice for the
life of the world (cf. Gal. 5:6; I Cor. 8:1–3; Rom. 14:14–15).
Paul's concept of charity does not allow any superficiality, for
instance, in the sense of supernaturalism which ignores the
dynamics of personal relationships. It has nothing to do with
the "charitable" actions of the "haves," who, out of snobbish-
ness or self-righteousness give alms to the "have-nots." Paul
could not even conceive of that individualistic "faith and char-

ity" which uses the poverty of others as a mere occasion for merits or self-aggrandizement.

Faith active in love radically defeats individualism and egotism; it is the harvest of the Spirit's presence in the baptized (cf. Rom. 5:5) which makes him a member of the one Body of Christ (I Cor. 10:17 and 12; Rom. 12:4–5; Eph. 4:2–6). On the contrary, Luther's concept of faith (*fides fiducialis*), which stresses one-sidedly the confidence that God will be a merciful God "for me," does not really liberate the believer from an anguished and individualistic concern for one's personal salvation; it is too self-bound and therefore cannot build community.

III. "FAITH ALONE," "GRACE ALONE," "FAITH AND REASON," "GRACE AND WORKS"

The historical period of polemics tended to label the doctrine of Luther by slogans such as "faith alone [*sola fides*]," "grace alone [*sola gratia*]," and "Scriptures alone [*sola Scriptura*]," while the Catholic Church was designated in the key of "reason *and* faith [*fides et ratio*]," "grace *and* works [*gratia et opera*]," "Scriptures *and* tradition [*Scriptura et traditio*]." For the moment, the problem of "Scripture alone" will be disregarded; we shall return to it later. These polemic placards failed to express the authentic Catholic vision. It would be unjust to reduce the complexity of Catholic doctrine to "reason as much as faith," "works as much as grace."

Although it is fundamentally engaging in polemics with the Reformation, the Council of Trent does not accept such a simplification; rather, it underlines clearly the primacy of faith and grace so that it would be unjust simply to place "human reason" beside faith or "human works" beside grace. "Given that the Apostle says that man becomes justified by faith and gratuitously, these words are to be interpreted according to the perpetual consensus which the Church has sustained and expressed, in such a way that it is said that we are justified through faith inasmuch as faith is the beginning of human salvation, the fundament and root of all justification, 'and without faith it is impossible to please him' [Heb. 11:6], and to arrive at the communion of His sons; and in a way such that it is said that we are justified gratuitously, insofar as nothing of that which precedes justification, be it faith or deeds, deserves the grace of justification; 'if it is by grace, then it does not rest on deeds done, or grace would cease to be grace' [Rom. 11:6]."[7]

Salvation thus comes to us uniquely from faith in Jesus Christ and it is the fruit of grace.[8] Man's intellectual efforts, human wisdom, good deeds, human traditions assume value only in the light and under the judgment of faith in Christ Jesus.[9] This means that we are to accept the intellect and good deeds of man and appreciate their true worth, not resting content to place them *beside* faith and the grace of Christ. Their subordination can be understood if one considers the analogous relationship found in Christ's human nature and divine personality. To assert such an ordering in no way diminishes the dignity and freedom of human realities; just as in Christ the maximum liberty and dignity of human nature is assumed by the Word, so will human wisdom and good deeds, in their dependence on faith and grace, grow in freedom and dignity.

Within an orthodox interpretation, the Catholic can accept the expression *"sola fides"* without devaluating man or evincing any contempt for him. The human *"ratio"* and the *"speculatio theologica"* have value but only if viewed in the perspective of faith, in the existential surrender of believers and the whole Church to Christ. Likewise, Christian morality is not a reality juxtaposed to faith: it is the product of faith by means of the Spirit in Christ Jesus. But such a statement does not exclude a diversity of psychological ways for arriving at salvation; it does not rule out the possibility that a strong experience

[7] Council of Trent, Sess. VI, C. 8; Denzinger-Schönmetzer, No. 1532.
[8] Council of Trent, Sess. VI, C. 7; Denzinger-Schönmetzer, No. 1528–31.
[9] Council of Trent, Sess. VI, C. 3; Denzinger-Schönmetzer, No. 1553.

of ethical values can constitute a valid way to acquaint oneself with and to open oneself to Christ.

IV. A VISION OF FAITH INCLUDING THE WORLD

We first began by delineating the situation in which Paul
formulated the doctrine of salvation "by virtue of faith" and
then proceeded to present the similar yet different circumstances in which Luther returned to Paul. If today we mechanically repeat the same formulas without an awareness of the
current historical-social context, we endanger truth itself by
alienating the Good News from life. Before stating or devising
new formulas, it is mandatory that we study carefully the distinctive differences marking the present situation from that of
Paul or Luther.

Countless are they who, today, through their critical and
anti-institutional formation, accuse all Christian churches of
being responsible for the removal of Christianity from a committed testimony to the risen Christ and from real life. Similarly, strong charges are leveled at the theologians who no
longer witness to Christ or who prove themselves incapable of
announcing to modern man that faith which saves. The
churches and the diverse theologies would thus bear the burden for having alienated the believers from life: from the joys,
hopes, and social commitment of humanity. Such accusations
are not aimed solely at those who presumably protect "the
purity and the integrity of holy faith" by means of unchangeable formulas, repeating the responses contained in Denzinger
(even if they are no longer in Latin). The condemnations also
extend to those who presumably respond to the grave problems
and doubts of modern man with literal quotes from Holy
Scriptures.

Should a Lutheran preach "faith alone" and "Scriptures
alone" in a style of the Reformation without reflecting on the
fact that the mentality and experiences of his listeners are very
different from those of Luther's contemporaries, he will be

speaking to empty churches. The same fate would await the Catholic moralist who proposes solutions and statements addressed to the peasants, fishermen and artisans of the seventeenth or eighteenth century but which are certainly devoid of meaning for the sociologists, psychologists, economists and urban planners of today. The abyss between religion and life is widened and deepened not only by a piety ascribing too much importance to indulgences, places, vestments, sacred stones, relics and miraculous images, but even by the literal repetition of formulas like *"sola fides," "sola gratia"* and *"sola Scriptura,"* and by the vestiges of seventeenth- and eighteenth-century controversies.

Catholic as well as Protestant theologians feel vividly today the conspicuous dichotomy between theology and life. Think only, for example, of the work of Richard Niebuhr, Paul Tillich, Dietrich Bonhoeffer[10]; without forgetting the great applications of the Reformation, they speak a new language, studying attentively the problems and horizons of the world of today. The theology of the "death of God," however, when it assumes the form of "Christian atheism," turns in a vicious circle; it formulates a "theology" of man alienated from God and, at times, alienated from life. However, the expression "God is dead" does not necessarily denote a doubt relative to the existence and dynamic presence of God, but can represent a protest against those theological forms and institutions which testify to the absence of a living faith, which no longer

[10] Bonhoeffer, D., *Gesammelte Schriften*, 4 vols., Bethge, E., ed. (Munich, 1965).
——, *Sanctorum Communio. Eine dogmatische Untersuchung zur Soziologie der Kirche* (Munich, Kaiser, 1954).
——, *Wiederstand und Ergebung* (Munich, 1970).
Niebuhr, R., *An Interpretation of Christian Ethics* (New York, 1935).
——, *Pious and Secular America* (New York: Scribner, 1958).
——, *The Kingdom of God in America* (New York, 1959).
Tillich, P., *Biblical Religion and the Ultimate Search for Reality* (Chicago, 1955).
——, *The Courage to Be* (New Haven, Yale University Press, 1952).
——, *The Shaking of the Foundations* (New York: Scribner, 1964).

respond to the life of the man of today and witness even less to Christ, Lord of history.[11]

Moral theology must urgently seek that language and approach which allow believers in a secular and even secularist milieu to remain faithful to the one faith in Christ. Theology is now committed to span the long-standing gap between Church-religion and modern life. The language and assertions valid for men secure in their faith because living in an environment permeated by it can no longer respond to the exigencies of those who appreciate social and cultural values and who, in the name of humanism, suspect monopolistic tendencies in institutionalized religion.

The demand is now for a moral theology concerned about those who still find security in religion through a system of formulas and norms but also a theology relevant for the ever-increasing number of "secular" believers who feel their primary task to be the building up of the secular city. In addition, there is need to remain faithful, as far as possible, to the *"sola fides"* while constructing sound contemporary bridges for a religious encounter with men of the twentieth century. These grave questions are of fundamental importance.

Paul announced and explained faith according to the needs of his listeners. Luther not only responded to the particular contingencies of his own epoch but he even restricted the Pauline vision of faith by his individualistic concerns and polemical emphases. Confronted by the new situations, we cannot relinquish the claim that faith is the root of salvation; however, we must express such truth in a living and vivifying way today.

Teilhard de Chardin is by now a classical representative of

[11] Altizer, T. J., and W. Hamilton, *Radical Theology and the Death of God* (New York: Bobbs, 1966).

Altizer, T. J., ed., *Truth, Myth and Symbol* (Englewood Cliffs, N.J.: Prentice-Hall, 1959).

Cooper, J. Ch., *Radical Christianity and Its Sources* (Philadelphia, 1968).

Edwards, D. L., ed., *Honest to God Debate* (London, 1963).

Vogel, A., *The Next Christian Epoch* (New York, 1966).

the particular effort to bring faith closer to contemporary humanity. Fascinated by evolution and progress, he saw the whole history of the cosmos and of humanity finalized in the point Omega. This final and finalizing point is Christ Jesus; Teilhard sees the meaning of history in the light of God's manifestation in Christ. He does not view faith in Christ apart from all that is fascinating to modern man; most of all, faith is not set beside all those realizations which render man justly proud of his own capacities. Rather, Teilhard delineates a vision of the world in which faith unveils the ultimate value of all reality. The marvelous evolution of the cosmos becomes the hope and expectation of Christ; the whole of history derives its deepest significance from Christ and in Christ.[12]

Teilhard sings a hymn of gratitude to Christ, who, according to the Apocalypse, is the only one "worthy to open the scroll and to break the seals" of the great book of the history of the world and of humanity (Rev. 5:1–10). In the light of Christ, all events become signs of the dynamic presence of God, a manifestation of him and a revelation of his divine plan, a message, a gift, an appeal and grace.

In the biblical message, faith is envisioned as the joyous, grateful and humble acceptance of Christ and of salvation, which is offered to us in him. The salvific message is a person; it is the messenger who can therefore say of himself: "I am the way, the truth and the life" (Jn. 14:6). Acceptance of Christ implies a total and radical opening of oneself to him; it is an existential mode of listening and responding with the intellect, mind and heart, with the will and all of one's passionate energies. Faith is the powerful dynamics which gathers all the strength and capacities of the person to serve the unity of all men in Christ.

If we speak of salvation coming to us by faith, we can never stress sufficiently the uniqueness of the revelation in Christ. The strong affirmation of Peter before the elders and leaders re-

[12] Cf. H. De Lubac, *La pensée religieuse du P. Teilhard de Chardin* (Paris, 1962); R. Gibellini, *La discussione su Teilhard de Chardin* (Brescia, 1969).

mains forever valid: "This Jesus is the stone rejected by the builders which has become the keystone—and you are the builders. There is no salvation in anyone else at all, for there is no other name under heaven granted to men, by which we may receive salvation" (Acts 4:11–12).

A post-Christian era is either pure nonsense or it is an epoch closed to salvation unless such expression refer simply to a new socio-religious situation marking the end of old "Christianity" in the socio-political sense. Of course, our negative judgment does not extend to those sincere individuals submerged in and suffocating from "post-Christian" tendencies.

We must not forget, however, that the unique revelation in Christ becomes obscured not only by panreligious syncretism but by all abstract theology. There are forms of religiosity and theology which place Christ *beside* instead of *at the center of* the world's history, forgetting that "in him everything in heaven and on earth was created, not only things visible but also the invisible orders of thrones, sovereignties, authorities and powers: the whole universe has been created through him and for him. And he exists before everything, and all things are held together in him" (Col. 1:16–17).

The "yes" of faith to Christ implies a deep assent to all the works of God, particularly the "yes" to his revelation in creation and the history of salvation, in Abraham, Isaac, Jacob, Moses and the prophets. In spite of the imperfection of some of their ideas and attitudes, the prophets' faith is the door to salvation because its source and end are in Christ. This fast and profound relation to and dependence on Christ only became clear, however, with the Lord's coming in the flesh (Heb. 1:1–2; 11:39–40).

From the viewpoint of salvific faith, the letter to the Hebrews includes not only the people of Israel and Christ's ancestors from Abel to Noah and Abraham but even non-Israelites like Rahab: "By faith the prostitute Rahab escaped the doom of the unbelievers because she had given the spies a kindly welcome" (Heb. 11:31). Matthew places Rahab and Ruth (who were not Israelites) in the genealogy of Christ

(Mt. 1:5). Further, the Old Testament integrates many sayings of sages who did not belong to the chosen people, especially in its books of "wisdom."

Whatever is true, good and holy in the various religions comes from God, Father of the Lord Jesus Christ: "for us there is one God, the Father, from whom all being comes, towards whom we move; and there is one Lord, Jesus Christ, through whom all things come to be, and we through him" (I Cor. 8:6; cf. Phil. 4:8–9; I Thess. 5:21). Wherever non-Christian religious communities help man to find true love, liberation and salvation, all this comes from Christ and glorifies his redemption. We are thinking not of any hidden presence of Christ but of that efficacious presence of his grace which sustains goodness, justice and peace, and manifests itself in the sincere religious and/or moral attitude of man, whatever be his religion. If we call this "analogy of faith," we speak of the dynamic of a life which honors God. Every monotheistic religion pleads for and seeks to arouse in its faithful a basic attitude which bears the character of faith, at least up to a certain point: a humble listening to and searching for truth, seeking to elicit a grateful "yes" and commitment to the good and the true, a dynamic toward unity of mankind.

Therefore we can do justice to all the works of God and to the whole of human history when we say "faith alone." Only faith can save, but faith intended in the broad, profound and vital sense and not as a sterile repetition of formulas or selfish preoccupation with "saving my own soul." It is a faith which praises God in all his works and which, according to the measure of grace and of knowledge granted liberally by the Spirit, adheres to the design of God, Creator and Redeemer, for the restoration of all things in Christ, "on whom faith depends from start to finish" (Heb. 12:2). Therefore, we cannot seek faith in one God and Father, or an analogy to faith, in people who are staunch supporters of apartheid, racial discrimination or exploitation, even if externally they profess Christian faith. On the practical level they are either polytheists or atheists.

The commitment to "fostering unity and love among men, and even among nations" (NA, Art. 1) is always an essential part of faith in Christ. It renders us capable of sensing the presence of salvation which comes from faith even in those cases where man, in spite of all his good will, does not yet know explicitly the ultimate source and value of his commitment of love. It therefore comprises the affirmation of Vatican II: the Church "has this exhortation for her sons: prudently and lovingly, through dialogue and collaboration with the followers of other religions, and in witness of Christian faith and life, acknowledge, preserve and promote the spiritual and moral goods found among these men, as well as the values in their society and culture" (NA, Art. 2).

Catholic theology has always given ample space and importance to creation and history in the perspective of faith. But it is duty-bound to ask itself if it has always witnessed adequately to the human and cosmic dynamism of salvation in Christ. Max Scheler severely criticized a "natural theology" centered in God as efficient "cause" and "proofs" of the existence of God, based on mere causality. In his vision, the "*analogia fidei*" begins only there where one succeeds in perceiving, admirably and adoringly, the will of God manifesting himself in his works.[13]

Scheler does not deny the validity of reflection on diverse "causes" but he does negate "causality" being a religious category by itself, having an affinity or an analogy with the existential structure of faith. Philosophical reflection should realize that it cannot grasp the religious phenomenon except through categories open to God's design to reveal his love and to man's desire to perceive and to listen to such a revelation so as to respond by overcoming his own limits in total gift of self.

In the biblical vision, in fact, all the works of the Creator and Lord of history are presented in the one perspective of salvific faith. Man's world exists by the Word of God. Since creation and all happenings are a wonderful message of the love

[13] M. Scheler, *Vom Ewigen in Menschen* (Leipzig, 1921).

of God, that man is wise who listens and meditates on this
reality, and responds with praise expressed in a generous commitment for his neighbor. Instead, all too often he moves away
from or closes himself to God, who incessantly calls him to
communion in brotherly unity; in an egotistical way, he ab-
solutizes his own strengths and capabilities, manipulates his
brethren and turns a deaf ear to their needs.

Rudolf Otto performs a remarkable task when he casts all
religions in the light of faith, or, better, in the light of Luther's
doctrine on "faith alone." It must be recalled that Otto insists
primarily on the "irrational" quality of religious feelings as an
existential response to mystery. The religious man remains
conscious of the limits of every rational category when he
stands before the mystery of the living God; however, he is
also cognizant of the need to open oneself totally to the
"Thou." Such an opening is characterized by amazement before the *mysterium tremendum,*" by joy before the *mysterium fascinosum."* When man presumes to be able to define
religion precisely according to the categories of human reason,
he fails to perceive its elements and thereby destroys faith.
This is very evident in the whole vision of Otto even though
his approach is most serene compared to Luther's indignation
over the *meretrix ratio."*

Otto also weighs importantly the mode by which the sense
of the sacred or mystery meets with ethical imperatives in the
various forms of religion and religiosity. He expresses confidence in being able to demonstrate historically that whenever
religiosity is profound in any of the great religions, there exists
an internal dynamism toward ethical commitment. Such religiosity assumes the customs and ethical experiences within
its sphere and gives them a "sacred" sanction ("sanctioned
ethos"). Its dynamism, however, decreases or disappears when
the sense of the sacred does not attain a dynamic harmony between *mysterium tremendum"* and *mysterium fascinosum,*"
between fear and joy, between wonder and jubilation.

A "feeling of the numinous" and a certain way of perceiving
it in sacred things, making salvation dependent on them, can

express a tendency to alienate from the great problems of humanity. It then becomes a "faith" deprived of dynamism toward commitment for justice, love and peace. Such faith, however, is not authentic; even Luther would have accused it of evasion, although this was not his dominant preoccupation. Not only within non-Christian religions but even in the history of Christian spirituality do we find such failures. We ought to recognize honestly how, even within the Church today, the vision of faith and morality does not always attain that synthesis which Paul classically expresses in his letter to the Galatians: a faith that reveals its dynamism through love (Gal. 5:6).

Modern humanism has developed and fostered attitudes which often coincide or correspond to forms of Christian morality which, at the practical or theoretical level, were structured along the lines of the "*et . . . et*," namely, those forms of morality not profoundly imbued by faith or characterized by the bipolarity of faith itself: listening and responding, gift of God and reciprocal gift of self. Other forms of contemporary ethics show at least traces of the "*analogia fidei*."

The commitment of moral theology ought, then, to pursue a twofold direction: it should be structured in such a way as to reflect clearly and openly testify to that faith from which its form and strength are derived; it should build strong bridges with the mentality and language of secular man, accepting and developing those elements of a humanistic ethics which have preserved some analogy with the contents and existential structure of faith.

V. "FAITH ALONE" AND THE ETHIC OF RESPONSIBILITY

Initially Karl Barth directed a sharp criticism against the *analogia entis* (the analogy between all that exists) of the scholastic theology by designating this doctrine as Anti-Christ. His thinking proves herein to be an extension of Luther's despisal of the *meretrix ratio* (reason as whore). However, in time, Barth concentrated his interest toward the salvation of all men of good will. Where Karl Rahner speaks of the "anonymous Christians" he found a solution on the basis of analogy of faith (*analogia fidei*).

Barth focuses on faith as total obedience (*Glaubensgehorsam*), thereby finding an analogy of faith in all those who, on the level of fundamental option, manifest an attitude which, with respect to sincere submission to the good, is similar to the radical submission of the believer to the Word of God. In fact, Barth sees moral life as the fruit of living faith, and since faith is for him mainly characterized as "obedience" and submission, he can find in the sincere dedication to truth and goodness a real analogy of faith. The Barthian approach does not neglect the gratuitousness of faith and morality's dependence on it, but, while proclaiming peace and salvation to all men of good will, he remains always a prophetic voice against human pride, which inclines to determine the good arbitrarily, or do "good works" just for self-enhancement.

It is evident that "obedience of faith" as a main perspective of moral life has different emphases and dimensions depending on whether it comes from a theologian of the Reformation or from a Catholic, and, most of all, on whether or not the latter has a juridical-casuistic mentality. The contemporary situation poses a fundamental question to both: what will be the consequences of dialogue with secular man if one continues to predicate "obedience" as conceptual basis of the whole Christian moral discourse?

In the reformed tradition, there is insistence on the freedom of conscience which should characterize compliance to the Gospel; however, it did overemphasize obedience to Christian princes (*usus politicus legis*). In the Catholic tradition, the "obedience of faith" includes submission to the Magisterium and acceptance of dogmatic formulations; in the moral domain, it insists too much on a necessary dependence on ecclesiastical authority in the formation of conscience.

Very often, the concept, exigencies and extension of the obedience of faith are presented in such a way as to leave little leeway for creativity and the spirit of initiative which should characterize a conscience guided by faith in the Gospel of freedom. The humbling experience of the submissiveness of so many "Christians" to inhumane regimes (as that of Hitler) has awakened a strong critical attitude toward theological statements bearing on the morality of the "obedience of faith." Dietrich Bonhoeffer was one of the first to recognize and to insist on the necessity of new perspectives to be presented in a new language. Today, some go to the other extreme; they explain the "spontaneity of faith" in a way that makes "fantasy" the fundamental characteristic of morality.[14]

Many Protestant and Catholic theologians concern themselves with closing the gap separating religion and life; they strive to express existentially Christian morality and faith in an attitude of listening and responding, in a radical opening of the mind and will to God and neighbor.[15] My approach to moral discourse follows a similar direction and endeavors to synthesize the applications of the biblical-theological renewal with those derived from ecumenical dialogue and encounters with contemporary man.[16] The fulcrum of the whole discourse lies in the unity of faith and morality, but a faith which gives perspective and form to morality and a morality which "bears the fruit of faith for the life of the world" (OT, Art. 16).

We must never lose sight of the strong aversion of Karl Marx and his followers, as of many of our contemporaries, for theological-philosophical systems and religious practices which beget a closed "religious world" folded upon itself, one that has nothing to do with the human community and the great social problems of the day. If we speak of proofs of the existence of an all-powerful God, deducing them from the categories of physical and finalistic causality, or even if we speak of a "feeling of the numinous," this all remains incredible to our contemporaries since this vocabulary is not sensitive to

[14] D. Sölle, *Phantasie und Gehorsam. Überlegungen zu einer künftigen Ethik* (Stuttgart-Berlin, 1968).
[15] R. Niebuhr, *The Responsible Self* (New York, 1963).
[16] Häring, *The Law of Christ*, Vol. III.

man in his concrete life. When faced by so many controversies on the *"sola fides,"* they will immediately think of an individualistic flight, of a stingy and selfish religion that makes believers oblivious of the true responsibilities for the future of humanity. A keen awareness of our contemporary situation will also lead us to identify and to discard whatever tends to divide Christian churches.

Cynics abound who think that this fate befalls modern man either because he is not a religious genius or because modern culture constitutes a continuous and insurmountable temptation to forget God. I prefer to see our secular age more as one of restlessness analogous to that at the basis of the Old Testament prophetism. If today we succeed in expressing the evangelical message in an effective love for man, modeled on that of the Prophets and of Christ's compassion for every man, especially the weakest, in hunger and thirst for injustice inspired by love of God, then the prevailing disquiet of man and the whole contemporary civilization can be transformed into a new blossoming of Christianity and religiosity.

A prophetic vision of the *"sola fides"* and of morality as an inseparable unity and fruit of a faith capable of restoring all things in Christ ought to be alert to another timely difficulty. Modern man is very suspicious of a theology and of a Church which presume to determine everything; he fears in it a monopolistic mentality and an undue extension of its competence. He is jealous of the autonomy of the culture and of the competency of the secular city, and he resents any impingement by theology or religious institutions.

I am sincerely convinced that only a stance of moral theology and Christian life in the key of personal and communitarian responsibility will be able to overcome the dangers of schism between faith and life. In fact, it will free us from serious misgivings of monopolistic tendencies. Such an approach does accept and appreciate the Magisterium, as intended by Christ, especially insofar as it leads the faithful to shared experience, shared reflection, discernment and co-responsibility.

Faith is the most sincere and most existential force in seeking liberation, peace and justice, because it implies a total opening to Christ, the Liberator and Peace, and thus to all manifestations of justice and love. When, in seeking that love which alone can save the world, the believers make visible the God of love; then the search itself grows in spontaneity and generosity, in gratitude and vigilance as well as in effective and courageous commitment. The God who reveals himself in Christ calls man to himself; he wishes to dispatch him, in the greatest freedom, as a messenger of peace to his brethren. He is to stand as a peacemaker, laden with unlimited enthusiasm for man, fully dedicated to the attainment of unity and solidarity of all mankind.

If we speak of "faith alone," we ought to exercise vigilance with respect to the expression of and witness to all the dimensions of true faith. Faith is never a matter of a God-soul encounter on a romantic isolated island of personal solitude. Faith always entails an encounter with the God of history, who, through his Spirit of love, creates and maintains everything in existence by his Word. The "yes" to Christ means assent to the Lord-Servant, the recapitulation and unifier of humanity and of the world; it is a "yes" which makes us sacraments of his Lordship in the service of our brethren. The true believer is a man who keeps himself attuned to the evolution of the world and of humanity. He is a vigilant man ever alert and attentive to perceive and recognize, in every historical event, the *kairos:* the gift of salvation in Christ, who calls to a more generous commitment to peace and love.

Particularly should it be noted that our faith that testifies is never "perfect"; it is the faith of a wayfarer, a faith ever in need of deepening, a faith that sincerely accepts the darkness surrounding the search for more light. It is the faith of a Church that will attain her full perfection in the glory of heaven when the time of final restoration of all things will have come. It is then that the human race with the entire world so intimately related to man and achieving its purpose through him "will be perfectly re-established in Christ" (LG, Art. 48). It is the faith of a Church "at the same time holy and always in need of being purified" (LG, Art. 8), which "realizes that it is truly and intimately linked with mankind and its history" (GS, Art. 1).

Today it would be more dangerous than ever before to define and to live faith in a prevalently intellectual way. Believers are faced by many questions, uncertainties and difficulties. If faith is rightly seen as a total opening to Truth (to Him who is the Truth and who is eschatologically given to us), if it is renewed as full surrender of oneself to God and, at the same time, as an opening to all human truths in full commitment to the search and realization of love and justice with the whole of humanity, then the difficulties, uncertainties and darkness will not constitute such a danger; they will rather serve as a precious admonition to authenticity. If, on the contrary, faith is considered as a perfect system of formulated truths, then it will soon become either an unbearable burden or something with which we no longer know what to do.

On the other hand, a morality of personal and social responsibility based on faith gives great security while, at the same time, it implies risk. Such a morality entails the courage to take those risks inherent in genuine human life. God asks our father in faith, Abraham, to leave his own people and his fatherland to go toward the unknown. Today's moral theology has the task of helping the believer and the community of believers to understand and to live their own calling, which, like that of Abraham, has something of the unknown. They are always open to the newness of life and initiative. A truly Christian morality does not want to abolish the risk of love.

The man of today looks for certainty and security in religion and faith but he is also aware that they cannot mean closed-mindedness and immobilism. If in the past the teaching office in the Church was often linked to a security characterized by stability and standard formulas, today the new human and ecclesial situation demands that it be more prophetic. The specific task of the Magisterium would seem to be that of "pioneering," and not of "braking," to point to the road ahead, to stimulate on the journey, to sustain and encourage while recognizing the charisma which the Spirit gives to whom he wants and when he wants.

VI. NATURAL LAW IN THE LIGHT OF FAITH

Concern for purity and maturity of faith obliges us to distinguish carefully salvation truth revealed in Christ from all the various doctrines which are the result of human traditions, of shared experience and co-reflection, marked by the historical situation. However, it would be simplistic and even erroneous to put reason and faith side by side according to the slogan "reason as well as faith." This would not only lead to a dichotomy but also belittle the uniqueness of faith. We have to look for a synthesis between salvation truth and natural law in a perspective of God's active and revealing presence to human history. I understand as "natural law" what is inborn in man, and in no way imposed from without. Natural law doctrine is, then, the result of shared experience and shared reflection ("reason" in the broadest sense). For believers it is faith which determines at least the whole vision. Faith (understood as *fides qua*) is total openness not only to the Scriptures, but also to all events and efforts in history of men in which we can discover an "ongoing revelation" of God in his works and through faithful men who, by grace, are his "co-revealers." Of course, we call human history an ongoing revelation only in the light of Christ. Since he alone is the center and goal of history he alone can open the scroll of history.

In past years I have devoted various studies to the relationship between natural law and the "law of Christ"; therefore I can here refer to them.[17] I reiterate some fundamental observations only insofar as I consider them essential to a discourse on faith and morality in an age of secularization.

[17] B. Häring, *Morality Is for Persons; The Church on the Move;* and "Dynamism and Continuity in a Personalistic Approach to Natural Law," in *Norm and Context in Christian Ethics* (G. Outka and P. Ramsey eds.) (New York: Scribner's, 1968), pp. 199–218.

(a) "Natural Law" is to be cast in the light of God and seen in the dynamism of his economy of love for man. Even in natural revelation, there are gradations and a progression. Therefore, to reduce "natural law" to immobilism and static formulas is to depreciate it. Historicity is a fundamental dimension of natural law which keeps it from ever being fossilized in lazy and abstract formulas.

(b) Humility and solidarity are vital to research, listening and meditation. Personal experiences and reflections ought to be inserted responsibly into the common effort lest they become sterile and deprived of value. Particularly should the Church and the Magisterium be actively and humbly inserted in the solidarity of research, the experiences and reflections of the whole of humanity.

(c) The whole effort of research and reflection ought to be guided and inspired by a passionate love for the total good of man and all men. This love, in fact, is a requisite on the divine plane.

(d) The whole process of inserting the "natural law" within the "law of Christ" requires grasping and underlining the "*analogia fidei*" proper to natural law, especially for that which concerns the listening, constant docility, humility and solidarity in research which allow the gathering of all the experiences and reflections of humanity on its destiny and historical character. If we come to understand such "*analogia fidei*," we are then capable of synthesizing an enthusiastic love for man with a wholehearted love for God.

(e) The dynamism of the "natural law" leading toward the light and judgment of Christ should be evident in the way theology and the Magisterium align their own reflections with the Gospel, adopting as central criterion: service to the total good of man for the glory of God, the one Creator and Redeemer.

CHAPTER 6

SANCTITY IN THE WORLD

The incarnation of Christ, Son of God, and his choice of the level and style of life common to the men of his culture constitute the fulcrum of the Christian vision of sanctity in the world. God, alone holy, shares with us his sanctity in Christ. Christian holiness, therefore, is the gift-promise of the God-Love in Christ through the Spirit. It manifests itself essentially in a "new heart" that lives the daily life of glory of the one Father, in a redeemed and redeeming love toward all creatures, and in an oblative commitment for a world more just, more humane and more brotherly in Christ.

Paul writes to the Corinthians: "Whether you eat or drink, or whatever you are doing, do all for the honor of God" (I Cor. 10:31; cf. Rom. 14:6–9). He frequently exhorts believers to exult with him in joy even in the midst of suffering and sorrow (cf. Rom. 12:14–15; I Cor. 9:19–23). He incites the Philippians: "Fill up my cup of happiness by thinking and feeling alike, with the same love for one another, the same turn of mind, and a common care for unity. There must be no room for rivalry and personal vanity among you, but you must humbly reckon others better than yourselves. Look to each other's interest and not merely to your own" (Phil. 2:2–4).

This vision of "sanctity in the world" is deepened by Paul and the primitive Church in fidelity to the words and desires of Christ. Christ did not shirk daily burdens nor did he give rise to a privileged sect, separated and closed in on itself like the ascetics of the Qumran, for example. He did not belong to the religiously superior class; he was son of "poor people."

Confronted by his wisdom and miracles, his fellow-citizens ask themselves in amazement: "Is not his mother called Mary, his brothers James, Joseph, Simon and Judas? And are not all his sisters here with us?" (Mt. 13:55–56).

Christ chooses for himself "the nature of a slave, bearing the human likeness, revealed in human shape" (Phil. 2:7–8). When faced by his "too worldly" style of life, the Pharisees, scribes and priests are scandalized: "He eats with tax-gatherers and sinners!" (Mk. 2:16; cf. Mt. 9:11, Lk. 15:2). They also classify him as "a glutton and a drinker" (Mt. 11:19).

The sanctity seen in and preached by Christ is simultaneously the most transcendent reality and the most immanent. Having "come from God" (Jn. 16:30) and having fulfilled his earthly life, Christ returns to him (Jn. 17:13). By this *coming from* and *returning to* the Father, he sanctifies us and gains for us "eternal life," which already begins here below in fraternal love to the glory of the Father. John writes in his Gospel: "This is eternal life: to know thee who alone art truly God, and Jesus Christ whom thou hast sent" (Jn. 17:3); but in his first letter he specifies: "Dear friends, let us love one another, because love is from God. Everyone who loves is a child of God and knows God, but the unloving know nothing of God. For God is love" (I Jn. 4:7–9).

Christ is the Emmanuel (Mt. 1:23), the Lord (Jn. 20:28) and friend (Jn. 15:15); yet the servant (Jn. 13:2 ff.), the Holy One of God (Mk. 1:24) and the man perfect in love (Jn. 15:13). The call of Christ frees man from the "world" (even religious) characterized by pride and egotism, and sends him to the neighbor to make of him "the salt of the earth" (Mt. 5:13). The vocation of Christ does not separate him from communion with his brethren and the cosmos but unites him deeply and thoroughly in a redemptive way (Jn. 17:15–19).

If we are to arrive at a correct vision of sanctity in the world, it is imperative to keep in mind all that we have enucleated up to now with regard to the Christian concept of "world," the "sacred-profane" relationship, the interpenetration of religion and life, faith and the ethic of responsibility.

Only a balanced synthesis integrating all these diverse elements will render possible and valid a discussion on Christian holiness.

In this chapter, we shall touch upon a few specific problems and by so doing, more or less summarize all that has preceded. We shall speak of the universal vocation to holiness as well as particular vocations; consideration will be given to the new image and new style which the priest must take on in a secular world and in a community of believers rediscovering the value of their own participation in the priesthood of Christ. There will be mention of contemplative life in its traditional and modern forms; conjugal-family life as a prototype of "holiness in the world"; the Christian witness in the political, economic, artistic life and in other fields where "sanctity" is particularly difficult but all the more urgent, and the presence of believers in the contemporary world. Our discourse, however, can only attempt to delineate the attitudes with which one is to face such problems.

I. THE UNIVERSAL VOCATION TO HOLINESS

After pausing on the mystery of the Church and its structuralization, the Dogmatic Constitution *Lumen Gentium* devotes a whole chapter to "The Call of the Whole Church to Holiness" (LG, Chapter V, Art. 39–42). In it, the Council overcomes all sacralization of a monopolistic kind and every vision of holiness tending to create privileged classes and discriminations: phenomena often encountered in most religions, e.g., sects of the Qumran, Pharisaism, the initiates in the mystery cults, Buddhist monasticism. Christian holiness pervades daily life. However, the Council also reacts by loyally recognizing those "profanity" tendencies more or less accentuated which, within the Church, have tainted daily life. They arose from Christianity's anxiously binding itself by the limitations inherent in sacred things, in rites and in "sacred" formulations of truth.

"Thus it is evident to everyone that all the faithful of Christ of whatever rank of status are called to the fullness of the Christian life and to the perfection of charity. By this holiness a more human way of life is promoted even in this earthly society. In order that the faithful may reach this perfection, they must use their strength according as they have received it, as a gift from Christ. In this way, they can follow in His footsteps and mold themselves in His image, seeking the will of the Father in all things, devoting themselves with all their being to the glory of God and the service of their neighbor" (LG, Art. 40).

The people of God, constituted in unity through Christ by the Spirit to the glory of the Father, stand at the very center of this perspective. The purpose of the vocation to faith is sharing in the priesthood, prophetic mission and Lordship of Christ-Servant. "In this way the Church simultaneously prays and labors in order that the entire world may become the People of God, the Body of the Lord, and the Temple of the Holy Spirit, and that in Christ, the Head of all, there may be rendered to the Creator and Father of the Universe all honor and glory" (LG, Art. 17).

Within man's vocation and in keeping with his dignity, the Council explores the value and significance of the particular charisms and special ministries. All believers come together in the same call to salvation, in the same commitment for salvation which consists essentially in a faith bearing fruit in love for the life of the world. The faithful actualize this faith-charity differentially, and it cannot be rightly assessed save in the light of the *diakonia* for the unity of the community. Even on a strictly methodological plane, the way in which the Council has broached the subject and directed its whole discourse is important. "In the various types and duties of life, one and the same holiness is cultivated by all who are moved by the Spirit of God, and who obey the voice of the Father, worshiping God the Father in spirit and in truth. These souls follow the poor Christ, the humble and cross-bearing Christ, in order to be made worthy of being partakers in His glory. Every person should walk unhesitatingly according to his own personal gifts and duties in the path of a living faith which arouses hopes and works through charity" (LG, Art. 41).

The Christian envisions holiness as appropriate to all states and all forms of life. To be holy, there is no need to imitate or copy the order and plan of life peculiar to distinct groups within the people of God; all that would be dangerous. Instead, a Christian is to live the concreteness and the exigencies of his own vocation and state of life in faithfulness, searching for and realizing God's plan for salvation of the world. The role and vocation of the priest and of religious men and women are in no way evaluated if seen in this perspective; they are placed on a firmer footing and will be more genuine and fruitful for all if freed from all monopolistic tendencies. The religious men and women as well as the priests fulfill their ministry for the whole people of God and, indeed, for the whole world, and come to their identity as witnesses of faith and servants of the vocation of all to holiness.

The various vocations within the unique people of God are illumined and visibly reinforced by this vision. The charism and vocation to celibacy for the kingdom of God can only be validly understood when considered alongside conjugal love, in the light of the sacrament of love which salvifically unites Christ to the Church. If their vocations are perceived in the fundamental dimension of testimony and service within the people of God, the priests and religious succeed in overcoming the temptation of conceiving and realizing their religious state as a privileged "world" in that pejorative sense which John applies when referring to the pharisaical-priestly caste of Israel as godless world. The ministry proper to Christian priests firmly links them to their neighbor by placing them totally in the service of the fraternal community. The charism does not allow pretexts of a superior class or any individualistic absenteeism (Jn. 13:12–17; Lk. 10:30–37). However, their definitive religious commitment certainly demands recollection, detachment and time for prayer.

II. THE NEW IMAGE OF THE PRIEST IN THE SECULAR WORLD

Christ's discourse on the priesthood is fundamentally desacralizing for what was regarded as "priestly class" or "priestly privileges." However, Christ bestows the highest dignity on the priesthood through its particular sacramental participation in his own. Christ does not belong to a priestly caste or family, nor does he learn the "sacred knowledge" in a priestly school; he is simply "the carpenter's son," a layman (Mt. 13:55). He is the Chosen and the Anointed of God for a testimony of total love toward all men and the whole world. Christ attains the perfection of His priesthood on the cross, in the supreme act of testimony and of love: "the blood of his sacrifice is his own blood, not the blood of goats and calves; and thus he has entered the sanctuary once and for all and secured an eternal deliverance" (Heb. 9:12). The priesthood of Christ excludes all empty ritualism separated from love of neighbor: "the argument becomes still clearer, if the new priest who arises is one like Melchizedek, owing his priesthood not to a system of earth-bound rules but to the power of a life that cannot be destroyed" (Heb. 7:15-16).

In referring to his own apostolic vocation, Paul stresses primarily his commitment to evangelization in a love which surmounts every barrier between men. "Set apart for the service of the Gospel," he worships the Father, "preaching the gospel of his Son" (Rom. 1:1-9). He therefore writes to the Corinthians: "I am a free man, and own no master; but I have made myself every man's servant, to win over as many as possible. To Jews I became a Jew to win Jews; as they are subject to the Law of Moses, I put myself under that law to win them, although I am not myself subject to it. To win Gentiles, who are outside the Law, I made myself like one of them. . . . To the weak I became weak, to win the weak. Indeed, I have become everything in turn to men of every sort, so that in one way or another I may save some" (I Cor. 9:19–22).

When there is question of choosing a successor for Judas, Peter expresses himself in this manner: "Therefore one of those who bore us company all the while we had the Lord Jesus with us, coming and going from John's ministry of baptism until the day he was taken up from us—one of those must join us as a witness to his resurrection" (Acts 1:21–22). The apostles, then, are *witnesses* invited to proclaim the Good News and to follow Christ closely. They are men whose faith makes them "light of the world" (Mt. 5:14) in Christ and for Christ. The calling does not make them a privileged class; it sets them unreservedly in the service of all and commits them to be everything to all while heralding the message of the Lord.

Vatican II has underlined over and again how the charisms of the episcopal and priestly vocation tend essentially to the proclamation of the Gospel: "Among the principal duties of bishops, the preaching of the gospel occupies an eminent place. For bishops are preachers of the faith who lead new disciples to Christ. They are authentic teachers, that is, teachers endowed with the authority of Christ, who preach to the people committed to them the faith they must believe and put into practice" (LG, Art. 25). Thus the priests "have as their primary duty the proclamation of the gospel of God to all; in this way they fulfill the Lord's command" (PO, Art. 4).

The liturgical renewal has contributed significantly toward informing believers of the kerygmatic value of liturgical celebrations. Today, these are structured so as to give more emphasis to the proclamation of the Lord. The whole celebration ought to extol the death-resurrection of Christ and the final hope of his return in glory. It follows that the priesthood itself is to be seen mostly as "proclamation" of the Lord Jesus.

The office of the bishops and presbyters is to be imbued with the spirit of Christ's priestly prayer: "May they all be one: as thou, Father, art in me, and I in thee, so also may they be in us, that the world may believe that thou didst send me" (Jn. 17:21). The bishops and clergy constitute, within the people of God, a "college" of service and testimony to unity in Christ so that the whole Church may be ever more clearly and effectively the "sacrament or sign of intimate union with God, and of the unity of mankind" (LG, Art. 1). The characteristic priestly function lies in the promotion of unity which is realized in the diversity of gifts, charisms, languages and cultures. The priesthood itself, therefore, necessarily demands a sane pluralism respectful of the variety of historical-cultural situations.

The world of today is marked by many tensions, by frequent and even organized outbursts of violence, by difficulty in effectively rising above personal and group egotisms; more than ever should priests strive to be messengers of peace. They ought to make their own the program of Paul: to announce the Gospel of Christ which beats down selfish divisions (even if "sacred") among the various human groups in view of realizing the one Body of Christ. They ought to be promoters of encounter and dialogue for peace and solidarity. In the midst of polarizations, they are expected to be Christ's ambassadors in the "ministry of reconciliation" (II Cor. 5:18–20).

Throughout the history of the Church, the priestly ministry has always been looked upon as a function of reconciliation. However, too often it has been restricted to "sin" and the "soul"; the priest has thus become uniquely or predominantly the minister of reconciliation of the soul with God. His ministry is then deprived of the dynamism toward reconciliation in brotherhood. Today, it is important that he be committed to the testimony and promotion of forgiveness and fraternal reconciliation without which it is pharisaical to ask forgiveness to the Father as in the prayer taught us by Christ: "and forgive us our sins, for we too forgive all who have done us wrong" (Lk. 11:4).

Witnessing to reconciliation and to peace is not synonymous with defending the status quo. The proclamation of reconciliation and peace remains strictly connected with the prophetic courage which defies the powerful by announcing to them: "Weep and wail over the miserable fate descending on you. Your riches have rotted; your fine clothes are moth-eaten; your silver and gold have rusted away, and their very rust will be evidence against you and consume your flesh like fire. You have piled up wealth in an age that is near its close. The wages you never paid to the men who mowed your fields are loud against you, and the outcry of the reapers has reached the ears of the Lord of Hosts" (James 5:1–4).[1]

The modern process of secularization can constitute an effective help in the search for the true physiognomy of the Christian priesthood. There is certainly no need to underrate the dangers and risks of atheism, secularism and horizontalism; notwithstanding, secularization is a *kairos* even with regard to a more evangelical priesthood. It is a grace and a summons to overcome all transient forms of sacralization which have studded the centuries in the form of the "sacred Roman Empire" or the *"Eigenkirchen"* of the Germanic world.

Latin has already fallen as a "sacred language"; the "sacred vestments," clerical privileges and halo of social-cultural superiority are taking the same course. The partially superstitious attitudes which, in the eyes of the people, have sometimes surrounded the figure of the priest with a quasi-magical aura are likewise disappearing. There remains for priests of the twentieth century the task of making more visible the life of faith, the witness and commitment for unity-charity which is open to all needs and pregnant with new possibilities, but a life specifically devoted to the service of the poor and the oppressed.

[1] *Populorum Progressio* presents a dynamic vision of peace which ought to be a source of reflection for all: "To wage war on misery and to struggle against injustice is to promote, along with improved conditions, the human and spiritual progress of all men, and so the common good of humanity. Peace is not reduced to an absence of war, fruit of the ever precarious equilibrium of forces. It is built up day after day, in the pursuit of an order wanted by God, which involves a more perfect justice among men" (No. 76, *AAS*, 59 [1967], p. 294).

The sacraments lose nothing when deprived of a climate of "mystery-secrecy" and "sacralism" (in the sense of "sacred things"). On the contrary, they gain much by becoming limpid expressions of the mystery of salvation in Christ. They reveal the faith of a community dynamically intent on a fraternally holy life through the power of Christ, a force that conquers "sin." Such a remark likewise holds for the priesthood and for priests; an age of secularization is a powerful call to purification and authenticity so that a greater transparence of essentials can be hoped.

In an epoch of rapid transformations, the new image of the priest cannot be immediately and precisely delineated, nor is it judicious to think of a unique "cliché" valid for any length of time and for the whole Church. We need to accept the anguish of searching and the risk of new experiences, many of which are destined to failure. There will have to be a greater pluralism with respect to types. The biblical-theological renewal along with a more active and more mature participation of the laity in the apostolate provide a sufficiently clear glimpse of some fundamental lines. The study of modern secularization, then, and the results of psychological, sociological and anthropological research will be of great assistance in delineating the concrete form which responds better to the new exigencies and emerging opportunities. Certainly the new image of the priest will set higher demands on him. Devoid of all the social-cultural factors which have, up to now, favored affluence to the priesthood (sometimes without true conviction), the new role definition will discourage whoever does not want to follow Christ until death in the service of the brethren.

Even the primacy of faith and prayer in a priestly life will be more evident than in the past because of the incontestable need for prayer and faith within the Church today. *Optatam Totius* recommends: "By sacred ordination they will be molded in the likeness of Christ, the Priest. As friends they should be used to loyal association with Him through a profound identification of their whole lives with His. They should live his paschal mystery in such a way that they know how to initiate into it the people entrusted to them" (OT, Art. 8). The priest ought to be master of prayer and faith. The need is great, however, to find those forms and structures which will render him first a man of prayer and of authentic faith (see the following chapter).

III. CONTEMPLATIVE LIFE AND SEPARATION FROM THE WORLD

Vatican Council II voices great praise for "those communities which are totally dedicated to contemplation, whose members give themselves to God alone in solitude and silence through constant prayer and ready penance" (PC, Art. 7). There is no doubt that the world of today has great need of the art and witness of contemplation. In our secular if not secularist context, there is a particular need for faith to be meditated, and a considerable urgency for testimony to the primacy of grace and prayer. The process of secularization, however, poses difficult problems with regard to the mode and forms of contemplative witness.

According to the decree of Vatican II on the renewal of religious life, the *aggiornamento* of communities dedicated uniquely to contemplation is to be undertaken "according to the . . . standards of appropriate renewal though their withdrawal from the world and the practices of their contemplative life should be maintained at their holiest" (PC, Art. 7). Such a principle generates a number of questions. First of all, what value would the term "world" have in the context of this quote? In the light of the biblical-theological vision of the world which we tried to delineate, there is need to analyze and specify in what sense one can speak, within Christianity, of a "separation from the world." Further, there would be need of serious self-questioning on whether it would be possible, Christianly speaking, to be interested in a life with God without serving him in the neighbor. Would the diversity of charisms reach the point of demanding that part of the Christians have contemplation as their unique goal? What value or significance would contemplation have in this total isolation from the brethren?

An adequate response to such fundamental questions demands an analysis of the extent to which the philosophical-religious movements of a spiritualistic impression have influenced Christian contemplation's "withdrawal from the world." A related query would be: to what point can contemplative persons humanly and Christianly do without closeness and contact with the joys, sufferings, hopes and anxieties of the Church and humanity today?

I am of the opinion that a sound and realistic response to the timely challenge is coming from the recent but recurring experience of the institution of contemplative houses within religious bodies devoted to the apostolate.[2] Certainly there is a great difference between institutes given uniquely to contemplation and these new forms; however, both share the profound conviction of prayer and meditation's eminent value. The "House of Prayer" seeks that psychological climate which favors contemplation without "separation from the world," save in the sense of separation from the world dominated by sin, the closed, pharisaical, formalistic and egotistic world. A number of congregations in the United States, England, Brazil and the Philippines have already realized Houses of Prayer.

The house of prayer is intended to be a school of prayer for all members of the religious institute; it seeks to assist them in becoming ever better witnesses of a life inspired by and deriving its dynamism from faith. Within the Houses of Prayer, there can also be constituted nuclei of religious given permanently to contemplation but ready also for other forms of apostolate. Their specific task would be to animate and help co-members who, for limited periods of time, gather in prayer and medita-

[2] See Bernard Häring, *Acting on the Word* (New York: Farrar, Straus, 1968), pp. 204–9. Also Bernard Häring, "A Contemplative House," *Review for Religious*, 26 (1967), pp. 771–78.

tion. The Houses of Prayer, however, would gain by being open to the laity and to priests who are not members of the religious institute. The first experiments of Houses of Prayer for diocesan priests have met with success.[3]

Houses of Prayer ought to foster prayer and contemplation in forms that make them alive and with accents meaningful to modern man. We must be mindful of both the difficulties and the new possibilities which the contemporary world offers for evangelization and be willing to discard every prayer form that smacks of neo-Platonic dualism. Especially should the religious involved in the House of Prayer movement keep in sight the totality of man within the aggregate of all of God's creation. The predominantly contemplative communities of religious have a well-grounded contribution to make in the search for a worthwhile synthesis between contemplation and apostolic commitment. The quest for synthesis is especially urgent today and it calls for the commitment of the whole Church. Learning contemplation and prayer in forms and a language adapted to our rapidly changing period is mandatory and claims the total effort of all members of the people of God.[4]

The Houses of Prayer and all similar initiatives undertaken today should be models for an integration of prayer and life; consequently, greatest attention should be directed to the living synthesis of fraternal love and contemplation. The Houses of Prayer are aspiring to be schools of contemplation in fraternal charity, fully consonant with the exigency for believers to incarnate themselves in daily life. In any case, the effort to which the whole Church is summoned for a renewal of the forms and language of prayer would be futile if one were to take no account of the extension and depth of the phenomenon

[3] See: *Exploring Inner Space,* by the Clearing Center for the House of Prayer Movement (Monroe, Michigan, 1970). Also: *Praying—Sharing—Living,* Report of Priests Experiencing Shared Life and Prayer, by Priests' Senate (Detroit, 1970).

[4] Very hopeful steps in the same direction have been taken by the Association of Contemplatives; see their *Contemplative Review* (Redemptoristine Monastery, Esopus, New York).

of desacralization with its new perspectives and new language.[5]

IV. SANCTITY IN MARRIAGE AND IN THE FAMILY

The Church has always jealously defended the sacramentality of Christian marriage against all assaults. In the course of her history, the sacramental vision of the Christian family has been a strong testimony of the vocational reality of the whole Church to sanctity. In many instances, however, there is need to recognize how unenlightened theological tendencies and certain types of false sacralization veiled the depth of the family's sacramental vocation.

The moral-theological juridicism has unilaterally emphasized the contractual dimension of marriage. The traditional manuals viewed the juridically conceived and stipulated contract as the sacramental reality.[6] Without denying the contractual dimension, the Christian marriage as an efficacious sign of salvific love binding Christ to the Church certainly cannot be reduced to a simple contract, even if most noble. Classical moral theology has spent a major portion of its energies depicting the conditions for the contract validity of marriage and for the proper liturgical celebration. Its other central preoccupation lay in the vindication of ecclesiastical competency in whatever concerns marriage and the family.[7]

[5] G. C. Milanesi, "L'uomo moderno di fronte alla preghiera," *Presenza pastorale*, 3 (1968), No. 11–12, pp. 987–1003.
[6] "Christ the Lord elevated to the dignity of sacrament the marriage contract among baptized. For those among the baptized whose marriage contract cannot be valid, there would be no sacrament," in I. Aertnys, C. Damen, and I. Visser, *Theologia moralis, secundum doctrinam S. Alfonsi de Ligorio, Doctoris Ecclesiae*, 18th ed., Vol. IV., no. 91, p. 85.
[7] "Marriage being, by its own intrinsic nature and significance, a sacred reality, it is logical that it be upheld and moderated not by the power of princes, but by the divine authority of the Church, which alone has the teaching office relative to sacred things" in Leo XIII, *Arcanum Divinae Sapientiae, Acta Leonis XIII*, Vol. II, p. 23.

The pastoral constitution *Gaudium et Spes* attests to the fact that the Council has positively avoided referring to the term "*contractus*," preferring instead that of covenant, "*foedus*." The sacrament of matrimony is an alliance, a covenant, a perceptible sign of love, an intimate relationship of the spouses with Christ which needs and wants to be ever more configured by his love: "the Savior of men and the Spouse of the Church comes into the lives of married Christians through the sacrament of matrimony. He abides with them thereafter so that just as He loved the Church and handed Himself over on her behalf, the spouses may love each other with perpetual fidelity through mutual self-bestowal" (GS, Art. 48).

The grace of matrimony is not a "sacred quantity" dissociated from life: it is the living presence of Christ's love which enables the spouses to love each other mutually. Where reciprocal love is wanting, there is no reception of grace. Without authentic love, there cannot be realized the visibility and truth of the pact of redeemed love. With much decisiveness also the Council has overcome all tendencies of the Church to monopolize family life as being within the compass of her own competency. This is not only intended to better serve the family but realistically and humbly, it acknowledges how other services can be rendered by the secular city only. The Church can no longer operate high-handedly in matters of marriage jurisdiction; she now becomes the promoter of a common commitment for the good of the family, respectful of the competencies of everyone else (GS, Art. 52).

Another grave danger in traditional moral theology has been the separation of conjugal love ("charity") from affection and sexuality. In the discussion which preceded the definitive approval of the chapter of *Gaudium et Spes* devoted to matrimony (GS, Part II, Chapter I, Art. 47–52), some Council Fathers still manifested in their interventions a strong influence of the Augustinian tradition, which restricted conjugal love to spiritual friendship only, and the conjugal act to procreation or to a remedy for concupiscence, *"remedium concupiscentiae."*[8]

Happily, the document approved by the Fathers recognizes how the whole life of the spouses is assumed by redeemed love: "Such love, merging the human with the divine, leads the spouses to a free and mutual gift of themselves, a gift proving itself by gentle affection and by deed. Such love pervades the whole of their lives. Indeed, by its generous activity, it grows better and grows greater. . . . This love is uniquely expressed and perfected through the marital act. The actions within marriage by which the couple are united intimately and chastely are noble and worthy ones. Expressed in a manner which is truly human, these actions signify and promote that mutual self-giving by which spouses enrich each other with a joyful and thankful will" (GS, Art. 49).[9]

The way in which Vatican II presents the sacramentality and sanctity of marriage and family life can be a logical point of departure and a valuable paradigm for catechesis on every Christian's vocation to holiness, especially for our contemporaries having little or no inclination to superficial sacralization. It advocates holiness in daily life, not one disdainfully aloof from everyday activities. Christian sanctity means responsibility and a commitment of love in our relations with God and all our brethren. The vital personalistic dimension always defended by the Church ought to be witnessed today in a more enlightened way, namely, one that brings out better the totality of the person as body and spirit, the product of history and of the environment, but also responsible for the environment and future generations.

[8] See Bernard Häring, *Love Is the Answer* (New York: Dimension Books, 1970); also: Häring, *Paternità responsabile* (Roma, 1970).
[9] There is need to recognize, however, how in the Council, the tensions between *"caritas coniugalis"* and sexuality were not fully overcome. Besides the texts like that quoted, others can be found in which the tension is still present, most of all when it is a matter of adjusting the exigencies of love with those of responsible parenthood; e.g., see Art. 50. Even more so are some formulations of Pope Paul VI in his encyclical *Humanae Vitae.*

V. ARDUOUS VOCATIONS

Medieval spirituality restricted the term "vocation" to the priestly and monastic states only. Martin Luther extended it to every honest state of life and to professional activities, but he held a fundamentally static vision of social life. The Christian attitude was characterized by acceptance of the status quo, man's resting content with his own profession and social situation in a spirit of passive submission to Divine Providence. Calvinism held a more dynamic vision of professional life and the whole concept of vocation but it did not always avoid the fascination of "success" in professional life. The whole theology of predestination has formally "sacralized" economic success. Contrariwise, the Catholic and Lutheran concept of vocation has often remained anchored to a predominantly static vision precluding a full and wholehearted commitment to socio-economic reform.

The vision of the universal vocation to holiness elaborated by Vatican II in its constitutions *Gaudium et Spes* and *Lumen Gentium* has completely reassessed the presence of Christians in the economic, social and cultural life. Remembering the words of the Lord, "If there is love among you, then all will know that you are my disciples" (Jn. 13:35), Christians can desire nothing more ardently than to serve with greater generosity and effectiveness the men of the contemporary world. Therefore, while adhering faithfully to the Gospel and benefiting from its strength, united with all those who love and search for justice, they assume an immense task on this earth: "concerning this task they must give a reckoning to Him who will judge every man on the last day" (GS, Art. 93).[10]

---

[10] "In the plan of God, every man is called to development, because every life is a vocation. At birth, all are given germinally the attitudes and qualities to be unfolded; in their full development, fruit of time of the education received and of the environment and personal effort, everyone

The salvation of man, although having a fundamentally transcendent perspective and dimension, remains intimately connected with the conditions of life in which the person develops and, therefore, with the commitment for the well-being and progress of the whole human community. Vatican II notes: "Many elements make up the temporal order: the good things of life . . . as well as their development and progress. All of these not only aid in the attainment of man's ultimate goal but also possess their own intrinsic value. This value has been implanted in them by God, whether they are considered in themselves or as parts of the whole temporal order" (AA, Art. 7).

It is an undeniable fact that the Catholic morality of the last centuries considered the world and the human environment of believers mostly from the perspective of proximate and remote danger of sin. Believers thus displayed an excessive sense of defensiveness and mistrust; they envisioned saints as people living marginally to real life, even if true saints often radically disproved such an image.

Moral and pastoral theology have given little attention to vocations for positions of responsibility in the life of the secular city and have restricted themselves to cautioning against risks, true or imagined, making demands for a more or less emphatically monastic life. This resulted in a striking absence of fervent Catholics in the political, artistic, journalistic and other professional fields. Even more serious was the fact that such an absence was justified and fostered by members of the hierarchy, and by priests who in a concerted effort tried to blackmail the earthly city.

The world of today assigns great importance to those who mold public opinion by means of the arts or the media of social communication. Equally influential is the work of pioneers in the fields of medicine, the social sciences, psychology

will be allowed to orient himself toward the destiny proposed to him by his Creator," Paul VI, *Populorum Progressio*, Art. 15, *AAS*, 59 (1967), p. 265.

and urban sociology. For believers, every field of endeavor can be the object of a genuinely divine vocation: a vocation which requires dedication, generosity, responsibility, courage, prayer —a vocation to which it would be a grave error not to respond.

In an essentially dynamic era, greater dangers and heavier damage result from a unilateral ethical conception which is an alienating expression of a static state of affairs that wants at all cost to avoid, for the believer, any risk of pioneering. "Holiness in the world," on the contrary, involves primarily responsibility and co-responsibility for the future of the world, and therefore implies the risk of initiatives which dares to blaze new trails. The eschatological hope of the Christian can be expressed in many forms. In a dynamic, future-oriented and strongly communitarian culture like ours, it ought to be a source of effective presence in the best positions of responsibility such as those deciding on the future of the human race, the possibility and capacity of living in love, justice, peace and openness to decisive values.

In speaking of sanctity, the accent should therefore be on responsibility toward the world, on an active presence in it, on a loyal commitment to it on the formation of true competence in the different sectors of life, on faith-charity as a commitment of salvation for the world and humanity. Only in this context will the discourse on the obligation of avoiding disproportionate dangers be truly important and valid.[11] This vision does not diminish the appreciation of those who make the proclamation of the Gospel their main concern. The Gospel will provide the strongest inspiration and set clear direction for the "arduous vocations."

[11] Bernard Häring, *Marriage in the Modern World* (Westminster, Md.: Newman Press, 1966). See especially Part I: "Sociology of the Family in the Service of Theology and Life," pp. 15–70.

CHAPTER 7

PRAYER IN A SECULAR AGE

Prayer is not a happening lifted out of life's context nor is it appended to life; it is not even a significant experience as long as it is peripheral to life. Rather, prayer permeates life and diffuses itself in, between, around and within every corner of living. Prayer is man's true language throughout life, a breathing forth or speaking to the Father day by day, an utterance in that life-giving peace of God (Sabbath) in which man comes home to the origin of true life. Man regrettably alienates himself from life when he removes prayer from its center.

Prayer forms the main orientation of life through which man gradually becomes aware of his existential dependence on God since he is a creature coming from the Father and a pilgrim son who, through his brother, Jesus Christ, is going back home to him in the mystery of the Holy Spirit. In genuine prayer, man realizes that the strength of the Spirit is with him personally, taking hold of him and guiding him to a greater knowledge and sharing of God's creative and redemptive love. In prayer, man becomes ever more a sharer of the very life which God celebrates in his triune love and which he manifests constantly in all creation. Through prayer, man can become a co-creator and a co-sharer in God's love for all men and the whole cosmos. When man's prayer does not emanate from the center of life, he voices only estranged "prayers" meshing mechanically like cogs in a wheel. He evidently becomes much like the people of the "Enuma-Elish" epic, a product of all the tensions in the world and a producer of new anxieties and novel forms of alienation, hatred, violence and war.

In the ancient Gilgamesh epic preserved in various literary forms, Marduk, the strongest of all gods, slaughtered the mother god Thiamat, and other gods. From their blood flowed the oceans and the rivers; from their bones, he made the dry land. Therefore, the tensions and struggle for life increased in nature, in mankind, in the family, in cultures and nations. This vision offers no escape for man; he is thoroughly ensnared in the painful dialectic. The author of the Enuma-Elish epic is somewhat of a Marxist but one with an absolutely "sacralized" outlook. The outcome is the same: there is no way out for man; he has to live with the tensions and he becomes godlike to the extent that he excels in strife and hatred. Gilgamesh is searching for a magical formula; however, all his art and efforts are fruitless. He cannot succeed, as the malevolent powers are inborn, "sacred" and "divine" qualities of creation.

Against this background, the inspired author of Genesis reflects that no created thing is taboo or sacred in that sense. There can be no "sacred" fate; therefore, there is no need of magical rituals. Man's calling demands that he make his life a full response to God since his personal talents and all things entrusted to his care are a gift and message of God. "God spoke and it was." Everything bespeaks a loving word to man, who is created to the image and likeness of God. God is always in his repose (Sabbath) and all creation invites man to seek his peace and tranquility in him. The principal message of Genesis (Chapters 1–3) is that man can be a free steward of the world around him and a worthy co-creator in God's universe if he is at home in God's Sabbath. The Sabbath is a "day" without evening and morning, the day that should give shape and meaning to all days. Man finds his freedom and dignity if he is a true adorer of the Lord in all of life's exigencies.

The man who does not pray or one who alienates his prayer from life through formalism and ritualism, is surprisingly well described by Karl Marx. Obviously Marx is misguided when he expects mere economic and social structures to free man finally from the vicious circle of a barbaric dialectic, of a hateful and frustrating polarization. "There is therefore no possible defence for their conduct; knowing God, they have refused to honor him as God . . . and their misguided minds are plunged in darkness. . . . Thus, because they have not seen fit to acknowledge God, he has given them up to their depraved reason" (Rom. 1:20–28). Yet the Spirit within man has been crying out continually, teaching him over and over again that ineluctable new orientation toward the world and fellowman. Finally, Christ the Redeemer and great Rabbi has wrought redemption in a total reorientation of life to the praise of the Creator. He teaches man to approach the Father, to pray to Him and adore Him in all of life "in Spirit and in Truth."

Man's prayer then becomes a yearning for interior freedom and for wholeness; it pleads for deliverance from an indurate and closed heart, from a dissipated heart darkened by hatred and violence, from self-centeredness, and from a heart weighed down by collective prejudices and power-mongering. Equally, man yearns to be free from the frustrations of endless rituals, dead formulas and empty-worded theologizing. Man implores the Spirit of Truth to pray within him, to help bring about the interpenetration of life and religion, to show him how to utilize his creative abilities and to share his gifts in all the circumstances of his personal and social life. This is prayer at the center of life. If the Spirit truly prays in and through man, the whole world will come within his compass and will somehow find its wholeness and redemption. Man gradually attains a holistic outlook and comes to psychological wholeness by finding God as the center of all life. In prayer he finds all the essential dimensions of living.

I. PRAYER: YEAST IN THE DOUGH

Man becomes the "salt of the earth" or the yeast in the dough of human life to the extent that he remains in Christ and allows Christ's Word to dwell in him. Therefore, no serious revision or renewal of personal and communal prayer life can take place without a painstaking study of the signs of the times, without apprizing the quality of today's dough before inserting a proper measure of yeast. Unquestionably, prayer reflects abiding values and sets an essential direction to life. Yet there are accents which are necessarily shifting to keep rhythm with the times, and expressions that have to be harmonized with the diverse cultures.

The complex phenomenon of secularization is obviously one of the outstanding characteristics of today's world. Therefore, the concern for wholeness in prayer impels man to study the mutual interdependence of secularization and the opportunities afforded by it for a genuine prayer life. This can be accomplished in any number of ways. Some major questions could well be asked: How does secularization influence religion, the Church, her formulation of dogma, her teaching methods and, above all, her prayer life? How can the Church become more aware of this process of secularization and its implications? Whatever be the answers, the thesis remains: the Church needs to exert a more conscious and generous effort in reading the signs of the times. She has paid a high price in suffering for having been remiss in this duty for so long.

Ours is an era of rapid secularization. Definitions of secularization itself must first be explored as well as the opportunities and challenges offered by it to the Church; secondly, the dangers must be discerned and appropriate countermeasures adopted for man's assistance. Since the secularized world is the dough into which prayer is to be inserted as the yeast, the renewal of prayer must represent a grateful response to the timely challenges of the secular world and a healing action for the faults and dangers inherent in the life situation of today.

It seems more appropriate to me and also a sounder methodological course to focus first on the positive aspects of secularization and to render thanks to the Lord of history for his graciousness before we single out the dangers of certain forms of secularization.

II. THE POSITIVE CHALLENGES OF SECULARIZATION

The phenomena I am about to suggest are not necessarily by themselves a triumph of man over evil nor do they constitute an unfailing help for growth in genuine faith and prayer. Yet they are events and signs of a period of secularization which, if rightly understood, *can* elicit a response to a challenge or opportunity for growth, especially on the part of those who are sincerely searching for greater genuineness and depth in faith.

A. Desacralization of "Holy Things" and "Sacred Traditions"

Many things considered sacred in earlier centuries because of their symbolic meaning are no longer accepted as such today. In many instances, they signify nothing other than an ossification of a past language and tradition. Hence they have become taboos or obstacles to a living faith; consequently, they constitute a separation from religion and life, and become a real cause of alienation.

An era of desacralization challenges man to rethink and to re-evaluate the emphasis on "sacred things" and "sacred traditions" in the Church. There is a long list to be reviewed: sacred signs, vestments, rubrics, precepts, laws, formulations, language, "authority," devotions, novenas, and down to the minutiae of "sacred" living. Is it not possible to have a totally new and fresh experience of the "You alone are holy, You alone are Lord"? Cannot the Church be brave enough to test all her "sacred" paraphernalia against the one and only God? Can she not be honest enough to discard whatever obscures or blocks this message, yet doing so sincerely by retaining what can contribute to a new life?

Desacralization does not necessarily imply the destruction of all religious traditions, ecclesial institutions, authority, laws, symbols and doctrines. It can happen that a total loss of the sense of the sacred, or an all-out battle against everything thought to be sacred, happens because both the proponents and the opponents of the "sacred" traditions cannot distinguish the abiding values of faith from the changing and sometimes very imperfect forms of religious belief and practice.

The process of desacralization profoundly affects mostly the understanding and practice of personal and communal prayer. Those who insist on imposing the stereotyped forms of the past are perhaps the worst enemies of prayer life. Happily, vigorous renewal efforts are not limited to a theoretical reevaluation but there are also many spontaneous movements for the revitalization of worship. The liturgical renewal in the Catholic Church and in great parts of the reformed Churches is but one of these felicitous events. Often, however, renewal efforts are still hampered by either inflexibility or angry reactions against any attempt to contain the liturgy within new legislation and restrictions. I trust that the liturgical renewal of worship will bear fruit and open itself to the needs of a vital faith, especially in view of the many extra-liturgical movements of renewal of prayer.

There are thousands of groups throughout the world who spontaneously come together in quest of life's ultimate meaning; they begin by praying together. One of these movements, that of the Catholic Pentecostals (or "the charismatic renewal" as many call it), has penetrated almost every sector of life. Its great impact on countless persons has led them to a renewal in their personal life style.

A probably equally important movement is that of the "House of Prayer," initiated by a number of religious communities of women and which has now importantly influenced priests and laymen. In the past few years, hundreds of groups of sisters, often joined by laywomen, dedicated six to eight weeks of their summer months exploring "the inner space" in view of their Christian mission to be "the salt of the earth." Dozens of permanent Houses of Prayer are now in operation; they are alike in one respect only: they all refuse to be simple copies of the traditional contemplative cloisters. Those who

open themselves to this new way of prayer are searching together for means of revitalizing man's response to the universal
call to holiness and wholeness.

The House of Prayer movement is a new "institution" if you
so wish to call it, but it functions without walls; the whole
concept revolves around openness, flexibility and variety. It
represents a fresh approach to learning; it offers a possibility
for meaningful experimentation within the framework of a
Church that understands herself as a "House of Prayer" in a
pilgrim situation. No single House of Prayer is a sacred cow, a
model so perfect as to deserve being copied. Each House of
Prayer has a significant and unique gift to offer others. It lies
in constant readiness to share, to take on new forms and to
evaluate its experiences, all of which cannot be achieved in
the restlessness of a prayerless world, or within an unpraying
theology. Its aim is adoration, meditation, prayer that bears
fruit in love for the life of the world. It is a quest for a
meaningful synthesis of adoration and daily life.

Again, this is accomplished without "holy grills" but always
in a context of peace and love, in freedom from anger or
bitterness toward the existing framework which has weighed us
down for so long. The participants hope that a new spirit of
community will flourish as they labor together and listen to the
voice of our times. The House of Prayer of today is built from a
singular blueprint; founders are convinced that a simple re-
modeling of old forms of religious life, either contemplative or
active, would not succeed in finding a new synthesis between
a life of prayer and a life of dedication to fellowmen in the
direct apostolate. They are impressed by the Lord's warning:
"No one sews a patch of unshrunk cloth on to an old coat;
for then the patch tears away from the coat, and leaves a
bigger hole. Neither do you put new wine into old wine-skins;
if you do, the skins burst . . . No, you put new wine into
fresh skins; then both are preserved" (Mt. 9:16–17).

While there is concern for continuity, there is no less of an
awareness that new times call for new ideas and a fresh
search for a novel synthesis. The House of Prayer is part of

a broad concern to adore God "in Spirit and in Truth" (Jn. 4:23), to renew religious communities, families and the Church in a way that honors the One God and Father. One of the basic convictions is that renewal of prayer life and renewal through prayer deserves high priority, and this is not possible without energetic efforts and great freedom in experimentation.

B. The New Emphasis on the Sacredness of the Human Person

When so many things are desacralized and submitted to a most critical and serene evaluation, what is there to offer as criterion? What remains holy on earth? The humanist tradition in the Church and outside of organized religion responds: the absolute value of the human person in his capacity to love, to promote justice, peace and brotherhood. The desacralization of taboos is meaningful only if it opens the horizon to the fullest resacralization of man in his dignity as God's image and likeness. At this point, we can build on the great tradition of ethical prophetism in Israel and in Christianity.

The prophets struck out forcefully against trust in the so-called "sacred things." They pointed to God, the one Creator of all things, and came to affirm man's dignity in his image and likeness to God. The powerful do not remind us of this profound sacredness, nor do those who can reward us, the beautiful, or those with whom we would terribly like to fall in love. Rather, the cogent revelation of man's dignity comes from those who have nothing to offer us save their human "creatureliness," their being made to the image and likeness of God; these are the test cases. Christ, the Redeemer, came for the sick, the sinners, the poor, the lepers, the discriminated against, the outcasts; Christ even desacralized nationalism (the holy people of Israel) and caste systems (the holy priestly class) in his parable of the Samaritan. The man of the "schismatic and heretical" nation who helped the Jewish casualty was the truly holy man.

Our secular age does not so much desacralize as sharpen our criteria relative to the quality of real saints. Man is grateful for their example, for they reflect God's perfection and orient him to the Creator of all goodness. This process of secularization has also helped to develop the concept of "analogy of faith [*analogia fidei*]" with emphasis on the self-transcendence that points to God's creative and redemptive presence, transcendence to the neighbor not because of utility but simply through respect for the human person and concern for the common good, for justice and peace. We believe that it is the Spirit who prompts man to be open-minded, sincere, unselfish and truly dedicated to others. These are the miracles, the handiwork of God that turn our attention to him and call us to genuine consecration in service to our brethren.

Respect for the person, the most basic of all human experiences, can enrich faith and prayer by bringing both to a greater depth of understanding. Our faith in one God and prayer to the one Father are revitalized when we begin to experience the uniqueness of man, his dignity, his freedom, whatever be his race. Under all circumstances, we respect him for his upright conscience, his yearning for unity and solidarity with the rest of men. It is a faith that strengthens the conviction that peace and love are possible when one person is able to acknowledge the uniqueness of the other, to recognize in a brother or sister God's sacred masterpiece. Whoever opens his eyes to the beauty of the human person, particularly the mature and loving person reflecting God's image, will more easily live in a spirit of adoration. Nothing turns us more directly to God than respect and love for all men.

This is the course whereby man can find a vital synthesis between religion and life, between prayer and everyday activity. We stand ready to see the promptings of the Spirit not only in an explicit "faith active in love" but also in all forms of generous, self-transcending love of neighbor so vital for seeking God. An example may better convey the idea I seek to express.

In a leprosarium of India, I met the benevolent companion

of a member of a religious community who helps most generously in the rehabilitation and adjustment efforts of these afflicted and needy people. It is her way of searching for "ultimate meaning." This young French lady is convinced that if a God of love exists, he can only be found through dedication to one's fellowmen, because prayer and faith are actualized in such love.

Does it not suggest that we should vary more often the formulation of our Creed? Instead of repeating day after day and week after week the same stereotyped formula, we can preserve the purity and vitality of faith if, in the liturgy and communal prayer, we express our Creed in such a way that the sense of God and the great human values of conscience, freedom, solidarity and peace find a life synthesis. Allow me to sketch such an expression of the Creed which, in an existential way, points to our constant commitment to the glory of God in loving solidarity.

WE BELIEVE in one God and Father of all men. We believe this truth in spirit and in truth if we honor and respect each human person created to the image and likeness of God and help each other to attain the full stature and maturity of persons in community.

WE BELIEVE in God, the Creator of all visible and invisible things. We believe this in spirit and in truth to the extent that with our unique capacities and with all that we have received from God, we commit ourselves to the service of our brethren in order to build a community of men in justice and brotherhood.

WE BELIEVE in one Lord, Jesus Christ, who came not to please himself but to be the servant of all men. Therefore, we believe that there is no salvation for us in Christ unless we too commit ourselves with him for the whole world, for a saving community. We can be rescued from the dark powers of evil, from the deleterious solidarity of egotists only if, like Christ, we also make ourselves servants of salvation in brotherly unity.

WE BELIEVE Christ was born of the Virgin Mary, the humble maiden who is pleasing to God by her humility, her willingness to serve; she thus sings her constant Magnificat to God, who has ranged himself at the side of the New Israel, his Servant that his Church might, with her, follow Christ, the Servant. Therefore, we are true believers and belong to the New Israel if we praise God in humble service of our fellowmen.

WE BELIEVE that Christ has borne the burden of all, has taken upon himself the heavy load of the past in order to transform it and give it new meaning. So we believe that we can also transform the suffering and frustration in our world into a saving power if we bear the burdens of one another in the same spirit as Christ Jesus.

WE BELIEVE that Christ gave his body to be bread for the life of the world, that he made himself available to the point of giving his life for all. That is why the Father gave testimony to him and manifested him as Lord by raising him from the dead. We believe, then, that we will find our true selves, our real fulfillment by giving ourselves to the service of our neighbor and community if, in redeemed love, we use all our talents, all our God-given charisms for the building up of the Body of Christ.

WE BELIEVE in one holy, Catholic Church; therefore in receiving the body of Christ, we recommit ourselves over and again to a constant conversion. Thus are we to become more fully the body of Christ if we strive untiringly toward Christian unity so that the Church may become more effectively and more visibly a sacrament of unity for the whole of mankind. The world can then believe in one God, the Father of all men.

WE BELIEVE in the one baptism which Christ accepted when he gave his blood for all, that all may be brought together in a real blood-brotherhood where one bears the burden of all. We are baptized into the saving solidarity of Christ. We believe firmly and truly in this baptism if we live

accordingly and commit ourselves ever anew to solidary
efforts in the pursuit of peace, justice and love.

WE BELIEVE in everlasting life, in the communion of all the
children of God. This faith and hope is truthful and will
not deceive if we manifest the one hope that is held out
for us through unity and solidarity. By putting to death
all selfishness and group egotism, we look forward to the
resurrection from the dead and everlasting joy in the communion of the saints, for the concelebration of God's
triune love.

Similar expressions of our creed will inspire a constant
prayer of faith: "Lord, we believe; help us wherever our faith
falls short." A similar form of the creed directed to the main
issues of our life can also serve as outline for a particular
examination of conscience and a prayer for forgiveness. Besides, it moves to thanksgiving and praise in prayer and in
our prayer life.

Other creeds can likewise be composed encompassing the
same basic truths but on a variety of themes: the *dignity* of
each human person, the genuine *freedom* for which God
has created all men and for which Christ has redeemed them
as children of God; the *conscience* that God awakens creatively,
the conscience that frees for full sensitivity, that is vivified by
the Spirit, that unites all men in the search for truth, goodness
and justice while grappling with the problems of personal and
social life; the yearning for *peace*. These timely topics and
others that the man of prayer discovers will truly be "sacred"
to the believer, for they promote the development of the
human person while manifesting the dynamics of faith.

In such forms of prayer connected with life, a believer comes
to a deeper knowledge of God and fellowman through a vibrant religious experience and these happenings of faith can
help one mature in the fortitude of a man of God; man then
"comes of age."

C. Possible Resacralization of the Whole Creation

In his determination to make certain things or groups of people sacred and privileged, the "religious man" of the past all too often forgot the merely symbolic value and the dynamic value of these things. He thus removed "sacredness" from all of God's other creations and circumscribed it narrowly. In such a sacralistic culture, e.g., "holy water" became so holy that the great symbolism of water, its goodness as a gift of God was easily forgotten. A few things were totally set apart by the priest who made them holy or sacred by precise "blessing" formulas. There arose much discussion on valid and non-valid "constitutive" benedictions and the like. Yet already the first chapters of the Book of Genesis are prophetically desacralizing taboos; for everything is sacred in the sense of being a message and gift of God, while nothing is so holy as to make it untouchable or cause it to be withdrawn from meaningful use. All of creation is entrusted to man, who is called to use all of God's gifts freely for the benefit of his fellowman.

In a scientific age where man, with the greatest courage, discovers the marvelous play of all kinds of causality and puts even an imperfect determinism to the service of development, we had better renounce presenting God with classifications of "prime causality" and "secondary causality" which were never truly good religious categories. We no longer entertain the myths of a God who, by his interventions into the realm of secondary causality, would fill the gap left by scientific insight and "the possible." Instead, the prodigious history of evolution and above all, the new knowledge relative to the history and further possibilities of human development, invite us to admire the on-going creation and to discover as co-revealers of God's love and creativity, an "on-going revelation," a continuing presence of God's creative word and love. If man never ceases in his efforts to transform the world in which he lives into a beautiful haven of goodness and justice for his own benefit and that of his fellowmen, then he truly becomes a co-creator and co-revealer of God's love, using his every gift and almost infinite capacity in praise of the Creator. Then can he truly communicate God's love and remind others of their calling to love.

In the historical periods preceding secularization, man was unremittingly reminded of the reality of religion through a thousand and one sacred signs, processions, holy places, devotions and holy pictures. The man of today does not find religion therein; he is not impressed by such an emphasis on external "sacredness." Rather, modern man wishes to emulate him who worships his God "in Spirit and in Truth," for such a man adores God by knowing how to love, how to be just and how to befriend all men. This is the kind of religion contemporary man views as real. No longer can he believe that only certain consecrated persons know effective formulas for blessings, some of which automatically achieve an invisible consecration of the world. Modern man has come to accept that the witness of a faith operative in love, in an ongoing and unique revelation in Christ, constitutes the only true consecration of the world.

Modern man does not deny the value of sacred places, processions, holy days and novenas; instead of sacralizing them, they approach them soberly in their capacity to foster an atmosphere of recollection, of common worship and spiritual encounter, of a relaxed and attentive attitude to the Lord. In these celebrations, the creative and imaginative qualities of man are set free and a new religious awareness is awakened. Each religious experience can therefore be weighed thoughtfully as to whether or not it serves for a deepening of love, produces fruit in love for the life of the world.

Modern man must realize that the harvest of love is not immediately forthcoming. He is only a beginner in prayer. From past generations, he has learned that there is a time to sow and a time to reap, but his urgency to act in the present, to produce here and now superabundant fruit impels him to begin now and to yearn constantly for a richer harvest. Only by abiding in Christ and trusting in him can his efforts be deeply rooted. In that trust, man will listen attentively to the Word and prove his readiness to be formed by it and to act upon it. Whenever modern man accepts this challenge, he patiently grows in Christ and in the love of the Father; quite spontaneously and soon, he will be offering the fruits of the Spirit to others in wholeness, integrity, and concern for peace and justice.

D. New Understanding of Consecration and Holiness

Our secular age pays little attention to the so-called "objective consecration" such as an ordination, a religious profession, a marriage ceremony and official blessings if these formalities do not truly express a total consecration to God and to the service of man; only then do they matter. I am not implying that there is no room for ordained priests and consecrated religious in a secular age, but the emphasis of the day is on the necessity of giving witness to a selfless commitment.

Man has lived too long in a Constantinian age which recognized only the clerical state and religious life as "states of perfection" (sanctioned by canonical privileges and protection), while persons choosing different walks of life belonged to "the world." The priest and religious were therefore separated from their families as if these would be a part of an "unholy world." This was especially so for the cloistered contemplatives, irrespective of whether or not their families lived holy Christian lives.

Our secular age has done away with expressions like "states of perfection," for the true believer reaches out for a total sanctification of his own life and of the world in peace and justice to the honor of God. He is more urgently pressed to leave behind him the "godless world" of the Pharisee with its self-conscious and narrow formalism, and the "impious" world of the Gnostic, who refuses to share the redeeming love of Christ for a visible world in which he can live honestly.

Since the universal vocation to holiness appeals to all mankind, religious life must therefore be an intensification of this

call, a constant adherence to this vocation. Hunger and thirst
for holiness and for a deep union with God is what allows
religious to be sharers of God's own active love for all his
children. God discloses his holiness in his salvific love, his
mercy and compassion through Christ, who is totally consecrated to reveal the depths of the Father's saving justice and
mercy. He also prays for his apostles and disciples that they,
too, may be fully consecrated in truth (Jn. 17:19), totally
dedicated to work for that peace and unity among men for
which he came.

What criteria will be set for the religious life of the future
is still to some extent an unanswered question, but one knows
with certainty that they will entail more than personal privileges acquired once and forever. Religious life will demand the
witness of a profound union with God, but one which will
issue naturally into solidarity with all mankind. In his high
priestly orison, Jesus prays that the apostles be one so as to
reflect his own union with the Father, and that through their
witness of word and life, all believers may come to give the
same testimony of dedication to unity and peace so that "the
world may believe." Christ convincingly testifies that the "consecration in truth" consists of a mission to give authentic testimony to unity, and that this mission arises from a profound
union with God. This call to holiness, to which the apostle is
summoned to be servant and witness, is infinitely greater and
more demanding than a mere ritual consecration and "holiness."

The legalism of the past, encumbered as it was by minutiae,
brought real anguish to meditation and contemplation, to
prayer and the liturgy. Today, there is no obsession relative
to ritual validity. The breviary, the sacraments, the Eucharist
itself are free more and more to develop in an atmosphere of
great openness to the Spirit. The concern is not so much for
ritual validity as for a growing union with God, an integrated vision of life, a living synthesis between hearing the
Word and acting on it. This is a beautifully hopeful return to
the great prophetic tradition.

Man needs a new orientation to prayer in view of his mission of unity and solidarity. The old definitions of lay people as "world," hierarchy and religious as "members of states of perfection," resulted in a concept of prayer and training in prayer geared primarily to monks and cloistered nuns. This spirituality was a narrow base on which to build universal prayer. Yet the diocesan priests were directed to adopt the monastic breviary, much like the contemplatives "who had left the world." Where did this leave the poor layman in his quest for God? The favorable moment, the *kairos* has now come. The desacralized world has challenged the clergy and religious to learn how to pray with mothers and fathers, children, youth and all who are committed to the humanization of the world. The laymen and religious of today must search together for God.

E. *Miracles and Prayer of Petition Revisited*

Many things which earlier provoked awe and religious fascination, fear or trembling as an immediate experience of God's extraordinary miracles and signs of his powerful presence are explained today by science and research. Phenomena and events once propounded as miracles, proof of God's existence or his direct intervention are now unveiled scientifically and have lost their enchantment and wonder. The two French theologians who declared the rhythm of fertile and sterile days within a woman's cycle as "the sexual mystery" will no longer provoke religious wonder among average laymen in a secularized age; the reaction will likely be one of laughter or a gentle invitation for further scientific verification of facts, causes and results for the benefit of human beings.

Modern man's well-developed religious sensitivity can admire the marvels of the world of biology, zoology, astronomy, but, at the same time, he will be careful not to cause religious "short circuits." He more easily understands that prayer, vital faith in God and religion are not at all an effort to move God to do our will but a living response to God, who reveals his love to man. This knowledge leads man to center his attention on God's masterpiece, the human person, on his wonderful presence in him who is created to his image and likeness. He will then look to man as a co-revealer of God's abiding love, wisdom and intimate life. He will be grateful for this continuing revelation of God's mystery in himself and in others. He will pray that the great miracle, namely, genuine love among men, be perpetuated; he will be eager to act according to this prayer.

The style and object of prayer are markedly affected by the progress of science, technology and organization. What in earlier days man sought to obtain either through magical rituals or trustful prayer is now immediately attainable. Scientific research and modern technotronics have thus extended man's own responsibility. The temptation grows weaker to make God a kind of "filler" between what is and what could be, a stopgap in a natural process. In relation to contagious disease, famine and war, man can no longer pray sincerely, "Spare us, O Lord," without at the same time pooling all his knowledge, competence and energy in working as God's instrument for liberating love, mercy and justice.

Sociology and history have well documented what constitute the main causes of war. Man is coming to realize that armed force can never ensure peace where there is no understanding of man, his freedom and his needs. When man prays for peace, he opens himself to a deeper realization of his mission as an instrument of non-violence, of reconciliation in charity and justice; he learns to influence public opinion; he discreetly uses his civil rights. He cannot pray for the millions of starving in India and East Pakistan without investing his best effort for international co-operation.

The miracles of health for which man prays today are not meant to prove that natural laws can be dispensed with, but fall more in the realm of kindness, gentleness, generosity and graciousness that reveal God, who is Love. Man needs to ask for the miracle of recognizing God's presence in the least of his children; he needs to ask for patient dedication to the poor and to those suffering from discrimination. This is the adoration of God "in Spirit and in Truth" that modern man recognizes as genuine. Prayer will then take a new turn, looking more and more toward God in all moments of life. Man can then discover the true meaning of suffering, even the import of the cross; he will learn to trust in God's grace, in the healing power of the Divine Physician's love while at the same time availing himself of the means of medical science. Man will come to realize that the source of all healing is the Lord himself, and that all else serves as God's instrumentation; he will pray for that love and gentleness which prove to be the greatest healing power for those in the throes of frustration and neuroses. In his prayer of petition, he will learn how to use to the fullest the gifts of God in the service of his neighbor. These few observations demonstrate how prayer can attain a broader scope and lead to a deeper experience of petition and adoration in a genuinely secular age.

F. Autonomy and Emancipation of the Modern World

The age of secularization has emancipated science, art, economics, politics, in fact, the whole temporal sphere from clerical domination and even from the Church, in a broader sense. Often in the past secularization went hand in hand with an anti-clericalism, which easily led to anti-religious feelings and attitudes. This has been and is today a positive challenge to the Church to proclaim Christ's reign by renouncing totally thirst for power and self-importance. Such a renunciation will instead express humble service of brethren in sincere recognition of man's freedom and the autonomy of the secular world. This purity of intention and urgent appeal to the whole Church for complete conversion to Christ, the Servant, is the challenge offered by the secular world of today. Only in prayer and union with God can man become this humble servant while simultaneously using his gifts in simplicity and love. Thus the prayerful person will understand the first beatitude as a rule of life: "Blessed are those who by the Spirit know that they are poor, for theirs is the kingdom of heaven."

The recognition of man's dependence on God for all created gifts and his constant joy in honoring the One Creator and Father through the generous use of all created things in the service of mankind are the harvest of the Spirit. Prayer becomes the simple response of the servant listening attentively for ways to be of service, to become an instrument of peace and witness to God's all-embracing reign, while respecting the unique personal freedom of fellowmen. The House of Prayer movement gives substance to this kind of prayer in its daily experience and search for simple forms suitable for clergy, religious and lay people. As St. Paul suggests (Rom. 8), prayer promotes the genuine freedom of those who listen to the yearning of the entire creation for a share in this freedom. Prayer establishes readiness to respond to this call.

While capitalizing on the insights provided by the behavioral sciences relative to man's sensitivity and yearning for wholeness, the man engaged in meditation, in listening to the Word in silence and in shared prayer, can achieve a synthesis enabling him to plumb the depths of his own creative Life. He is, then, able to proclaim God's all-embracing reign, having renounced any desire to domineer with direct or indirect claims over the temporal realm or paternalistically to tell the human society what has to be done in the various fields of human activity, as if he were the master and knew all the answers. The best he can offer the world is an integrated vision of life as he grows in the knowledge of God and of man. A mature prayer life, a deeply felt experience of God's living presence in the world and in man's innermost being, an encounter with God's grace will make him gracious, gentle, single-minded, generous, creative, spontaneous and sensitive. He will be a credible servant of God and a witness of God's kingdom as a free servant of his fellowmen.

III. DANGERS OF SECULARIZATION COUNTERACTED BY GENUINE RENEWAL IN PRAYER

One cannot disregard the ambivalence of secularization. The awareness of this fact stresses the need to give prime attention to the positive challenges, which is the most effective way to counteract its hazardous elements. Not fight nor an anguished outlook but immunization through the good use of the present opportunities by a style of prayer which is faithful to the prophetic tradition is our approach. However, this does not dispense us from denouncing and unmasking the dangers which are inherent in a part of today's secular culture in order to seek for adequate remedies.

A. Secularism and Horizontalism

Secularization is not the same as secularism. The man of the secular age can be fully attuned to the signs of the times without ignoring God, as does secularism. Neither is secularism always identical with atheism. It does not militate against religion and faith in God; it does "simply" ignore God and religion in the ordering of life, while atheism shows at least a negative interest in faith.

A milder form of secularism finds its ways even into the life of the clergy and religious communities in the form of horizontalism: no time for prayer, only for activity. Prayer is then considered a waste of time. Leisure and activity in loving concern for others become the new slogan for "secular prayer." However, while the self-transcending love of the humanist may well be an "analogia fidei," a path toward faith in a personal relationship with him, horizontalism moves away from explicit prayer. It reflects a gradual loss of existential interest in God; the need to praise him unreservedly and to speak out one's heart to him is either no longer felt or is disavowed.

This danger cannot be counteracted by a one-sided verticalism or by a contemplation of the Neoplatonic or Gnostic type. Only that relationship to God which enkindles a strong, pure and free interest in man, in his longing for integrity and total freedom can be a valid and convincing witness for people tempted by a secularism that has lost the dimension of wholeness, including transcendence. The quest for ultimate meaning will not appeal to modern man if it fails to shed light and meaning on daily living. Ultimate meaning must be incarnated in human relationships and in the building up of a better world. The religious capacity, latent in both the humanist and the horizontalist, must be awakened by the prayerful person who gives to life a wholeness and integration of vision and action.

B. Fragmentation of Life and Education

Student unrest all over the world epitomizes man's hunger and thirst for an integral approach to formation and education. Many of the protesters and their contemporaries are already deeply affected by the fragmentation of today's life, particularly in the public system of education. Distraction is a striking phenomenon of the day; it is almost an institutionalized temptation resulting from the breathless society where commercialization (even of man's leisure) is taken for granted. In spite of their better selves, people live on the level of the present moment but without any great perspective of the meaning of the here-and-now. What is lacking is a creative continuity with the past and an eye to the final expectation in responsibility for the future.

Only people who know the tensions of modern living and who live at the same time in deep union with God—thus giving full meaning to everything and creating genuine vigilance for the wealth of the here-and-now—can touch those people who live on the horizontal plane and in the fugitive moment. In other words, only prophets who enjoy a profound sense of both God and man, and who come from involvement in life and return to it, can be appropriate "voices" calling men home to wholeness and holiness. At the heart of the various contemporaneous movements which promote a new style of prayer and meditation is the experience and conviction of the imperative need for wholeness.

C. Degrading Utilitarianism

There are humanists today who, although they have not found conscious faith and prayer, are not characterized by utilitarianism. In the sense of Karl Rahner, they are truly the "anonymous Christians," or, stated differently, those living the "analogy of faith." But admiration of these generous humanists cannot blind us to the phenomenon of others who follow an expedient philosophy and psychology, who have institutionalized a utilitarian life style and a superficial pragmatism in economics, politics, sociology and medicine. Life and death have also become pawns in this pragmatic game.

When man seeks remediation, he ought not overlook that part of the secular world or those non-religious humanists who promote the dignity of each person. The remedy that can truly cure the evils of our times is a Christian community and Christian people whose life is impregnated by a spirit of thanksgiving and praise, admiration of beauty, reverence for the uniqueness of each person in the sight of God, the healing power of mature human relationships and an unselfishness resulting from adoration, and therefore is not withdrawn from life. It takes prayerful people to bring life to the praise of God and to shape it in the spirit of thanksgiving and adoration.

To achieve this goal, mankind needs time, people and places from which assistance is forthcoming. Surely, God can send these helpers from the desert or anywhere else. But again, the man of the secular age does not ask for miracles but uses God's gifts to create environments, beginning with small groups and communities, where this spirit of integrated living can be fostered in authentic sharing and searching. Only thus is his prayer that God send us persons who can teach us how to pray fully sincere.

D. New Idols of the Secularist World

Man is a worshiper by nature. If he does not adore the true God, he will bow before substitutes of his own making and become enslaved to them. The idols which man raises for adoration are varied: power, violence, power structures, economic and political success, social status, crusades against the unborn (as though they were the greatest threat!), depreciation of the old, segregation, racism, apartheid, belief in indiscriminate sex experiences, and confidence that technology alone can build a better future.

Again, only the man of prayer helped by a community of faith, by the mutual trust and inspiration of those who share the spirit of faith and praise can unmask these idols as they emerge. At the same time, the Christian must realize that he himself is exposed to these various forms of idol worship. Individually, therefore, and in community, he will bring his whole life before God and beg for the help to be transformed until, finally, all that he is, desires and does can be praise and adoration of God "in Spirit and in Truth." Shared prayer joined to common action can liberate man on all levels, freeing him from those prejudices which are so easily accepted as a part of "good conscience" or tradition.

E. Demythologizing Versus Dry Rationality

Religious people of all ages have expressed deep experiences of mystery by myths, midrashim and so on. They knew quite well that the words or images they used and the picture stories they told could not express the whole reality of the mystery. They did not and could not use arid rational concepts that would give the impression that this was all they had to say. The myth is not "true" in the realistic sense of a story of purely authentic human events. It bespeaks truth in a much stronger sense, namely, it points toward an absolute mystery that is infinitely greater than all words and images.

For some time now, man has been exposed to a dry theology that has expressed religion, prayer and faith in stereotyped rational words, all the while draining him of a true filial sense of religion. In an age of secularization which is simultaneously an age of technology, rationality and utility, some well-intentioned theologians endeavor to make faith acceptable and so proceed to a radical demythologization. All too often, they fail to state clearly that the myth, from the very beginning, was only an allegory pointing to the ineffable mystery; they thoroughly do away with it, or translate it into dry concepts to the point where the mystery is practically negated and the sense of mystery greatly impaired if not destroyed.

The elaborate language and ceremony of the solemn liturgy of yesteryear also served the function of a myth, creating a consciousness that man could not adequately express in everyday language and simple style the greatness of God's mystery of self-revelation. For the past few years, many (including churchmen and religious women) have tried to replace all myths and mystery by rationality and rational instruction about life.

There is no way back to naïve mythology or to the overstylistic Latin celebrations, but there are other ways of experiencing the mystery of God's redemptive love. For many, shared prayer is a helpful witness to a spontaneous faith that responds to the mystery of God's abiding love. Here, in community, imperfect man can express his faith in the ever great God in very simple words, often with a stutter and a stammer. Here, in community, he can receive a new revelation from people who accept each other in their human predicament and who desire to search together for new and creative ways of praising their God. In all this, there is a new openness to the mystery of the Word, a searching for and sharing in the deeper and ultimate meaning of life, love and redemption. Besides, there is a genuine commitment to praise the Father in community. In humility and acknowledged self-insufficiency, this kind of prayer points not merely to mystery and to an open future but also to that fidelity, courage and vigilance which proclaim the mystery of God, who was, is and will come.

Many small communities of sisters, priests and laypeople in the Houses of Prayer as well as groups of Catholic pentecostals (charismatic renewal) experience in a sober way a new sense of mystery. (Admittedly, some pentecostals are not too sober in their extravagant exuberance!) Youth can turn to these groups or pilot communities to seek a life in love and faith; they do not have to resort to psychedelic drugs and the creation of mysterious montage to experience or transcend the aridness of a certain kind of rational religion.

F. Misleading Autonomy

It was necessary for the secular world to come to grips with the problem of an overly condescending and paternalistic clergy who did not, in many instances, realize their incompetency in secular matters; autonomy of the secular world is good *per se*. But in the secular age, the man who has lost contact with a community of faith falls all too easily into an arbitrary individualism solely concerned with his own freedom and his self-made "conscience"; the other possibility is that he fall prey to new forms of group egotism and collective prejudices while loudly proclaiming his autonomy. Again, the faithful's response to this problem lies in a common searching for a right conscience in prayer so as to discern God's will and follow it in love. This is best done in community, since the Spirit works in all, through all and for all.

G. Danger of a New Pelagianism

Church historians depict Pelagius as a man of strong will, an ascetic who called for a radical Christianity in the imitation of Christ. His fault was "only" that he did not emphasize sufficiently the gratuitousness of redemption, the necessity of grace and prayer which his fellow-believers acknowledged.

Many modern men, including theologians, find themselves more tempted in this direction than was Pelagius himself.

Ours is an age of computers, of the technopolis, one of planning futurology, of the invention of inventions. Again all too easily, man can lose contact with that inner sanctuary where he senses God's gracious presence. Once man has lost the sense of gratuity of God's friendship, of his patience, gentleness and graciousness, he tends to become violent, even in religious matters. He has lost the awareness of Christ. The result cannot be other than impatience, angry criticism, violent polarization such as that of liberal against traditionalist, even within the Church. Each party takes itself too seriously because it has not learned to rely on God and to seek creative fidelity and constructive renewal in union with him, who is the source of all life and redemption.

There is definite need of a vigorous, coherent and visible affirmation of the gratuitous character of salvation as a basis for hope and trust in God's grace. Only when man is ready, with his fellowmen, to learn patiently and constantly to praise God, to render thanks, to submit humble petitions in trust and total dependence, can he transcend the meager attitude of the technocrat, the inventor, or the pragmatist and only then can he experience his undeserved dignity as co-creator, co-revealer of love and instrument of redemption. The relevance attributed to prayer and man's dedication to a life of prayer must be a visible and striking witness that there is a synthesis between prayer and action. Prayer, understood as communion with God, as listening and responding with heart, mind and action is the great prerogative of the redeemed man and a sign of redemption.

CHAPTER 8

ETHICAL DIALOGUE WITH THE SECULAR MAN

Christ did not entrust his Gospel to the Church to have her jealously guard it underground or preserve it in the secrecy of archives; he wished her to proclaim it to all men. Like the city situated on the mountaintop or the light on the candelabra (Mt. 5:14–16), the Church ought to make the Gospel visible to all; she must shout from the rooftop that which she has heard from the Master (Mt. 10:27; Lk. 12:3).

The message of salvation remains unchanged in its essential religious core, namely, the proclamation of the death-resurrection of Christ and the necessity of faith in him. However, the man to whom the Church addresses herself is forever changing in his experiences, in his culture, his language and mentality. The change becomes more rapid in some periods of history than in others. Today, it is necessary to be aware of the historical-cultural differences existing between the men to whom Christ and the primitive Church addressed themselves and those to whom we are sent. We ought also to be aware of the pluralism and of the diversities typical of our contemporary situation.

Starting from different perspectives, we have thus far reviewed the variety and complexity of the problems which our times pose for the testimony of Christ. As we conclude our work, we can now summarize the fundamental lines along which to initiate ethical dialogue with either modern secular man or the secularist humanist. A faithful proclamation of salvation and acceptance of the mission to transmit the salvific message in our time demand from us a sincere commitment to research and to the promotion of conditions facilitative of loyal dialogue with the secular humanist as with the most deeply secularized believers.

In our discussion of "faith alone," we have already indicated an ethic of responsibility-coresponsibility as one of the central points for dialogue. There are other equally fundamental issues such as the dignity of the human person seen in the totality of its complex dimensions; conscience and full respect for its sincere convictions; personal and communitarian freedom in its exigencies and promotion; and, finally, the solidarity of the human race and the unity of man with the world in the all-embracing vision of history since the beginning of time.

The dialogue will be true if believers see it as a service of pre-evangelization, as a commitment for the acquisition of greater knowledge of Christ and of man, and as a sincere contribution for the realization of peaceful coexistence. The collaboration of all men for the attainment of solidarity and peace in the world is an indispensable task today. The Church cannot drag behind; her credibility depends much on the sincerity, the generosity and humility with which she offers her full contribution. "Since God the Father is the origin and purpose of all men, we are all called to be brothers. Therefore, if we have been summoned to the same destiny, which is both human and divine, we can and we should work together without violence and deceit in order to build up the world in genuine peace" (GS, Art. 92).

Man's commitment includes the furtherance of personal dignity, sincerity of conscience, the freedom and liberation of man, the strengthening and deepening of the bonds of solidarity. There are options which, when sincere, bear the fruit and recollection of divine grace, i.e., they foster an attitude of openness to faith and a choice of "salvation" even when all the dimensions and presuppositions of salvation are not fully developed or conscious.

These remarks are not meant to imply that a man who so pledges himself to service finds an explicit "proof" of the existence of God. We are here compelled to underline the fact that man's commitment is an existential path to salvation: it constitutes a choice which, secretly and implicitly, duplicates in him the existential structure of faith in the one God, who created man to his own image, and belief in Christ, who redeemed man for brotherhood and unity.

Occasionally, the fraternal commitment of the secularist humanists is so absolute as to evoke the gratuitousness and absoluteness of an oblative Christian love, of the *agape*, fruit of faith and witness to the presence of the Spirit in the heart of believers. On the other hand, there is need to caution relative to the dangers to which these same values are exposed; when seen in an explicitly anthropocentric way with responsible exclusion of God, they become idolatry, i.e., they thwart our approach to the end goal and become a source of frustration.

I. THE DIGNITY OF THE HUMAN PERSON

Men of today, including those who neither consider themselves nor define themselves as believers in the Christian sense, manifest a great sensitivity for the dignity of every human person regardless of sex, color, race or social class. Often, Christians and secularist humanists are associated in the same struggle against various forms of discrimination which unfortunately still imperil the respect and rights of the human person.

The common commitment not only offers a link at the level of reflection but also at that of witness; it is a bridge for the dialogue that becomes life. By means of it, the secularist humanist can find the hidden fundament of his own commitment and of his "faith" in the values of brotherhood; he will encounter the Creator and Savior of all. It is necessary, however, that Christians realize a convincing testimony of their fraternal commitment and render transparent in an existential fashion how their effective and generous fraternity springs from faith in the God who created man to his own image and redeemed him, through Christ, in a solidary unity free of egotism, exploitation or discriminations.

Vatican II considers the dignity of every person a valid starting point for a fruitful dialogue with our contemporaries. Especially in *Gaudium et Spes* can numerous passages be found referring to this point. The fourth chapter of the Constitution opens with these words: "Everything we have said about the human person, and about the human community and the profound meaning of human activity, lays the foundation for the relationship between the Church and the world, and provides the basis for dialogue between them" (GS, Art. 40).

II. CONSCIENCE

In the Stoic concept of conscience (syneidesis), St. Paul found an influential current of ethical culture which can be compared to modern humanism. He gave greater depth to this concept by setting the sincere conviction of conscience in relation to faith. Very significant in this respect is the solution which he proposes on the pure-impure food dispute. He starts from the fact that the "kingdom of God is not eating and drinking, but justice, peace and joy inspired by the Holy Spirit" (Rom. 14:17). He is therefore "convinced as a Christian, that nothing is impure in itself" (Rom. 14:11). Nevertheless, he considers that "a man who has doubts is guilty if he eats, because his action does not arise from his conviction [conscience] and anything which does not arise from conviction is sin" (Rom. 14:23).

Wherever there is lacking respect for a sincere conscience there will be no human community based on the dignity of the person nor will there be any authentic dialogue: "In fidelity to conscience, Christians are joined with the rest of men in the search for truth, and for the genuine solution to the numerous problems which arise in the life of individuals and from social relationships. Hence, the more that a correct conscience holds sway, the more persons and groups turn aside from blind choice" (GS, Art. 16). For a fruitful dialogue with modern man, it is vitally important to clarify what is meant by "conscience." This constitutes the first essential step, one on which depend subsequent encounters and understanding.

The man of today is called to conscience-awareness when he protests: against the intolerance of certain individuals, against the psychological or physical pressures of groups or of power, against collective prejudices, against a legalism deprived of sensitivity for the exigencies of love and social justice, against blind obedience, against the cruel transgression of laws promulgated for the common good, especially by those destined to protect the fundamental rights of every person. In the name of conscience, contemporary man protests most strongly any and every attempt of brainwashing.

Twentieth-century man is considered conscientious when he displays a strong sense of responsibility in relation to himself, to his family and neighbor, when he proves to be dependable in his professional life and social-political commitment, e.g., in the struggle against prejudice and discrimination. A responsible conscience today involves a vibrant and committed awareness of present opportunities and the actual needs of individuals and communities. The upright man is sensitive, vigilant, sincere and spontaneous. The rectitude of conscience becomes linked to the manner in which, at particularly crucial moments, one arrives at a decision in full responsibility not only for one's own integrity but also for that of his neighbor and future generations. The man come of age appraises above all a sincere and steadfast search of truth in sharing experiences and in co-reflection, passionate concern for human values and healthy environment, and, last but not least, a conformity of acting with one's own sincere convictions.

A man of conscience is worthy of trust. He matures his own ethical convictions, knows what is rightly expected of him and acts in conformity with his conscience without selfish calculations. He is open to self-criticism and accepts the criticisms of others; when mistaken, he becomes aware of it and he frankly recognizes his shortcomings.

Discussions on the dignity of conscience gain in depth when faced with religious problems. Today, the conscientious persons in religious matters are those who are personally convinced and sincere, more preoccupied with the loyal search for truth than the defense of institutions or religious group to which they belong. In a pluralistic and secularized society, one is judged not so much on the basis of his belonging to this or that religious group as by the sincerity and loyalty of the choices of conscience on which his belonging is founded, by the strength and quality of fraternal love which it arouses.

Looking primarily at the sincerity of choices, modern man succeeds more readily in appreciating those who belong to different faiths and religions. The fundamental attitude of tolerance so highly valued today is appropriately based on a firm respect for conscience. Unless there is evidence to the contrary, modern man is little inclined to doubt the sincerity of the convictions of others, whether or not they coincide with his own.

In the past, one often sought conscientiousness of the kind displayed by a servile preoccupation with the thousand and one subtle civil and religious prescriptions, even if one never questioned the meaning of individual norms in view of the common good and love of neighbor. Today, confronted by such a person, one would not even dare intimate "conscience." Today's believer does not condemn them disdainfully; he feels pity for them because of their deformed conscience. However, where legalism blocks the development and liberation of our fellowman, we protest just as Christ so strongly protested against the pharisaical world overly concerned with meticulous traditions but not much with justice and love of neighbor.

With ever greater frequency today, man appeals to conscience and to the right to follow his conscience when, by virtue of personal convictions he also actively reveals the laws and norms to be unintelligible in view of the common good. Great respect is due those who do it at considerable sacrifice because inspired by the principles of non-violence. They bring into evidence the real points of contact of human thought and Christian life. In many contemporary humanists there is present, at least to a certain extent, a permanent Christian heredity even when it is cut off from the original religious-ecclesial matrix and manifests a more or less intense secularization tending toward secularism. For fruitful dialogue, it would be unfair to begin by criticism or by the recognition of positives followed immediately by a series of "buts" and "howevers." It is necessary to appraise sincerely those aspects of thought and of modern practice which reflect Christian faith and charity; these form a valid basis of collaboration and, with the grace of the Spirit, true bridges toward faith in Christ.

When the humanist actively defends the integrity, wholeness and dignity of each man's conscience, his attitude reflects an essential aspect of the Christian vision of salvation since it presupposes and demands recognition of and respect for the integrity of the human person and commitment to its promotion. All this can, especially today, be a decisive step and opening toward the fullness of faith-charity.

In the Christian vision of conscience, a central value is assigned to contrition, which arises from the recognition of sin and a person's openness to and commitment for renewal. Analogously, some secularists recognize the necessity of confronting in absolute sincerity that which Erich Fromm calls the "dark forces behind our backs." Many of our contemporaries recognize and decidedly maintain that conscience is not a superstructure arising from or imposed on individuals by an aggregate of socio-economic factors only. Conscience consists in the person's intrinsic dynamism toward the fullness of being and maturity of love, his growing (*"per connaturalitem"*) by greater existential familiarity with goodness and justice in discernment of the good. Psychological studies demonstrate ever more convincingly that he who painlessly and unreservedly acts against his own intuitions and moral convictions disintegrates personality-wise.

Persons who wish to attain wholeness, integrity and interior security ought to grow in openness to the needs of people and to higher values, in readiness to put them into practice in daily life. By so actualizing himself, the person will feel himself drawn, from the depth of his heart, to the living source of all truth and goodness, and notice that his own integrity depends on a generous response to the good regardless how it is manifested, in the gifts which are offered, in the concrete opportunities for doing good and in the opening of oneself to the truth which presents itself. Every loyal, sincere and open conscience reveals signs of the dynamic presence of God, who gives value and meaning to history. Many of our contemporary humanists who are equally sincere, are not aware nor do they succeed in perceiving explicitly the religious dimension of conscience and its striving. Such ignorance reminds us of many believers whose underdeveloped conscience does not find a living synthesis between faith in God and generous dedication to mankind and the world.

Whether people are explicitly aware of it or not, no value can stand without a dynamic and true relation to God and Christ; every value is such because it reflects the presence of God, who creates man and the universe in Christ, who redeems it and recapitulates everything in Christ. Besides, the absence of an explicit religious dimension in the categories of thought and in the sincerity of conscience rarely originates from an outright rejection of God. Most of the time, it results from the hectic style of life and from a secularized environment exercising a fascination all the greater because of the absence of an authentic witness to God and to Christ in everyday life, especially at the level where the future of man is being decided.

The conscientious man who is sincerely open to others numbers among those who ask Christ on the last day: "Lord, when was it that we saw you hungry and fed you, or thirsty and gave you drink, a stranger and took you home, or naked and clothed you? When did we see you ill or in prison, and come to visit you?" And the king will answer, "I tell you this: anything you did for one of my brothers here, however humble, you did for me" (Mt. 25:37–40).

The dialogue on a vigilant and open conscience will become a pre-evangelization if not a full evangelization. All depends on our sincerity and capacity for witnessing to the strong dynamism of faith, a testimony which assumes, purifies and vivifies the values in which our contemporaries "believe." It is necessary that in our assertions as in our life, our testimony be respectful of the just autonomy of earthly values; it must be stripped of every design of power or superiority complex and fully witness to service, a service of love rooted in humility and in loyalty to Christ.

III. FREEDOM

One cannot speak of conscience without immediately touching upon the theoretical and existential problem of freedom, particularly in relation to conscience. In fact, the values of freedom and of conscience are interdependent and strictly bound together. A commitment for promoting the dignity of conscience always and necessarily coincides with the affirmation of freedom as a fundamental value and liberation as a primary task of man. Any discourse on the centrality of conscience would be pharisaical without a sincere commitment to see that our modern society be so structured as to leave room for the promotion of freedom in co-responsibility.

Faced by the perils which threaten freedom and confronted by all the new opportunities for its promotion, the Church (specifically moral theology) cannot inspire confidence unless she generously and disinterestedly participates in the concerns and sincere commitment for the liberation and freedom of persons and communities at all levels. It cannot suffice to point out specific dangers; action and positive testimony of the believers are needed. Words are meaningless without a sincere effort to institute freedom, to create life-convictions which foster the freedom of all men and a responsible use of it.

The pastoral constitution *Gaudium et Spes* speaks of the dignity of conscience (GS, Art. 16) and then pauses on the excellence of freedom, noting among other things: "authentic freedom is an exceptional sign of the divine image within man. For God has willed that man be left in the hand of his own counsel so that he can seek his Creator spontaneously and come freely to utter and blissful perfection through loyalty to Him" (GS, Art. 17).

If the image of God shines forth in our convictions and decisions (not only of *us* considered individually but also *us* as a community witnessing to Christ), making us promoters of freedom, we will know how to encounter and converse with the men of today who "make much of this freedom and pursue it eagerly, and rightly so" (GS, Art. 17). If we succeed in clearly testifying to our concept of and commitment to freedom as springing from man's being "image of God in Christ," we will realize very valid bridges for encounter and dialogue. We can thus become a convincing "proof" of the truth and of the validity of faith for many of our contemporaries, while a proof on a mere theoretical level does not move at all the man of the secular age.

IV. BROTHERHOOD OF THE HUMAN RACE

In the past, the too individualistic views of "eternal beatitude" wound up alienating many believers from a social commitment and led them to search for salvation "outside of the world." *Gaudium et Spes* loyally recognizes that a "false presentation of doctrine" and "defects" of a truly religious, moral and social life have made believers themselves a cause of atheism and secularism (GS, Art. 19–21). Instead, if the eschatological hope of the Christian is authentically presented in the biblical and eucharistic perspectives, it becomes a source of real brotherhood; it "does not diminish the importance of intervening duties but rather undergirds the acquittal of them with fresh incentives" (GS, Art. 21).

The "faith" of the secularist in the cosmic and fraternal dimensions of the person implicitly confesses the one Father-Redeemer of all men and of the whole cosmos. Today's man is particularly sensitive to justice and peace on all levels, particularly on an international scale, and stands fully conscious of their demand for steadfast solidarity among all men and all nations.

All this is Christianly positive; it may well be that we are touching here on the greatest possibility for speaking to the secular world about one God in its own secular language. It is nevertheless necessary for believers to become aware of all aspects of the modern striving toward cosmic and human unity including the diversified attempts and the numerous experiences. Only in this awareness will it be possible to present the Christian life-truth in such a way that the intimate relationship of faith with the desire for unity in freedom will be clearly perceptible.

The dialogue on solidarity and the common commitment of all men for the realization of justice and peace in freedom and brotherhood will seem all the more effective and credible, and will be all the greater if there is found "within the Church herself mutual esteem, reverence, and harmony through the full recognition of lawful diversity. Thus all those who compose the one People of God . . . can engage in dialogue with ever-abounding fruitfulness" (GS, Art. 92).